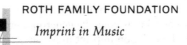

ROTH FAMILY FOUNDATION

Imprint in Music

Michael P. Roth

and Sukey Garcetti

have endowed this

imprint to honor the

memory of their parents,

Julia and Harry Roth,

whose deep love of music

they wish to share

with others.

The publisher and the University of California Press
Foundation gratefully acknowledge the generous support
of the Roth Family Foundation Imprint in Music, established
by a major gift from Sukey and Gil Garcetti and Michael
P. Roth.

The publisher also gratefully acknowledges the generous
support of the Director's Circle of the University of
California Press Foundation, whose members are Stephen
and Melva Arditti, John Geiger, David Hayes-Bautista,
Arlene Inch, Deborah Kirshman, R. Marilyn Lee, Donald
Mastronarde, and Meryl and Robert Selig.

Publication is further made possible in part by a grant from
the Barr Ferree Foundation Publication Fund, Department of
Art and Archaeology, Princeton University.

Mirror in the Sky

Mirror in the Sky

The Life and Music of Stevie Nicks

Simon Morrison

UNIVERSITY OF CALIFORNIA PRESS

University of California Press
Oakland, California

© 2022 by Simon Morrison

Library of Congress Cataloging-in-Publication Data

Names: Morrison, Simon Alexander, 1964– author.
Title: Mirror in the sky : the life and music of Stevie
  Nicks / Simon Morrison.
Description: Oakland, California : University of
  California Press, [2022] | Includes bibliographical
  references and index.
Identifiers: LCCN 2021062927 (print) | LCCN 2021062928
  (ebook) | ISBN 9780520304437 (hardback) | ISBN
  9780520973091 (ebook)
Subjects: LCSH: Nicks, Stevie. | Singers—United States—
  Biography. | Rock musicians—United States—
  Biography.
Classification: LCC ML420.N6 M67 2022 (print) |
  LCC ML420.N6 (ebook) | DDC 782.42166092
  [B]—dc23
LC record available at https://lccn.loc.gov/2021062927
LC ebook record available at https://lccn.loc.gov
  /2021062928

Manufactured in the United States of America

31 30 29 28 27 26 25 24 23 22
10 9 8 7 6 5 4 3

For Billie, the biggest star

Contents

Photographs follow page 116

Introduction

Crystal Visions

It's November 5, 1979, at the Checkerdome in St. Louis. Stevie Nicks, on tour with Fleetwood Mac promoting their album *Tusk,* performs a new song, "Angel." She sports a claret-colored beret that can hardly contain her mass of blond curls, and a layered party dress reminiscent of the Roaring Twenties. The tune evokes a giddy dance hall ditty, made giddier when Nicks's bandmate and former romantic partner playfully throws his arm around her shoulders during the chorus. She lights up, he bathes in her glow, then she breaks free and the band shifts—maybe even struggles, just a bit—to keep up with her, to match the might of her voice. She imbues the song with such possibilities of form, meaning, and purpose as will only be revealed after listening again and again to different versions captured on tape and film. That night, on stage, she grabs the mic and quickly looks to the left, smiling in delight; then, before the final shout-out, she treats the audience to something unexpected: buck-and-wing dancing, blending steps from the Mashed Potato and the Charleston, channeling the Follies. A real show. The steps seem hard to pull off in her platform heels, but she delivers, rotating her hips and pumping her fist, immersed in the power of her presence.[1]

A thousand moments like this define the career of Stevie Nicks, who sings of divination, moon goddesses, the stars of the silver screen, her grandmother Alice and *Alice in Wonderland,* Joan of Arc, sibyls and sylphs—channeling all their energies into her songwriting. Her music reflects and refracts desire, need, and regret; the most beloved tracks attest to an artist of profound knowing, unapologetic instinct, and much hard-won wisdom. In her ballads, she's often the truth-teller capable of transgressing boundaries, honoring that part of herself that hurts the most and forming from that acute act an intense bond with her audiences. Today, Nicks remains loyal to the heroines who lit the way for her and the audiences who have cheered her on for some fifty years. The artist and her career are generous and optimistic and fierce. Her music matters.

Steeped from childhood in her grandfather's country songs, Nicks formed her first group, a Mamas & Papas–style quartet called Changing Times, while still in high school. After college in the San Francisco Bay Area and four years with a group called Fritz, she and her partner, Lindsey Buckingham, relocated to Los Angeles. Their album *Buckingham Nicks* (1973) did not sell especially well but caught the attention of drummer Mick Fleetwood, who invited Buckingham and Nicks to join Fleetwood Mac.

Nicks wrote hit after hit with Fleetwood Mac, as did Buckingham, a singer, virtuoso guitarist, and innovative producer. Their arrival marked a change in geographic location as well as style. The group had been based in England, soaking up American vernacular and producing occasional singles like the ballad "Need Your Love So Bad." Guitarist Peter Green founded the original Fleetwood Mac, joining drummer Mick Fleetwood and bassist John McVie in 1967 for a debut at Great Britain's National Blues and Jazz Festival at Windsor. Christine Perfect, "voted one of Britain's top girl singers" (along with Petula Clark) in the late sixties, sang with a rival blues band called Chicken Shack before marrying John McVie and, after a brief solo turn, becoming part of his band.[2] She had perfect pitch, conservatory piano training, and a clear singing voice. She produced singles for Fleetwood Mac after Nicks and Buckingham joined—not before.[3]

As a California band, Fleetwood Mac occupied the same commercial space as acts like the Eagles, but with richer syntax. The rebelliousness of rock and the angst of the blues were tempered by harmonic Novocain, pulsed ambience, and melodies that rose and fell like the orbs in a lava lamp. Nicks added a playful diablerie to the mix, and the listener feels the strength of her will even as part of a languorous vibe. *Rumours,* her second record with Fleetwood Mac, is remarkably still on the charts, thanks to the enduring appeal of her song "Dreams," Buckingham's "Go Your Own Way," Christine McVie's "Don't Stop," and the magical effect on all the tracks of the layers and layers of overdubs. Not all the great music made the final cut. The song Nicks cared about the most at the time, the love-hate anthem "Silver Springs," was excised for logistical reasons. (In addition, Buckingham was embarrassed by the intimate circumstances that inspired it.)

In remarks for the 2013 deluxe edition of *Rumours,* Buckingham called the process of making the album "organic."[4] It is a synthesis, perhaps, but not a product of effortless growth, given that most of the songs went through multiple late-night drafts. Nothing just grew; the album was meticulously cultivated, and the process proved personally as well as professionally fractious. As Jessica Hopper of *Pitchfork* puts it in her review of the rerelease, the production is as close to perfect as twenty-four tracks can get. *Rumours* is "so flawless it feels far from nature," she writes. "It is more like a peak human feat of Olympic-level studio craft. It was made better by its myopia and brutal circumstances: the wounded pride of a recently dumped Buckingham, the new hit of 'Rhiannon,' goading Nicks to fight for inclusion of her own songs, Christine McVie attempting to salve her heart with 'Songbird.'"[5] The success of *Rumours* was breathtaking, topping the billboard charts for thirty-one weeks and selling ten million copies in its first year. Warner put the album on the cover of its 1977 annual report.

The popularity complicated the making of a sequel to the point of creative paralysis. It could not be topped, but the band was under pressure to at least equal it. *Tusk,* the double album follow-up to *Rumours,* takes experimentally anti-*Rumours* license. Dissonant pitch clusters and suggestive noises recall what modernists of earlier times called *flaques sonores* (sound puddles). The title track, referencing male genitalia, involves a marching band—excess for excess's sake, given the remixing required to wrestle the trumpets and trombones playing the stinger chords into tune. The result was a commercial flop that has been extensively analyzed, with Nicks often bearing the brunt of critical censure.[6] "All the weakest songs on *Tusk* came from her pen," music critic Geoffrey Himes declares, condemning "Angel" along with the rest.[7] His claim becomes accurate when negated; the strongest songs are hers.

The most successful commercial band of the seventies created, in the final year of that decade, a brilliant album whose brilliance rested in its absence of commercial appeal, and *Tusk* gained cult status as a decadent Los Angeles response to the punk movement.[8] The albums that followed, *Mirage* and *Tango in the Night,* are, as the first title suggests, simulacra produced in the mid-eighties to sound like Fleetwood Mac in the mid-seventies. But the moment had largely passed. Production technologies could not replace the beating heart of musicians singing their songs. Only Nicks's track "When I See You Again" adds some sense of sincerity to an otherwise over-polished recording that makes clear the band members were never in the studio at the same time.

Nicks's later solo career—inspired by country music, synth pop, Tom Petty, and Prince—commands less attention in the mainstream media than the murky prism of half-truth, biography, and reporting that defines the legacy of Fleetwood Mac.[9] She is twice, however, a member of the Rock & Roll Hall of Fame, with her second induction in 2019 a testament to the space she has carved out on her own and with those who believed in her being on her own. The picture of her career, the facets of her success, becomes all the richer when her demos, alternate and extended mixes, and duets with others are taken into account. On her retrospective box set *Enchanted* (1998), the process behind familiar songs is presented for all to hear, and the less familiar songs have their own stories to tell.

Popular music experts are careful to preserve the distinction between the "real person," a "persona," and any given "character" when talking about songwriters and their songs. Nicks consciously blurs these categories.[10] In "Landslide," she expresses her own feelings about aging; she sometimes dedicates her performance to her father. "Gypsy" allegorizes an intense childhood friendship, and "Mabel Normand" forges a parallel between herself and a silent film actress. "Rhiannon" is an example of another sort. The song, Nicks shares with her audiences, is about an "old Welsh witch," obscuring the more immediate inspiration of a 1973 novel of the occult, Mary Bartlet Leader's *Triad*.[11] Nicks's "Rhiannon" persona is far removed from the everyday, and yet, according to occult expert Kristen Sollée, "Nicks has done more for the mainstreaming of witchcraft than most out-and-proud witches have."[12] In 2014, for example, Nicks guest-starred in an episode of *American Horror Story: Coven* titled "The Magical Delights of Stevie Nicks." She served as the model for the character Misty Day, an outcast who roams the bayous of Louisiana in communion with nature before her supernatural gifts are discovered and she is taken into Miss Robichaux's Academy for Exceptional Young Ladies, a safe haven for goth femmes. Day meditates, listens to "Rhiannon," and bring souls back from the dead. Nicks, appearing as herself, gives Day a shawl that she has worn on stages around the world. Nicks's attraction to the fantastic has been portrayed as somehow adolescent or guileless. Yet when Led Zeppelin, Blue Öyster Cult, or any number of metal bands delve into the mythic, their fantasies are indulged, even revered.

And while Nicks's creative power can seem inseparable from her sexuality, her femininity dominates her literary imaginings, her musical textures, and her deviations from girl-in-the-band compliance. Femininity has a fraught relationship with rock 'n' roll as chronicled by men. Much writing about the popular music industry exalts male artists, including those at the console adjusting inputs and outputs. Yet nothing can detract from her singular asset: her gold dusk voice and its gothic impurities, described by music critic Amanda Petrusich as a "strange, quivering contralto" denoting "the gloaming—that lambent, transitional moment between night and day."[13] The voice consoles, Petrusich adds, and offers "shelter" from music's current interest in confrontation. Too often, compromise is misread as capitulation, and acknowledgment of vulnerabilities mistaken for weakness, a willingness to sacrifice agency.

Likewise, women's creative energies are often dismissed as immature, except when they inspire a man who hones his craft, his talent, on her feelings. Nicks's contributions have been reductively portrayed as skeletal, the bare bones of an idea to be fleshed out, then coveted, by others. She has been portrayed as the muse, not the artist. As feminist scholar Sara Ahmed has argued, female imaginings have historically been limited to a "narrow horizon" that prevents them from becoming a threat.[14] Nicks's songs ultimately trouble the tales of women as muse, lover, ingenue, accessory by insisting on the importance of her own imagination.

Stevie Nicks will tell her own story one day with the poems and diaries she has bequeathed to her godchildren.[15] She has talked about sitting down "with some of my girlfriends who have been there for a lot of it, putting on a tape recorder, and speaking from the very beginning."[16] Respecting her long-term intention, my accent falls on her public side, and on demos, songs, styles, and recording techniques, reflecting on my earliest and most recent impressions of her hits. The artist's life is but the scaffold for my discussion of her music.

Technical analysis, historical data, critical theories, first- and second-hand accounts, assertions backed by evidence—all have their limits. I have kept the narrative chronological, detailing how her itinerant childhood forged her art, how she synthesized her influences as she matured, how her attachments and creative impulses shaped Fleetwood Mac, and how that group became greater than the sum of its parts. I trace her solo career through the eighties and nineties to the present.

Part of what follows is aesthetic and analytical, part factually biographical, and part journalistic. I conducted interviews with musicians and producers and quote from them. I reference books, magazines, academic publications, photo shoots, videos, fan sites, and legends and literature from different cultures to explore Nicks's artistry. Hers is a most American story, and it begins in that most American place: the West.

CHAPTER I

Stephanie

Where she was is who she became. At the start, she was in the Arizona desert, looking at the horizon and seeing nothing looking back at her, nothing to measure the distance.

Stephanie Lynn Nicks was born at Good Samaritan Hospital in Phoenix on May 26, 1948, and her younger brother, Christopher, in Los Angeles on December 18, 1953. (He would marry one of his sister's backup singers, Lori Perry.) Their father's ambition and success meant a peripatetic childhood and even adulthood for Nicks; his hard-driven life guided her own. By the time she finished high school, she had lived in Arizona, Southern California, New Mexico, Texas, Utah, and Northern California.

As a toddler she couldn't pronounce her name. "Teedee" became "Stevie."

Her parents were devoted, highly protective, and, over time, became well to do. Neither of their own childhoods started out that way. Nicks's mother, Barbara Meeks, was born in the old copper-mining town of Bisbee, Arizona, on November 12, 1927. The town developed in the 1880s as a backstop to the Copper Queen Mine, part of a rich system of excavations in Tombstone Canyon and the Mule Mountains. Barbara was raised poor in tumultuous circumstances but tried to keep her cheer. Her mother, Alice, Stevie's maternal grandmother, was a singer who married Edward Neppel at nineteen. They had three children, and after an acrimonious divorce, Alice married Audy Meeks, a miner who died of tuberculosis in 1972.

As a child, Stevie took trips with her mother to visit her grandmother in Ajo, a town southwest of Phoenix bordering a cactus forest.[1] Nicks's 1989 album, *The Other Side of the Mirror,* is dedicated to Alice, who died on July 3, 1988. It was also indirectly inspired by Lewis Carroll's *Alice in Wonderland* and *Through the Looking-Glass,* which Alice had read to Stevie. In addition, Nicks wrote several songs that refer to the "lady of the mountain," a figure from miners' lore that points to both Audy and Alice. Stevie's family history—down to its smallest details, the low-grade ore of her biography—has shaped her songwriting throughout her career. What might have seemed superfluous at first, perhaps even to Nicks, often later emerged as valuable or even crucial experiences to be extracted in song. She claims not to remember much of her childhood and teenage years, but somehow her music does. There the past is everywhere, though not everything. Images from fables—doves flying out of towers, hair tumbling down walls—fill the gaps alongside impressions of more recent events. In a track with a hazy hook, "Rooms on Fire," she describes memories ensnared in "nets of white cloud."

Like Alice, Barbara married at nineteen.[2] A song that Nicks released in 2020, "Show Them the Way," obliquely references the fact that in her youth, her mother (the "shadow" referenced in the lyrics) worked at a Japanese American internment camp in Lordsburg, New Mexico, which closed in 1943.[3] In 1945, Barbara moved to Phoenix and enrolled in business college. There in July 1947 she met Jess; a month later they were married.[4] Barbara was penny-wise and pragmatic and held a number of office jobs while her children were growing up. But she also loved fantasy fiction and antiques, and in her later years opened a store called Silver Spring Emporium, which sold dolls, collectibles, and Fleetwood Mac memorabilia passed along by Nicks.[5] The store first opened in Scottsdale, then relocated to the Zane Grey area of the state, Payson, under the proprietorship of Barbara's niece Minette. Barbara also involved herself in philanthropic causes, supporting hospitals, veterans, and the Salvation Army.

Stevie's father, Jess (Aaron Jess Seth Nicks Jr.), was born on July 2, 1925, in Phoenix and attended school in Peoria and Glendale before serving in the navy between 1943 and 1946. He enrolled for two years at Arizona State University, technically majoring in psychology but actually, he boasted, in "fun and girls."[6] To cover school costs he worked part-time in the circulation department of the *Arizona Republic,* where Barbara also was employed.[7] After Stevie was born, Jess relo-

cated the family to Southern California. From 1952 to 1956 he operated a hole in the wall in Pasadena, Mickie's Tavern, perhaps with a
brother, while Barbara collected debts for a credit-service bureau.[8] The
family lived in Sierra Madre and Highland Park before settling in
Pasadena proper.[9] Running Mickie's got to be too much—Jess didn't
have time to spend with his little girl and baby boy—so he sold the bar
and took a job as a draft equipment technician with Lucky Lager. Soon
he began to rise up in the company, and after two years he moved into
sales for the Pasadena region, using his gift of gab and connections in
professional bar owners' associations to propel a career that embodied
the slogan "It's Lucky when you live out West. It's Lucky when you live
in America."[10]

Jess became vice president and then president of Lucky's parent company, General Brewing, and later an executive with the Greyhound
Corporation, which operated more than just buses: its holdings included
Dial soap and a meat products firm.[11] At age forty-six Jess was simultaneously serving as president of Armour (the meat products firm) and as
executive vice president of Greyhound, whose offices relocated, on his
initiative, to Phoenix in 1971. Jess became one of the power players in
Phoenix, holding positions on various boards of directors while net-
working at the Paradise Valley Country Club.[12] A lifelong athlete—he
set a state pole-vaulting record in high school—he rode dune buggies
for fun.[13] In March 1974 he had open-heart surgery and subsequently,
on his doctor's advice, took disability retirement from Greyhound.[14]
The experience motivated his involvement in the Arizona Heart Institute; he became chair of its board.

Late in life, Jess followed his daughter's (and his father's) lead by
moving into music promotion, running the Compton Terrace amphi-
theater in Phoenix's Legend City amusement park.[15] Her father hadn't
molded her childhood or encouraged her music, but after Nicks became
famous, Jess signaled his respect as he had been taught to do: by getting
in on the action. Fleetwood Mac performed a charity concert for the
Arizona Heart Institute in 1977, and Nicks did the same as a solo artist
at her father's request in 1996. She was "happy to support the cause,"
according to an attendee, "excited about playing a small, intimate audience." She wore "a long, flowing black dress and brown boots with
laces . . . a large cross around her neck and large cross-shaped rhine-
stone earrings. Her hair was completely straight and she was absolutely
beautiful; a hypnotic vision for the audience."[16]

A.J.

Stevie's earliest musical impressions came courtesy of her paternal grand-father, A.J., though the specifics of the grandfather-granddaughter connection are hard to pin down. Zoë Howe imagines "the two of them [being] inseparable," claiming that "A.J. would take four-year-old Stevie with him to taverns across the mid-West, where she would sing along with her grandfather and charm everyone, already quite the box-office draw."[17] Stephen Davis describes parties and saloons in the Phoenix Valley, with the tot doing sets dressed in a cowboy outfit. The sozzled crowds would cheer, and she'd earn fifty cents.[18] Nicks pointedly downplayed the influence in a 2019 interview: "My grandfather was a country singer, but I said, 'No, I'm full-on Top 40. I'm not country.' I'm dancing to all this crazy R&B music, singing, 'Sugar pie, honey bunch,' and my parents are asking, 'Where did she come from? She's an alien!'"[19] Still, Nicks also invoked her grandfather to shore up her authenticity as a songwriter. She had his grit, his passion.

Aaron Jess (A.J.) Nicks Sr. came from Marble Falls, Texas, not far from Austin. He registered for the draft for both world wars, his paperwork for the first listing him as a "laborer" but also, after he tried to avoid service, as a "slacker."[20] The second registration describes an "unemployed" forty-nine-year-old, with "blond hair, blue eyes, a light complexion with a height of 5'8" and weight of 140 pounds."[21] He and his wife, Effie, had three sons, but their marriage didn't last, and she relocated to Riverside, California. When Stevie was born, A.J. was living in a trailer in Peoria, Arizona. He got by with welding, farming, pool sharking, and riding the rails, picking and singing. His liquor intake increased, so his complexion reddened. Neither his 1974 obituary nor Phoenix community reports from earlier years mention musical activities—just his transience.[22]

A.J. involved his granddaughter when performing in her parents' presence and helped plant the showbiz bug in her. He appears in family photographs, hugging Stevie closely in one (she seems to be holding his cigarette) and watching her ride a donkey at an amusement park in another. He and Stevie sometimes performed together at Mickie's Tavern while her father tended bar and her mother served food.[23] A.J. would sing the lines "Are you mine? All the time?" from a song by country stars Red Sovine and Goldie Hill. Stevie would answer, "Yes, I am" and "Yes, sir-ree," toy guitar resting on her knee. Family lore has her standing up on tables to dance, and her grandfather playing forty-fives for her.

"He'd say, 'You're a harmony singer,'" she recalled. "'You're a perfect Everly Brother.'"[24] She looked back at it as a "heavy relationship," lamenting her grandfather's decision to abandon his family for music: "I mean he was too serious about it."[25]

After the success at Mickie's, A.J. proposed taking his granddaughter with him on the road. Her parents refused and there was an argument: she was obviously much too young for a Boxcar Willie lifestyle. A.J. disappeared for a few years to Bozeman, Montana, and Winona, Minnesota, then reappeared in El Paso, Texas, when Stevie was in fourth grade, and again in Arcadia, California, during her sophomore year of high school. He was of limited skill but wrote affecting lyrics, evident, Nicks says, in a remorseful song about his family called "Two Blue Stars."[26]

Nicks grew up listening to Patti Page, British Invasion hits, Motown, and several "girls' groups," including "the Chiffons, the Shirelles, the Supremes, Martha and the Vandellas." She "liked the sound of the Shangri-Las singing 'Remember (Walking in the Sand)'" and Carole King's songs, including "One Fine Day," which the Chiffons recorded.[27] The Loretta Lynn of "Honky Tonk Girl" must have been an influence, given the kinship in their singing styles: the sound of mild strain at the top, thin and strident for keening effect, followed by a descent, throat relaxed, and a trailing off at the end of phrases. The microphone elaborates their vibratos and belting tone. Lynn channeled the shame and pain of the "sexually charged atmosphere of the working-class juke joint."[28] Nicks did too, at a remove. As a member of Fleetwood Mac, she allowed the country element of her artistic persona to be tempered for a more mystical vibe. This element stayed with her, however, and is pronounced on her most recent album.

In between stints in California, the Nicks family lived in Salt Lake City, where Jess served as division manager for General Brewing. Stevie first attended public school at Wasatch Junior High, on the east side not far from her home on Jupiter Drive. She learned to twirl a baton in drum-major style at the football games—something reprised in 1979 in the video of the Fleetwood Mac song "Tusk"—and sang in a cappella groups. Tap-dancing in top hat and black vest and skirt won her a prize in the school talent show. She had "a lot of fun" at Wasatch, especially after befriending a girl five months younger named Karen Jean Thornhill. But when her grades dipped below the expected "B-plus average" at the end of ninth grade, her parents "whip[ped] me out of that school and put me in a convent," namely St. Mary of the Wasatch High School, the only one of its kind in predominantly Mormon Salt Lake.[29] Stevie kept Karen in stitches "imitating the nuns who taught her classes."[30] The laughter turned to tears when Stevie's father was promoted to vice president and head of operations at General Brewing, returning the family to California. Still, Stevie kept up with Karen and maintained the friendship through the height of her career. Karen would even decoy for her at concerts, allowing Nicks to sneak out the back before being ambushed by fans. She didn't envy her rock-star friend: "I've seen enough to know that I wouldn't want to trade places."[31]

The Nicks family moved into a newly built house at 1752 Alta Oaks Drive in Arcadia, a suburb of Los Angeles, where Nicks attended the local high school for tenth and eleventh grades.[32] By way of welcome, the Campus Pals club hosted a dinner for her and the other students new to the Arcadia School District.[33] Local diversions included the town swimming pool, drive-ins, marching bands and parades, the Pony Express Museum, and lawn bowling. The peafowl population was a subject of debate, likewise the appropriate hair lengths and clothing for school-age girls and boys. Nicks would have bought guitar strings at the Music Mart on Huntington Drive.[34]

In tenth grade Nicks met her closest confidante, Robin Snyder, and their friendship lasted through the end of Snyder's life. (She died from leukemia on October 5, 1982, just thirty-four years old.) The "it girl" at Arcadia High School in the mid-sixties, Robin belonged to the school's theater group, the a cappella choir, and the Orchesis dance troupe. The girls' bond endured through the ups and downs of Fleetwood Mac and the release of Nicks's first solo album, *Bella Donna*. Like Thornhill, Snyder was Nicks's sister, inspiration, and helper. "She was the one person who knew me for the person I really was and not the famous Stevie," Nicks recalled, adding that only her parents knew her better. "She kind of walked me through life." When Snyder died, Nicks dedicated a painting to her titled *The Gypsy That Remains*.[35] She committed to looking after Snyder's baby boy, born just a month before her death, and briefly married her widower, music promoter Kim Anderson, at the start of 1983. The marriage baffled her parents and lasted mere weeks before Nicks had her lawyers pursue an annulment; she helped support the child, her ex-stepson Matthew, through college. Other women have entered this circle of care over time, but the childhood friendships have remained Nicks's closest, manifesting ideals and desires that have worked themselves out in complicated ways. Her bonds with women have strengthened throughout her life, despite, and because of, her relationships with men.[36]

Snyder appears in the Arcadia yearbook in a photograph that freezes in time the eighty-plus members of the coed a cappella group. Nicks isn't pictured. She and three classmates at Arcadia instead formed a folk group called Changing Times, which lasted at least through the 1964–65 school year.[37] The most musically committed member was Tom Sipzer. While involved with Changing Times, he also sang with Choral Carousel, an Arcadia-based ensemble that played bluegrass music in casual settings and for Arcadia's Methodist Youth Fellowship. (The Choral Carousel recorded a double album in 1965.) His whereabouts, like that of the two other singers, Debby (Deborah) Thacker and Dave Nelson, are unknown. The group's biggest concert seems to have been a March 26, 1965, charity "shindig" held in nearby Monrovia High School's auditorium. It raised $1,100 for foreign-student exchanges, bringing in more than the senior class play and an American Field Service project. A total of 1,600 people attended, each paying two dollars a ticket to hear the San Francisco–based folk duo Bud & Travis, who performed patter songs and Mexican ballads. Nicks and Changing Times opened, singing "several rousing folksongs."[38]

One of Nicks's stories from this period involves her father arranging, through a contact at Twentieth Century Fox in Los Angeles, for her to audition with a record producer named Jackie Mills.[39] In 2011 Nicks told the *Guardian* that, during high school, she signed a five-year contract with Mills that was annulled after he left his company.[40] Mills (1922–2010) was a jazz drummer who became a jazz producer for, chiefly, Capitol Records. How and why the daughter of a beverage executive who played a few chords on guitar and sang like her grandfather would be of interest to him is unclear. Perhaps Changing Times was the real interest? Or perhaps the deal was signed with Liberty Records, which managed Bobby Vee, Willie Nelson, Jan and Dean, Gary Lewis and the Playboys, and the Nitty Gritty Dirt Band. Mills worked for Liberty in the early sixties, losing his job in 1963, when the label was sold. Nicks would have been fifteen at the time.

Nicks's father changed positions again, relocating the family to 68 Tuscaloosa Avenue in Menlo Park, a suburb south of San Francisco, so Stevie switched schools once more. In 1966 she completed her senior year at preppy Menlo-Atherton High, where many students had their own cars and their parents employed gardeners and housekeepers. The Menlo-Atherton yearbook, *XV*, describes Nicks as a popular member of the High Spirits glee club. A slightly awkward photograph shows her with someone named Dave Young at a senior dance (the music played

by the band included Cole Porter's "My Heart Belongs to Daddy").[41]
Nicks took English and drama with a beloved big-hearted teacher named
Lee Clements and turned an Edgar Allan Poe assignment analyzing
"Annabel Lee" into a song. Clements also taught Lindsey Buckingham.

Other photographs from the two California high schools Nicks
attended show her strumming a guitar at a sports night, her dark-blond
hair done up in beehive style, and singing (hair down) with her father at
a Valentine's Day concert. The guitar, a Goya, was a birthday present
from her parents after she had started lessons with a "Spanish-style"
guitarist, according to Stephen Davis.[42] Nicks composed a song on it,
"I've Loved and I've Lost and I'm Sad but Not Blue," after a boy she'd
been dating broke things off. "I was totally in tears sitting on my bed
with lots of paper, my guitar and a pen, and I wrote this song about
your basic sixteen-year-old love affair thing," she explains. "When I
played my own song that night, I knew that second on that I was not
going to do a lot of other people's songs. I had to write my own."[43]

The person who would go on to become Stevie's musical partner,
Lindsey Adams Buckingham, also appears in the Menlo-Atherton yearbook. He was born on October 3, 1949, in Palo Alto, and grew up in
Atherton, the third son of Morris and Rutheda Buckingham. Morris, an
aviator during the war, followed his father by going into the coffee business in 1947, running a cannery at 455 Alan Street, Daly City, for the
Alexander-Balart Company, owners of Alta Coffee. It was "small and
slowly not doing so well and eventually went under," according to
Lindsey. He and his older brothers, Jeff and Greg, had uneventful childhoods and became "golden, suburban jock types" in their teens.[44] Both
Jeff and Greg swam competitively in high school, and Greg won a silver
medal at the 1968 Olympics in Mexico City. Like their father, Greg died
prematurely of a heart attack.[45] Lindsey swam as well but preferred
music; he listened to his brothers' forty-fives and plunked a plastic guitar before obtaining a real one. An autodidact, his guitar-playing men-
tors included Dave Guard and Bob Shane of the Kingston Trio. His
parents supported his aspirations unfailingly but couldn't finance them.
After graduating from high school, Buckingham used an inheritance left
to him by his aunt Rhoda to purchase recording equipment and pay living expenses.[46] A rear room in the coffee-canning plant would become
the studio for the four-track recordings he made after hours with his
first band, Fritz, and those he made with Nicks alone.[47] "It was scary
there," she recalled of the gloomy gray building and the hours spent
getting her music right. "Good acoustics, though."[48]

Lindsey and Stevie saw each other in the cafeteria and halls of their school, and both remember meeting at a Young Life gathering in East Palo Alto. The organization spread the faith among clean-cut suburban teens, offering an excuse to get out of the house and mingle. It had distant origins in the eighteenth-century singing schools intended to improve the quality of congregational singing; New England choral composer William Billings established the first one. The youth of that distant time likewise flocked to the schools less for the Bible lessons and sight-reading practice than to catch a glimpse of the opposite sex.[49] Young Life served as a social club of sorts for the Menlo-Atherton population, allowing for casual girl-boy music making and interaction. Nicks is thought to have sung one of the Changing Times covers, "California Dreamin'," among other songs, and Buckingham sang with her while accompanying at the piano.[50] She liked him—"I thought he was darling"—but no connection was made until both were semiprofessionally gigging.[51] Her parents kept her close, imposing a strict curfew on school nights, and she and Lindsey were dating others.

The name of Nicks's folk group Changing Times references Bob Dylan's iconic "The Times They Are a-Changin'," from 1964. Dylan mentions that tune in later songs, including "Murder Most Foul," a seventeen-minute-long recitation dropped in the spring of 2020. The title refers to the assassination of President John F. Kennedy, but Dylan invokes other long-standing traumas, including the scourge of racism and the struggle of the civil rights movement surrounding the assassination of Martin Luther King Jr. The lack of a tune presumably symbolizes the existential crisis described by the lyrics. References to Charlie Parker, Patsy Cline, and Bud Powell mingle with Irving Berlin's twenties hit "Blue Skies" in a stream-of-consciousness survey of popular culture. Echoes of Americana include parlor sounds (old-time fiddle, piano, randomized drums, and cymbals) that drone on in the background, while electronic swirls point to the dreams and nightmares ahead. The recitation doesn't have a point, but that, according to critic Kevin Dettmar, might be just the point: Dylan is operating at the meta level, referencing the people, like him, who have "forged and preserved" the US experience in music, pro and contra and completely apolitically.[52] Farewell to the people of the late sixties, Dylan implies in his final lines, goodbye to "Love Me or Leave Me" and the Summer of Love fairy garden. The Everly Brothers are included in the lyrics, so too the Kingston Trio, Wolfman Jack, the Eagles, and Tom Petty. Woodstock is mentioned but not Nina Simone, the 5th Dimension, or the Harlem Cultural

Festival of 1969—since history, Dylan perhaps knew, has chosen to remember the Summer of Love, not the Summer of Soul. Instead, he mentions A.J.'s baton-twirling granddaughter and her future boyfriend too. Stevie Nicks's fame would equal Dylan's in the years ahead.

FRITZ

Nicks had no post–high school plans, but her parents insisted she pursue higher education, so she enrolled at the College of San Mateo.[53] Owing to a nearsightedness that "made the world blur at the edges like a wet watercolor," she avoided driving and commuted from her parents' house to campus with a friend.[54] She graduated on June 16, 1968.[55] Nicks then enrolled for two years—the fall of 1968 to the spring of 1970—at San Jose State during a period of intense campus activism (her studies were marked by protests against the manufacture of napalm and the founding, by a San Jose alumnus, of Earth Day).[56] She majored in speech-communication but did not graduate from the program, which involved courses in public speaking, ethics, persuasion, classical and modern rhetoric, and semantics.[57] She fell for a guy from Spain who gave her a poncho that later inspired some of her stage attire. Buckingham, meanwhile, completed high school and also enrolled at San Jose State, his parents' alma mater. He was much more absorbed in music than in his studies, and he practiced with the discipline of an athlete. He initially played electric bass with Fritz; guitar came later.

The original name of the band was the Fritz Rabyne Memorial Band, mockingly in "honor" of a German exchange student at Menlo-Atherton High School.[58] The group had serious talent and comprised four rising seniors: Jody Moreing, her cousin Cal Roper, Bob Aguirre, and Buckingham. Moreing was a devout Christian who would go on to earn a degree in composition from Mills College and cut four albums with the Christian group Street Called Straight, having "surrendered her life to God."[59] Fritz's "Next Time Around," which uses the same piano chords as Nicks's later song "Sara," and the group's "The Power" are both deeply religious.

The band rehearsed at Buckingham's house and in the banquet hall of an Italian restaurant. Their first concert seems to have been the high school graduation dance at Menlo Park Civic Center in mid-June 1967. Moreing headed that concert (she's in the photograph of the event) but soon departed the group.[60] Fritz's roster then became Brian Kane (lead guitar), Bob Aguirre (drums), Javier Pacheco (keyboards), and Buckingham (bass and guitar). Nicks successfully auditioned for lead singer that autumn. She appears in a photograph taken on December 15, 1967, at Ellwood P. Cubberley High School, not far from her own alma mater; Fritz had been hired to play at the Cubberley winter dance. The student newspaper "highly recommended" the show, held from nine to midnight in the cafetorium for $3.50 a ticket.[61] Nicks is shown in front of the drummer, wearing a flip bob and a proper Jackie O–style skirt suit.

On the surviving Fritz recordings, Nicks can be heard singing in the middle range beneath Buckingham's impressively precise falsetto. Her guileless air and modest two-chord tunes didn't initially endear her to the keyboardist, Pacheco, who wrote the band's most ambitious material. "Her early songs were too basic," he grumbled in the middle of a protracted online Q and A session with Fleetwood Mac fans. "She did use metaphor, but only slightly [despite] a knack for combining proverbs or sayings with . . . simple narratives."[62]

> The best I can say of Stevie at the very beginning of our Fritz hiatus is that she was considered a "cute chick." She was 19, and cute. Not sexy, nor sultry, nor fancy or shmancy, just cute. . . . When we first heard that people wanted to hire the band because they liked that "blond chick," we didn't throw up our arms and say, "Those heathen philistines don't know good music when they hear it!" We collectively said, "Great!" "They want us back." No one was jealous, we were satisfied that we had been remembered. And Stevie never did anything off-color or tasteless to get attention, she wasn't a "bump and grind" kind of girl. . . . The fact that she caused the band to get attention and that she contributed music to the band meant that her place in the band would become more secure. At the beginning, we didn't know Stevie, didn't know how long she'd last—she was new to rock bands. She also had her own insecurities.[63]

To this account Pacheco added, curtly, that she didn't seem rebellious (clearly, she didn't belong, as he did, to what Bibi Wein called the "Runaway Generation").[64] Her admitted political apathy—her disinterest in the Cold War, civil rights movement, Vietnam, and all the unrest and alienation that rock channeled—separated her from Pacheco.

Pacheco cared about music and current affairs, while Nicks cared about music and books and everything going on in her personal life: school, her first apartment (shared with friends in San Jose), and the relocation of her parents. (Jess joined Greyhound/Armour in the Midwest.) Before leaving Atherton, Barbara tried to dissuade Stevie from dropping out of college for full-time (as opposed to part-time) involvement in Fritz. Pacheco recalls, "Late 1967, Linds[ey] and I went to

[Nicks's] door to pick her up for rehearsal once, and her mom said 'Why don't you boys just go to Vietnam?' (To me, that was like saying 'why don't you go to hell!') It was funny but also chilling."[65]

Fritz acquired a manager, David Forest, and began to think about fame in greedy, "plastic" Los Angeles as opposed to bell-bottomed, "groovy" San Francisco.[66] Forest remembered first booking the band for $150 a show out of his dorm room as a freshman at Stanford, with $25 added on top as his cut. "I needed a band for a job I had, a frat party," he recalled:

> My friend, the social chairman of that frat house, had Greg [Buckingham] call me with his brother's number. I called Lindsey and went to see his band at practice at his parents' home in their garage. I was impressed with the girl singer (Stevie) and their great vocals. They also did songs that not all of the bands did, songs by Buffalo Springfield, Young Rascals, and Dusty Springfield, for example. I told them, however, that to do the frat parties they HAD to include "Louie Louie," "Satisfaction" and "Gloria" or the frat guys would be mad. They said "SURE."[67]

Forest became the "exclusive personal manager" for Fritz, according to his business card, using a post-office-box address at Stanford before relocating his operations to 11750 Sunset Boulevard in Los Angeles. After Fritz's breakup in 1971, he worked for the owner of the Fillmore in San Francisco, and later for music magnate David Geffen. The Carpenters became his clients, along with several hard-rock acts, although a television special featuring Alice Cooper almost ruined him financially. Forest's other interest—gay porn production—kept him afloat. He became an adult-films "super agent" in Hollywood; eventually, he was arrested and imprisoned as a prominent "male madam." Outrageous, unabashed, and excessively proud of his small part in Nicks's rise, Forest succumbed to diabetes before getting a chance to write his memoirs. He recalled Nicks's "Cher potential" and its realization: "Gay men have always loved their dance divas, but Stevie has always appealed to the gay guy rockers. It's the outfits, the twirling, the persona. The gay guys just really dig her," he chimed. She evinced this power even with Fritz, despite the boys in the band teasing her: "She was the 'show.'"[68]

Nicks brought her twang and rockabilly influences to the band, fusing those with its psychedelic and hard-rock (even metal) sound. In its early days, however, Fritz mostly played covers, like so many high school and post–high school bands. Among the crowd-pleasers were a faithful rendition of Steppenwolf's "Born to Be Wild" and an unfaithful (in terms of solo guitar modulations) version of Buffalo Springfield's

"Special Care," as well as Dylan's "If You Gotta Go, Go Now" and Ray Charles's "Georgia on My Mind"—this last a closer. After Pacheco joined as keyboardist, the band focused on original material. His eclectic jams were performed alongside a pair of songs by Nicks: "A Funny Kind of Love" and "Where Was I?" An image from an April 10, 1969, outdoor concert at Cañada College has her leaning over her guitar at the mic in mod Pucci-style attire.[69] The boys in the band were beginning to privilege facial hair. The number-one song in the United States that month was "Aquarius/Let the Sunshine In," by the 5th Dimension.

Nicks's music, Pacheco recalls of this period, had become more involved, less "basic." It was

a good contrast to the other more "metalish" type of music. When we got together, we all participated in writing parts for the songs. I was doing most of the music writing but everyone contributed something. Back then Lindsey was easy, but we were very fastidious about doing good work, we knew what the competition was doing, so we had to make every song as perfect as possible. We were sticklers for original parts—every part had to have something going on. Perhaps Linds got his perfectionism from this.

Pacheco also remembers Nicks's "emotive," "dramatic" onstage persona. "There was a song we did by Buffy Saint Marie (Codeine) in which Stevie cringed and doubled up and acted out withdrawal pains while she sang it. I used to complain about it because to me, it seemed all a big 'put on.'" But, he added, she "persisted" and "got noticed" and charmed the band's audiences with the opposite: the simple ballad.[70]

Pacheco has spent the last few years remastering the 1967–71 Fritz catalogue for downloading and streaming. The polished-up gems are available on Apple Music and Spotify. One song—"When We Love Again"—is comparable to Taylor Swift's recent sound; it was recorded on reel-to-reel tape in Nicks's parents' basement, with a pool game audible in the background. Other songs from studio sessions are fuss-free dance tunes. Fritz played in several styles, not just the free-for-all psychedelia of lore. Pacheco generally opted for a more disciplined sound, while guitarist Kane took to R&B. The musicians' range is no less impressive than the improvement in their sound as they rose from high school gymnasiums and graduation parties to the opening act at stadium shows.

Nicks's "A Funny Kind of Love" captures the rockabilly of the early sixties; it's up-tempo, with a solid pulse and tight harmonies. Buckingham's bass playing has strong attack and a booming sound; the strings are flatwound, the technique indebted to Jack Casady, famed bassist of

Jefferson Airplane. Pacheco's "A Dream Away" is a power ballad not far in melodic contour from Nicks's later hit single "Leather and Lace." Pacheco draws in the concluding freak-out section (highlighting Kane's raw, out-of-tune, overdriven guitar) from Jefferson Airplane's "White Rabbit," one of the most remarkable escalations in rock. "Take Advantage of Me," another Nicks song, has a Doors-style pseudoblues texture and a standout declaration: "I'm not your toy!" It's a demo, recorded at Action Studios in December 1968.[71]

"Wondering Why" is gloomier, grounded in minor chords with occasional chromatic sideslips; the sequential ascents in the chorus needed better harmonic support. The Byrds flutter in the background. Pacheco reports that it was also recorded at the studio in San Mateo, but earlier, in the fall of 1967, a month or so after Nicks joined Fritz. Pacheco's "Flames" amounts to "grown-ups are a drag." Buckingham sings on "Reconsider," which showcases Pacheco's Hohner Clavinet and Vox organ aptitude. "Sharpy," also by Pacheco, features intense Hendrix-like guitar playing and hard-to-hear lyrics (the song concerns music-business hustlers). It was recorded live at Aragon High School in San Mateo in 1970, when Fritz opened for the Youngbloods, the crowd doubtless gathering to hear that band's evergreen anthem "Get Together," itself a cover of an earlier Kingston Trio release, as well as "Product of the Times," a song by Love, which involves protospeed metal picking.

Pacheco's "The Power" is in a blues style, with the words "After you see Jesus, you let that light shine on in" defining the climax. Another religious song in the online archive is a slow, hard, blues-rock number by Brian Kane called "Oh Lord." "Eulogy," a ten-minute-long composition about rebirth, involves call-and-response singing between Nicks and Buckingham at the start, then a long Grateful Dead–style instrumental break, with the guitarist, keyboardist, and drummer soloing in sequence. Nicks dribbles a drumstick on a cowbell. The drummer halts the proceedings, then revs the band up for a concluding unison chorus with a gospel aspect. There's a smattering of applause and the announcement of a set break. "Existentialist" and the milder "Yellow" were also taped live at Aragon High School—it was quite a night of music. In "Yellow," Nicks and Buckingham sing in unison about the woes of the world as trumpeted in the press:

All the front-page stories
the war and all its glories
strife throughout the nation
the dollar and inflation

The singing is preceded by a stunning, pull-out-the-stops bass solo.

"Whirlpool" is fun but underwhelming, a pretext for "Wipeout"-style drumming with another virtuoso cowbell part. Buckingham introduces "Empty Shell" to an audience at Fremont High School in Sunnyvale with a joke and the line "It's dedicated to our friends: we need to practice."[72] It's a loose jam characteristic of California psychedelia with tremolo picking sounds on the bass. The tempo shifts are remarkable, especially the metric modulation before the keyboard solo. "Louisa Joy" is a loony love song with psychedelic lyrics reminiscent of "Savoy Truffle" by the Beatles, the food metaphors (butter and toast, etc.) explicitly sexual. "In My World" is the most psychedelic—in the sense of being unpredictable and open ended—of the songs. A studio recording, it is, according to Pacheco, a "capricious fantasy about secret corridors in the mind."[73] "Time Ago" is a lovely ballad, recorded at Pacheco's home in Menlo Park after the breakup of Fritz, but not for posterity: Pacheco was looking ahead to a career that never happened, overdubbing harmonies in earnest. Nicks's "Anybody There" might or might not belong to Fritz but anticipates her later songs about needing release. Fritz would have been lucky to have it. She sings with fuzzy melancholia over fingerpicked nylon strings, reaching a resigned, older-than-her-years apex with the words "good God almighty."

The musicians in Fritz had timing on their side and sensed the zeitgeist. The Bay Area was a hub of the music world, with Haight-Ashbury the mecca of the moment. Fritz resonated with the better-known superstar bands at the time and had brushes with Jefferson Airplane, the Grateful Dead, Quicksilver Messenger Service, and Big Brother and the Holding Company. Unusually for a largely forgotten group, Fritz opened for and played with the Steve Miller Band, the Moody Blues, Ike and Tina Turner, Chicago, War, Chuck Berry, the Youngbloods, Poco, Leon Russell, Moby Grape, Creedence Clearwater Revival, the Santana Blues Band, Janis Joplin's Kozmic Blues Band and Full Tilt Boogie Band, and Jimi Hendrix's Band of Gypsies; they also performed at the Earth Day Jubilee concert at Cal Expo (other acts included B. B. King and the Guess Who) and Bill Graham's rock concerts at the Santa Clara County Fairgrounds.[74] Four photographs survive from a run-out to Harveys Resort at Lake Tahoe on July 5, 1969: one places the band in front of a totem pole and other Indigenous artifacts; another has them on a ladder on the resort's roof, taking in the surrounding mountains. Buckingham is clean cut and wearing railroad-stripe pants (the other boys wore stripes too) and a white Henley shirt. Nicks prefers shift dresses. Earlier, in 1967, the band's look mimicked that of the Beatles on *Sgt. Pepper's Lonely Hearts Club Band.*

"You could not have been there at a better time," Nicks said of her experience with Fritz, "there" being the Bay Area.

> So we were a good band. So we got on, I mean we opened for everybody. So we opened for Janis at Frost Amphitheater at Stanford. When you open for them you get the perk of being able to stand on the side of the stage. So I got to be very close to Janis and watch her do an entire hour-and-a-half show. . . . On the other side of that, we opened for Jimi Hendrix at San Jose, no, Santa Clara Fairgrounds. 75,000 people. Now we were just little kids at this point.[75]

Nicks's recollection and its soothingly musical repetitions of the word "so" omit the detail that Hendrix played a song for her at the Santa Clara event, "Foxey Lady," after seeing a sudden gust of wind blow up her skirt.[76] A radio interviewer jogged her memory of Hendrix's shout-out, though she never mentioned the wind: "[Jimi] looked over at me and said, 'This is for you, babe.' And I'm like, 'You're awesome! You are so awesomely cute and handsome and you play so amazing and thank you, Jimi!'"[77]

Ultimately Fritz lost what became a Northern California battle of the garage bands.[78] The group simply couldn't break through as a headline act. Fritz's manager, David Forest, desperately called around in hopes of luring a producer to a concert. More and less seasoned people passed, so he dialed Keith Olsen, an aspirant at the back of the Rolodex. Olsen accepted the "free trip" to San Francisco from Los Angeles and heard the band at Aragon High School. The band was "average," he claimed decades later, but he was wowed by the lead couple, Nicks and Buckingham, and when he met them in Los Angeles in the summer of 1970, he proposed that they strike out on their own, sans contract.[79] (Fritz performed in Los Angeles at Whisky a Go Go, did a couple of recordings with Olsen at Sound City in August—"In the Dawn" and "Louisa Joy"—and presumably brought along their Action Studios material, but nothing impressed.)[80]

Terminating the four-year-long relationship with Pacheco and the rest of Fritz was protracted and painful. Pacheco seems to have taken it cordially if not happily; bridges weren't entirely burned.[81] He had witnessed the couple's deepening romance and gradual withdrawal, foreseeing both their exit and his band's dissolution. The cute Anglo suburban kids would move on; the Latino from a working-class background with leftist views would not. Olsen's aesthetic and the market's bandwidth were limited by prejudice, just as the blues and Latin-American styles were diluted by the studios and their overseers. Monochrome music had to be performed by monochrome musicians. Pacheco, a hard rocker who didn't look the part, was denied the chance given to Nicks and Buckingham. He lost out because of racism. Fritz ended just as it had begun, as a local group on the high school and college circuit.

Nicks and Buckingham contemplated their future in a room at the Tropicana Motel on Santa Monica Boulevard, near the Troubadour and Whisky a Go Go. The motel was a cheap hangout for musicians playing on the strip and those hoping to catch a glimpse of them poolside or at Duke's Coffee Shop.[82] The plan was to remain with Olsen in Los Angeles, putting together enough music to pitch to record labels. The plan was foiled when Buckingham became sick with mononucleosis, which kept him fatigued and out of sight for several months back in Northern California. Olsen proposes that the illness played a part in the breakup of Fritz—or at least provided a gentler reason than careerism for Nicks and Buckingham's departure.[83]

Buckingham used the time on his back to practice acoustic guitar, but Olsen claims, "He didn't have enough energy to strum it. He could only lay his arm on it and do that flamenco kind of shot. Now think about the style that Lindsey plays—that's how it happened."[84] Flamenco is energetic and intense and strumming one of the easiest things to do on a guitar, and Olsen seems to be referring to the honing of one through the other, with rockabilly elements added in. Buckingham's technical development after Fritz suggests concentrated repetition rather than capacity. During this period, 1971–72, he and Nicks lived partly with friends in Campbell, California, across from a shopping center called the Pruneyard.[85] The inheritance from Buckingham's aunt Rhoda helped keep them afloat, covering living expenses through the making of a clutch of demos. These were done at Morris Buckingham's coffee plant in Daly City, after the grinders and canners had finished their shifts. "It was just me and Lindsey and the Ampex," Nicks remembered of the highly caffeinated musical flourishing. Their stuff was strewn about the "floor of this tiny room." She recalls recording seven songs, then "we got in Lindsey's car and drove to LA, where every record company in the world passed on us. We were devastated, but we still knew we were good."[86] They trusted their producer to help make them stars. It took time, perseverance, and some tradeoffs, but the producer did.

VAN NUYS

Keith Olsen (1945–2020) came from far away (Sioux Falls, South Dakota) and, in terms of musical tastes, long ago. He trained in cello and learned basics of other instruments at the University of Minnesota while steeping himself in the eighteenth- and nineteenth-century orchestral music canon. He took to the music of modernist composer Igor Stravinsky and studied both tonal and post-tonal music theory.[87] He developed an interest in electronic music and, after he took up the bass, played with a band called the Music Machine, whose 1966 single "Talk Talk" offered a glimpse into a punk future. The available video is a comically weird juxtaposition of morbid complaining on the microphone and ecstatic go-go dancing on the edges of the set.[88]

Olsen came to producing in a roundabout way, pitching his services as an arranger to the Music Machine's opening acts. The popular-music industry was growing quickly, and thanks to a college friend he found a job with Columbia music president Clive Davis, who brought huge acts to prominence and helped transform production into an art. "A lot of record producers back then were 'stop-watchers' and budget minders," Olsen said. "Clive was interested in people who wanted to push the envelope."[89] Olsen moved from four- to eight- to sixteen-track recording on a 1968 album called *Begin,* a "quantum leap forward" that brought together musicians from different bands, including the Music Machine, under the name Millennium.[90] So began Olsen's quarter century in the studio in Los Angeles, followed in the nineties with work designing digital recording equipment. He retired in Hawaii.

The acts he championed ran the gamut from Aretha Franklin to Journey and Santana to Whitesnake. Rick Springfield's "Jessie's Girl" emerged from his soundboard, as did Emerson, Lake & Palmer's addled final album, *In the Hot Seat,* an uninspired flop to which Olsen contributed music of his own.[91] He had no tolerance for bad technique and less for narcissistic musicians who soaked in sweaty adulation on the road but couldn't generate a tune, much less entire verses and choruses, without hand-holding. He listened closely, in the dead acoustic he preferred, and rejected slop. He also took a hard line against narcotics in the studio, claiming, "I don't think drugs ever did a great recording."[92] A good sound for Olsen meant something marketable, and album-oriented radio in the seventies made him rich despite a dispute with Mick Fleetwood, then the band's manager, over missing royalties.

The Van Nuys studio in the San Fernando Valley, where Olsen earned his reputation, has a reputation of its own. The neighborhood was and is grim: burlap-colored apartment complexes, a Roni Macaroni food truck, a Denny's, a strip club, broken furniture piled at a school crossing sign, and homelessness. A converted U-Haul subs as a grocery store in front of a discarded couch around the corner from where Franklin recorded "Amazing Grace." The inside of Sound City used to look like the outside, with trash strewn about and shag-carpeted brown walls preserving the sour odor of long-expired cigarettes.[93] The murderous cult leader Charles Manson menaced a producer into securing a few hours at Sound City in 1969. When he arrived to collect his master tapes and was asked to settle his tab, he pulled out a .38 and fired at the receptionist. The bullet dinged a filing cabinet.[94] Manson died in jail, and the space has long since been scrubbed clean. Today the vibe is chill. Legendary producer Tony Berg is now the tenant, and the back room of Studio B is stocked with his wondrous guitar and amplifier collection. The 28- and 32-input Neve soundboards of the seventies, with miles and miles of hand-soldered wire, take pride of place; an autographed photograph of the Rolling Stones at their peak hangs on the wall, while a paperback of Dostoyevsky's fiction lies beside a Fender and a can of soda. Seasoned as well as up-and-coming artists hunker down there on Berg's invitation. He has made Sound City a haven in which groups can try out different instruments and re-create something like the feel of Laurel Canyon back in the day. He asks them to do crossword puzzles and acquaints them with modernist literature to sort out their heads and work out creative kinks. Berg idolizes Olsen for making it happen—"it" being a SoCal sound of permanent youth, manufactured in a nondescript square building on a square of asphalt located just off exit 65 from Interstate 405.

Olsen partnered with Tom Skeeter to set up a production company, Pogologo, named after his pet husky. From fall 1972 into 1973 Olsen turned Nicks and Buckingham's demos into album tracks on Skeeter's custom-made console. Sound City's mastering was handled at Crystal Sound in Hollywood, which is where Olsen met a gofer named Richard Dashut. When Dashut was dismissed by Crystal Sound, Olsen brought him to Sound City. Dashut did backroom prep work—cleaning and aligning tape heads—but rose up the ranks in the claustrophobic space.[95] Olsen, Dashut, and later, Ken Caillat would become essential to the post-1974 Fleetwood Mac odyssey.

On September 5, 1973, the record *Buckingham Nicks* was released on the Polydor label. It was unsuccessful in Los Angeles and California but

emerged as a surprising hit in the Southeast. An aspiring record executive, Lee Lasseff, is credited with brokering the deal, although the terms
were vague and promotion lackluster. The album demonstrates easy
command of southern tropes with bluegrass-like, banjo-based balladeer-
ing in the female voice and the guitar. Certain aspects of Nicks's mature
melodic writing—misalignments between the tune and accompaniment;
nonimitative, oblique, contrapuntal relationships; and expressive interjections, fragmentations, and disappearances that thwart cadences—are
anticipated on the album.[96] Buckingham, as its first author, made the
bulk of the creative decisions. The songs involve Nashville (high-strung)
tuning; elaborate word painting (hobbled rhythms for "Without a Leg to
Stand On," for example); some esoteric harmonic choices (the shifts
from Ab to Bb7 to A6 and B6 in the first verse of the Ab-major "Races
Are Run"); inspired dueling between Buckingham and the illustrious second guitarist on the album, Robert (Waddy) Wachtel; and all manner of
shuddering, staggering, stuttering, and stumbling effects—anything to
keep the guitar and vocal lines from sticking to the drumbeat, as opposed
to each other.[97] The melodies are broadly spaced from the harmonies in
the mix, as is the click-tracked drumming from the rest of the texture.
Buckingham Nicks has a self-indulgent element that ensured commercial
neglect, except in those musical centers that positioned themselves as
Other to the mainstream. Nicks and Buckingham found their ideal audience among the progressive kids on southern campuses.

Making the record involved twelve musicians, and the $25,000 Poly-
dor budget allowed for some frills—notably, string arrangements on
"Lola" and "Frozen Love," embellished by synthesizer. Gary (Hoppy)
Hodges, Buckingham, and Jorge Calderón messed around with percussion overdubs. "On 'Races Are Run,'" Hodges remembered, "the sound
you hear is a pair of pliers hitting the microphone base to make it sound
like an anvil. We would play on a chair with sticks. They didn't have
shakers back then, so we used sand in a matchbox. Lindsey had a real
unique way of doing percussion." Hodges adds that he visited the couple in their modest lodgings in the Toluca Lake neighborhood of the San
Fernando Valley. "Lindsey was studying this book of 5,000 guitar
chords when I met him," and Nicks was working on lyrics in her paja-
mas. "They were young and just vibrant and beautiful kids. And they
were in love."[98]

Nicks had a different take: "So many of these songs are about me and
Lindsey moving to LA in 1971, asking each other, 'Now what? Should
we go back to San Francisco? Should we quit?' We were scared kids in

this big, huge flat city where we had no friends and no money."[99] These doubts aren't audible on *Buckingham Nicks;* it's a confident record, brimming with ideas for other confident records. Richard Halligan, a famed arranger, participated, and seventies oddball Monty Stark—responsible for a funk-psychedelic reinvention of fifties children's music called *The Stark Reality Discovers Hoagy Carmichael's Music Shop*—somehow got involved on synthesizer. Parts of songs were repurposed in later years and Nicks's "Crystal" entirely redone. Fleetwood Mac rerecorded it in 1975, in a different meter, soft rock's preferred 4/4 instead of 3/4. Buckingham's lemon-drop paean to his girlfriend, the instrumental "Stephanie," is often considered the first draft of Fleetwood Mac's "Never Going Back Again." It also, however, goes back in time, revisiting Crosby, Stills & Nash's intensely alliterative "Helplessly Hoping" from four years before.

Success in love, more than failure, is the album's subject, and Nicks uses symbols from nature—sunflowers for adoration, trees for evolution, the sea and the tides coming in and out—to express headlong, heedless rushes of emotion. The lyrics of Buckingham's "Don't Let Me Down Again" seem banal in comparison: "Baby, baby don't treat me so bad / I'm the best boy you ever had." "Django" is an homage to John Lewis but also suggests "Lady Jane" by the Rolling Stones, though with string effects rather than dulcimer. "Lola" is a good-time tune suitable for line dancing.

The songwriting is half her, half him, with Buckingham's dexterity and self-indulgences on the guitar overshadowing Nicks's contributions. "Long Distance Winner" is an obvious example. She wrote the song, but she's barely heard. There are two, if not three, acoustic guitars at the start—then bass, and then an electric guitar, and then another one, the texture further enriched with guiro. The guitar parts are not that difficult compared to the solos on the album, but the cumulative effect is mesmerizing.

Nicks and Buckingham both wrote the final track, "Frozen Love," which is dramatic and forward-looking but, again, essentially a guitarist's showcase. The opening acoustic passage is fingerpicked, in a style more akin to that of the Kingston Trio than (to name three other sources of inspiration) Chet Atkins or Merle Travis, or the more classical fingerpicking of Peter, Paul and Mary. The solo that ends the song is so elaborate that only listening at half speed reveals if it is one guitar or two (it's one). The bass component fits the fifths pattern of Travis's picking, but everything Buckingham does melodically is unique to him.

The title is captured in the cool, fast vibrato and the brightness of the sound. Nicks's lyrics are compact and beautiful. Buckingham, perhaps abetted by Olsen, didn't give them the attention they deserved:

> You may not be as strong as me
> And I may not care to teach you
> It may be hard to keep up with me
> But I'll always be able to reach you
>
> And if you go forward (if you go forward)
> I'll meet you there
> And if you climb up through the cold, freezing air
> Look down below you; search out above
> And cry out to life for a frozen love
> Cry, love
>
> Life gave me you; yeah, the change was made
> And there's no beginning over
> You are not happy, but what is love?
> Hate gave you me for a lover

Nicks would force the guitar to serve her words in a later, much sadder song: "Landslide."

The semi-naked cover of *Buckingham Nicks,* photographed for Polydor by Lorrie Sullivan, is a source of regret. Nicks remembers spending her "last $111 [about $475 in today's dollars] on a beautiful, very sexy blouse" for the shoot, only to be told by a photographer to take it off. "'It was awful, you know. . . . And maybe that has a lot to do with why I went from that [points to *Buckingham Nicks* cover] to that [points to *Rumours* cover]. Because I said, 'All right, that's it . . . instead of going in the direction that a lot of the women singers are going in now, I'll be very, very sexy under 18 pounds of chiffon and lace and velvet.'"[100]

Outtakes have emerged, showing the cover that might have been. Buckingham reclines in jeans and an unbuttoned white shirt, coiffure fluffed, moustache extra virile, while Nicks rests a hand on his chest, expression soft and slightly doleful. Her silk blouse has sheer sleeves and a delicate pattern. Any of these would have sufficed; instead, Buckingham and the photographer went for titillation. That her parents were appalled was the least of it, and the shadow covering her chest beside the point. Beleaguerment in the service of desire is a hoary misogynist trope: there are countless examples, old and new, of the goodness and innocence of the maiden disappearing with the removal of a veil.[101]

Nicks wrote a song obliquely referencing the experience, "Garbo," in tribute to the Swedish American actor Greta Garbo (1905–90), who made pants fashionable for women in the thirties, and whom Nicks emulated in her refusal to wear revealing clothing.[102] Nicks's song addresses the pressures of stardom, imagining what life would be like should she, like Garbo, become a shut-in diva. (Divas, another actor, Marlene Dietrich, remarked, "didn't go out" and so didn't get to meet one another.)[103] Los Angeles is exposed as a "town full of fools," and Nicks explores longing, loss, and regret. She mulls alienation: "For you think you must do what you feel you do best / And you mustn't give it up for you're still but a guest." It's a slow, minor-mode waltz that slips like worn heels at the end of phrases. The double entendre of "miss what you lose / lose yourself" is especially poignant, and when Nicks sings,

I could be Garbo or even Marlene [Dietrich]
I could be Marilyn [Monroe] . . .
Or I could be alone,

she underscores that fame and loneliness are conjoined. She also mentions Venus, the goddess of love, whose attributes (love, wealth, beauty, desire) connect to the song's description of dolls being used up by guys. Venus is habitually represented naked. Marilyn Monroe was found dead in the nude.[104] The line "Venus doesn't glitter when she stands next to you" is sung in a neon haze. Buckingham plays guitar but doesn't share vocals with Nicks on the 1973 Daly City demo. The distant honky-tonk piano (on the recorded version), the sparse ending, and the Patsy Cline affect make for an unprepossessingly lonely song, a song that doesn't fit the script, a jukebox B-side awaiting accidental discovery.

When asked, after she reached stardom, to speak about the album cover, Nicks referenced "Garbo":

Alright, so on with my story. And also you guys, I've never done this before. This is probably the last night I'll ever do this. I've never really talked to the audience like this, and I get like, you know, "Am I saying too much?" but at the same time I really want to share this with you. So, the second song is about the infamous photo session for the *Buckingham Nicks* cover. Every time I tell this story, I feel like I'm depressing the audience, but at the same time I need to actually tell you what happened, so I went to do this. I was not happy about it. I got in a lot of trouble for not being happy about it. [mocking] "Don't be paranoid, don't be a child. This is art." You know? And, so anyway, I thought about it in my dramatic twenty-seven, twenty-three, twenty-five? twenty-four maybe—I was very young—dramatic way, I thought maybe the movie stars that came here felt this way, you know? Maybe they felt like they had to do something they really didn't want to do that much, but they did it anyway, for art, for music. So, I went home and I wrote this song, and it's called "Garbo."[105]

She admits to modeling her maquillage on Dietrich and Garbo and Monroe, having scrutinized photographs of them in books about Hollywood's black-and-white era and the silent era preceding it. In backstage footage from 1977, she is seen generously applying eye shadow. When pressed as to what she truly admired about the heroines of yesteryear, she went back to childhood: "Just the elegance. Just the total *Queen Christina* type of a vibe. As a little girl, my whole—things that I read about were old kings and queens and . . . that whole type of thing. Riding horses and riding habits. That was the thing that was most romantic to me as a little girl. And even as a big girl, still, is the type of thing that I really love."[106] The big girl was shamed in 1973 and resented it. So, as she informed *Us Weekly,* to regain control of her body, she concealed it under layers of fabric.[107]

ALABAMA

The *Buckingham Nicks* tour was brief: a show at the Starwood nightclub in West Hollywood, then opening for John Prine at the Troubadour for a week in mid-October. Robert Hilburn of the *Los Angeles Times* called Nicks "a promising vocalist" and heard "some excellent three-part harmony" in the set but thought the couple's cover tunes better than their originals.[108] At the time, success at the Troubadour could mean opening up the LA market, then the rest of California's, and then the US market and beyond. The market stayed largely closed. Two dates in Ohio followed on February 18–19, 1974, and then a half dozen at a now-defunct space called the Metro in New York City and five at Passim, a small venue for folksingers nestled behind the Harvard co-op in Cambridge, Massachusetts. Nothing further happened until an August 25 concert at Birmingham's Municipal Auditorium, with Hodges on drums, Wachtel as second guitarist, and Tom Moncrieff on bass.[109]

Alabama loved *Buckingham Nicks*, even if the rest of the United States did not. Radio station WJLN-FM put the LP, especially "Frozen Love," into its regular rotation and started a buzz in Birmingham that spread to Tuscaloosa—a humid, mellow town whose youth took to music with the same vibe. The racism in Alabama was real, enshrined in a crazily long Jim Crow–era constitution that covered everything from churches to bingo games to segregation, but the record-buying kids were more liberal than their parents. Ten thousand of the thirty-five thousand copies in the first pressing sold in a single week in Alabama. The duo returned to the state at the start of 1975 to enjoy interviews over home-cooked meals, audiences in the thousands, and much mutual admiration.[110]

But Polydor denied them a second contract, deeming their sound too "folk" for a major commercial label. Buckingham recalled "an odd New York meeting with a Polydor A&R type" who told them, "'I think you'd be better off, you know, if you did something more like this,' and put a 45 on his office turntable—Jim Stafford's crackerbilly hit 'Spiders and Snakes.'" Crackerbilly was a "one-way ticket to Palookaville" and the "steakhouse circuit" fob off, Buckingham decided, so no deal.[111] Most of the music he and Nicks recorded at Studio City for a second Polydor album went to waste. (Some of the tapes disappeared in a robbery.)[112] But not all: the draft of a tune called "Monday Morning" ended up on a Fleetwood Mac album, likewise the draft of "Rhiannon." The teens of Alabama heard these songs before the rest of the world.

Janitor, banker, English teacher, folksinger, and proudly eclectic music critic Rob Trucks was among them. He played *Buckingham Nicks* in the basement of his parents' house when he had girls over. "'Frozen Love,'" he jokes, was a "particular favorite among late-night Alabama disc jockeys in need of a bathroom break, as a kind of 7-minute warning."[113] Nicks joked too, about moving to Birmingham.

She didn't. Her future, and Buckingham's, belonged not to colleges and local venues and regular people but to the music business, which, in the mid-seventies, began to place the latest studio technologies in the service of escapism and enchantment. Popular music somersaulted from the "real," sounds that had an authentic element and drew from African American blues and white country ballads, to the "surreal," "pipe dreams," and "enlightened apathy." The difference between *Buckingham Nicks* and the records that followed reflects a broader political and cultural turn in the United States toward individualism and the pursuit of personal desires and aspirations. Politics and culture left the working class, the common good, and America's unhappiness behind.[114]

Nicks had had an authentically good time in Alabama promoting an album that gained cult status and has never been reissued.[115] The album didn't generate a single, and she and her boyfriend left it behind, returning to California to figure out what to do next.

CHAPTER 2

Stevie

Nick's father told her that should she decide to re-enroll in college, he would once more cover her expenses. Having that fallback, she decided to stick with music. Buckingham had burned through the inheritance from his aunt and quit his part-time job as a telemarketer. Nicks paid for groceries by cleaning producer Keith Olsen's Los Angeles house, where they had crashed during their first months in SoCal, and Buckingham helped her paint the studio. "She looked just like Carol Burnett. It was absolutely hilarious," Olsen said of her twice-weekly mopping and dusting of his house for $200 a month.[1] Her response, index finger cocked in the air: "I'm not going to be the maid for long, just so you know, just so y'all know."[2] She also—not for long—waited tables at the Copper Penny Family Coffee Shop on Sunset and La Brea and, for $1.50 an hour excluding tips, at a trendy singles bar in Beverly Hills called Clementine's. Nicks lasted a day in a dentist's office, longer as a host at Bob's Big Boy. The cleaning job and restaurant shifts are mentioned in Nicks's biographies, fan sites, and even an online tourist guide, but a precise chronology is unavailable.[3] Nicks's brush with working-class life lasted about half a year; meanwhile Buckingham smoked hash with the likes of Warren Zevon on her dime.[4] The couple moved around, from Olsen's house, to Richard Dashut's apartment (at 751 North Orange Grove in the Fairfax area of the city), a bungalow here, an adobe house there, with wall-to-wall carpeting and lacquered furniture. They were in love, and remained so despite the frequent upheavals and accumulating resentments.

"LANDSLIDE"

In the fall of 1974, Buckingham was hired by Don Everly of the Everly Brothers to play guitar and sing harmony on tour. The Everly Brothers had split up mid-concert on July 14, 1973, at the Knott's Berry Farm amusement park. Don was too inebriated to sing all the lyrics, leaving vast lacunae in the middle of songs. Partway through the second set, Phil Everly slammed his guitar on the stage and announced that he was through with the band. Don got sober, retreated to Nashville, and formed a group of his own, with Robert Wachtel on guitar and Warren Zevon on keyboards. He hoped against hope that the melancholic offerings on his first solo album, *Sunset Towers,* would be as popular as "Wake Up, Little Suzie" and "Love Hurts." Wachtel couldn't go on tour, owing to other commitments, and so recommended Buckingham. Rehearsals began in Aspen, Colorado. Members of the Everly "entourage" parked themselves in Crystal Zevon's parents' house to reduce costs.[5] Nicks and Buckingham drove up from Los Angeles in their Toyota, and while the band hit the road, Nicks stayed on at Crystal's invitation. She would use the time away from Clementine's to write some music.

The tour was a bust and ended early. Nicks recalls Buckingham returning to Aspen in a foul mood. She wondered if he'd been unfaithful on the road, and his mood soured even more:

> He was very angry with me—and he left me—took Ginnie the poodle and the car and left me in Aspen the day that the Greyhound buses went on strike. I had a bus pass 'cause my dad was president of Greyhound, I had a bus pass, I could go anywhere. I said, "Fine, take the car and the dog, I have a bus pass." I had a strep throat also. He drove away, I walk in and on the radio it says "Greyhound buses on strike all over the United States." I'm going, oh no, I'm stuck. So in order to get out of Colorado I had to call my parents and they *unwillingly* sent me a plane ticket because they didn't understand what I was doing up there in the first place. So I follow him back to Los Angeles, that was like October, it was all around Halloween, two months later Fleetwood Mac called on New Year's Eve.[6]

Before her parents bought her the ticket, she wrote out her feelings in song, and not just about her boyfriend. Her grandfather had died in August, her father had been diagnosed with heart disease, and he and her mother were hinting that life with Buckingham, and a life in music, might not have been the best choice.[7]

The song she wrote in Aspen, "Landslide," is a classic—a truly brilliant song. The words conceal and reveal, as does snow, blanketing specific details while revealing overall shapes. The tune outlines things buried below the surface. The narrator describes life's seasons and the past's reflection in the present and the future. She speaks of disappearing into a landscape of truths obscured by the world outside. The narrator looks at the mountain through a window and imagines climbing it only to fall back with the snow. The music sinks as the text dictates, with falling intervals for the word "down" narrating her emotional tumble. Fear of change comes with a harmonic change, while the guitar mutates beneath repeated lines of text, changing how she expresses the words but not the essence of what is expressed. G minor is dropped into the texture, then G minor 7—that seventh an added complication to the chord that captures the complexities accruing with experience.[8]

The nature of love is questioned in the verses, the answer found and feared in the chorus—hence, the minor undertow to the major. The guitar-solo bridge between verses is palindromic, the sound moving forward and then backward, from present into past into future. The lyrics mention "the child within [her] heart," and in the chorus she offers the basic sad truth that "children get older." The text is of course about physically aging as well as wising up with the years. "Landslide" speaks powerfully to the perils of maturation. The refrain, "the landslide will bring you down," rises at the end before falling, and the song ends with the first verse mulled anew and a fermata-like pause in the voice before the final descent. The conclusion is a declaration: some events can't be controlled, including relationships gone awry, years and regrets passing by, and slush that sullies the snow. Seasons change, and we all wonder what we can handle, yet the annular fillip in the guitar and the down-becomes-up reversals of tune suggest a certain resilience—a way to ski the slopes.

The song is easy to sing, because the melody forgives imprecision and encourages adaptation, as we would hope of life itself. Its status as a classic reflects how far and wide it has circulated and the "persistence" of its "sentiment," to quote the title of a wonderful book by Mitchell Morris about songs from the seventies that people love unabashedly and guiltlessly (if a touch sheepishly). Covers range from the Smashing Pumpkins (surprisingly reverent) to the Chicks (piercing the wounded heart of bluegrass) to Stacey Kent (jazzified, with stunningly precise diction). Most of the love is given to songs heard in youth, and growing old with them as new songs are made for the next generation is a tragic and beautiful reminder that, as Morris writes, "We become history along with the things we have chosen to love."[9] That's what "Landslide" is about: the beautiful tragedy of becoming history.

"RHIANNON"

The companion song that defined Nicks's career, "Rhiannon," was written around the same time. It is thought to have come into existence through an act of bibliomancy, of seeing the future in a randomly selected page of a book. In this instance, Nicks opened Mary Bartlet Leader's *Triad* (1973), "a stupid little paperback," she has said, "that I found somewhere at somebody's house, lying on the couch" around Halloween. Nicks has also said she bought the novel in an airport, perhaps en route back to Los Angeles from Aspen.[10]

Whatever the case, the story of this oddly compelling page-turner is as follows: a freelance writer, Branwen, has just lost her baby boy to sudden infant death syndrome. She and her husband, Alan, who often travels on business, seek a new start, so they purchase a rundown mansion on a lake to renovate. Another loss haunts Branwen, from her childhood: the death—accidental, but, the text hints, perhaps not entirely—of her malevolent cousin, Rhiannon, whom Branwen locked in an old freezer while playing hide-and-seek. The rusted handle snapped, and, unable to get out, Rhiannon suffocated. Now Branwen's house brings that loss back: speaking tubes that connect the rooms whisper Rhiannon's name, and Branwen—who fears that Rhiannon has returned from the dead, intent on possessing her—starts to unravel, repeatedly blacking out. Then Branwen discovers she is pregnant—or is Rhiannon? A psychiatrist decides that Branwen is suffering multiple personality disorder. Branwen gives birth, and her husband takes the child after Branwen is confined to an asylum with her alter ego. "At the worst," Branwen's narrative ends,

> I'll have to remain in an institution . . . for the rest of my life. But I have closed the door on Rhiannon. As long as I'm alive she can't escape.
> And yet, if there is someone—someone with uncommon insight—then perhaps the world will find a way to vanquish Rhiannon. I know this much—the veil between this life and the unknown beyond must someday be torn away, for that veil, which is our ignorance, is at once our protection and her weapon.[11]

The "triad" of the title is hinted at in the novel's epigraph: Branwen is the stand-in for Branwen, daughter of Llŷr, the king of the Britons. Branwen's marriage to the Irish king brings disaster for both kingdoms. Caradog ap Bran, Branwen's cousin, is the second member of the triad, and Ffaraon Dandde, a king whose son was murdered, the third.

The novel and its epigraph indicate that Leader knew of the medieval Welsh legends known as the *Mabinogion,* perhaps not in their original form but through popular retellings.[12] These Middle Welsh prose tales, eleven in total, are found in fourteenth-century manuscripts but seemingly date back to at least the twelfth century. They are of different dates and contexts and served as courtly entertainments with a moral purpose. Four of the tales are linked and are commonly known as the *Four Branches of the Mabinogi,* the latter word a scribal variant of the collective term *Mabinogion,* which came into fashion in the nineteenth century.[13] Branwen is the leading protagonist of the *Second Branch of the Mabinogi,* which tells of her ill-fated marriage to the king of Ireland, brokered by her brother, Bendigeidfran (Bran the Blessed). In Ireland Branwen is imprisoned and brutalized; she teaches a starling to speak and sends the bird across the Irish Sea to her brother, who invades Ireland to free her, an event that parallels the fate of Leader's hero, who is confined to the asylum. Nicks used the image of the starling ("And the starling flew for days") not in "Rhiannon" but in another song, "Sara."

The main character in the *First Branch of the Mabinogi,* Rhiannon is an otherworldly woman who marries Pwyll, the mortal prince of Dyfed (South Wales). Both in the *Mabinogion* and in the Welsh Triads, a collection of late-medieval story themes (which no doubt also inspired Leader's novel *Triad*), Rhiannon is associated with three songbirds who accompany her; mythographers have also associated her with the Gaulish horse goddess, Epona. Nicks became obsessed with the name Rhiannon and later, she claims, learned more about the figure's origins:

> I came to find out, after I've written the song, that in fact Rhiannon was the goddess of steeds, maker of birds. Her three birds sang music, and when something was happening in war you would see Rhiannon come riding in on a horse. This is all in the Welsh translation of the *Mabinogion,* their book of mythology. When she came you'd kind of black out, then wake up and the danger would be gone, and you'd see the three birds flying off and you'd hear this little song. So there was, in fact, a song of Rhiannon. I had no idea about any of this.[14]

At some point, Nicks read the four-volume novelization of the *Mabinogion* by the prolific fantasy writer Evangeline Walton (1907–96), sent to her by a fan. The second volume appeared in 1972 under the title *The Song of Rhiannon.*[15] Since the hero-goddess's origins are not specified in the *Mabinogion* or in the Triads, Walton settles on an aggregate. Rhiannon is the glorious night queen, the goddess of the moon and a symbol of female independence, magic, and power. As in the original *First Branch of the Mabinogi,* she rides a swift white horse and songbirds circle her head. She marries Pwyll and has a child with him. The god she was supposed to have married enacts revenge by framing her for the child's murder, Walton's modern twist on the source tale.

In 1977 or 1978, Nicks visited Walton at her "totally Rhiannon" home in Tucson. The writer was in her mid-seventies and suffering from an affliction that made her skin appear purple.[16] Nicks recalls Walton telling her "about her life and how she had been entranced by the name, just like I had. It's so interesting, because her last book was in 1974, and that's right when I wrote Rhiannon. So it's like her work ended and my work began."[17] Nicks acquired, gratis, the rights for a Rhiannon film from Walton. Although not yet made, she has written music for it.[18]

The lyrics of the song indicate greater knowledge of the Rhiannon legend than Nicks acknowledges. Perhaps she divined it, or perhaps she encountered the *Mabinogion* through the writing of Leader and Walton earlier than she contends. The line "She rules her life like a bird in flight" seems to have been inspired by the *Mabinogion,* and "Will you ever win?" echoes the ending of *Triad.* The similes and metaphors in the song are distinctly Nicks's own: Rhiannon is "a cat in the dark" but also "the darkness." The starling of the legend becomes a skylark in "Rhiannon," amid an erotic reference to a bell ringing in the night. "Dreams unwind/Love's a state of mind" is also Nicks's unique voice.

Work was quick: Nicks claimed the skeleton of the song came to her in a few minutes, as though an ancient voice were being channeled through her. An A minor chord against F, bumped up to C: the enchantress became a symbol of uplift as well as of the power of music to soothe. Nicks left the cassette draft for Buckingham. He found it by the coffeepot with a note: "Here is a new song. You can produce it but don't change it."[19] He didn't, and it became a hit that got her to a new place as an artist and provided her with creative opportunities to which she would repeatedly return.

GLUNK GLUNK

Fame was on the horizon, or just over it, as 1974 approached 1975. In December Mick Fleetwood heard *Buckingham Nicks* at Sound City. Nicks was there that day, recording a demo of "Rhiannon" for the hypothetical *Buckingham Nicks* sequel. She was not Fleetwood's focus, though he supposedly laid eyes on her.[20] He cared more about the epic guitar solo on "Frozen Love," which Olsen played for him along with two other songs from the record, one by Emitt Rhodes and one by Aretha Franklin. Fleetwood took to Olsen's production work on the albums—the orchestration of acoustic and electric guitars, the boosting of low ends of registers—and signed a deal with him. On New Year's Eve, however, Fleetwood called Olsen to report that guitarist Bob Welch had just departed Fleetwood Mac. He remembered "Frozen Love" and asked Olsen if Buckingham might be available.

> "So, that fellow in that band you played me—would you see if that guy would like to join my band?" And I said, "Well, they're going to come as a set. Because they're very much into their own thing, and the only chance of getting them to drop that would be to bring them both on." And he says, "Well, maybe that will work. Can you see if you can convince them to join my band?"
>
> I drop what I was going to do on that New Year's Eve [1974], take my date, and we drive over to Stevie and Lindsey's house. I said, "Hey, Happy New Year" and all of this—I brought over the obligatory bottle of bad champagne—and I said, "Can we talk? Mick Fleetwood would like you to join Fleetwood Mac."

Nicks was intrigued, but Buckingham blanched: "Oh, no, no—I couldn't possibly play anything as good as Peter Green did. How am I supposed to get up there and play 'The Green Manalishi'?"—a mescaline-tormented pileup of heavy-hitting guitar effects and spooky lyrics. But by the end of the evening, after five hours of cajoling, Olsen had convinced the couple to give Fleetwood Mac a go, with no obligation to play "Manalishi," if only for a few weeks.[21]

The tale changes with the teller. Drummer Eddie Ponder remembers Buckingham first hearing from Fleetwood in Washington, DC, at the end of the Everly tour—a two-week stint at the Cellar Door in Georgetown, a small venue that attracted diverse top-flight talent: "While we're walking down the street, Lindsey says, 'I just got a call from Fleetwood Mac, and they want me to join their band.' I said, 'Lindsey, are you out of your mind? You're making four hundred and fifty dollars a week, you've got all your expenses paid, you're working with stars. Why would you want to do that?'"[22] Fleetwood Mac, which was seldom charting and leaching personnel, seemed headed for oblivion.

According to Stephen Davis, Nicks bought Fleetwood Mac's records and thought she and Buckingham had something to contribute. Buckingham, however, hesitated: "Listen to me Stevie, a hundred fucking people have been through Fleetwood Mac. It's like a meat grinder"—a reference to the traumatic departures of Welch; of founding guitarist Green, who was diagnosed with schizophrenia; of Jeremy Spencer, who joined the Children of God cult; and of Danny Kirwan for professional and personal reasons, including drunken altercations with the others. "*We're doing this,*" Davis has Nicks countering. "I'm tired of being a waitress!"[23]

In January 1975, Fleetwood's aide Judy Wong arranged an introduction, which took place at El Carmen, a taqueria on West Third Street founded in 1929 that today still boasts of having the best margaritas in LA. Christine McVie recalls Mick saying to her, ahead of time,

> "Chris, if you *don't* like [Stevie], then it's *not* going to happen." I had never been in a band with another girl before, so it was important. So we met for Mexican food. First, right from their entrance, I was so struck by the way Lindsey looked when he walked in the door—I said to myself, *Wow, this guy is a god.* And then Stevie walked in laughing, *so* cute and *so* tiny, and I took an instant liking to her. She has this wonderful laugh and a fantastic sense of humor. So by the end of that evening, I said, "Mick, let's do this."[24]

Imagine the scene: Stevie rushing from Clementine's to El Carmen dressed in Gibson Girl vintage, flicking long gold hair from her eyes. She takes the hand of her boyfriend, Lindsey, the musician's musician, blue-eyed in jeans and flowy shirt, with mustache, goatee, and a mound of black curls. He has already met Christine, cigarette-breathed, dirty blond, casually dressed in a blouse and denim, both proper and profane in speech; and her jocular, defiantly unsober husband, John, dressed, as Nicks told Ann Powers of NPR, in "shorts, which is what he wore for 25 years, and tennies and a white hat and a little vest."[25] Outside, a white Cadillac making a "glunk glunk" noise pulls up and out pops Mick, tall, thin, bearded, dressed like a fop's alley regular. It was an evening of margaritas (served well past midnight at El Carmen) and laughter that dulled any sense of desperation: the older musicians were looking for another reboot; the younger sought a second chance to make it.

Nicks and Buckingham lasted for another month as a duo, performing four more times in the state that by fluke loved them most: Alabama. On January 28 the Birmingham Fairgrounds hosted them; the next night, Morgan Auditorium in Tuscaloosa, then Jacksonville State University, and finally Birmingham's Municipal Auditorium, where they had also played on August 25, 1974. Buckingham dominated, and during his guitar fantasias Nicks sometimes left the stage for a sip of wine. University of Alabama electrical engineering student William Alford made a reel-to-reel recording of the Tuscaloosa concert through the console. "Lola" sounds terrific—tighter, faster, and giddier than the album version.[26] Nicks also premiered "Rhiannon." Alford's tape is one of two bootlegged recordings of the song from the Alabama run. Nicks told the Tuscaloosa crowd of six hundred that "Rhiannon" was inspired by a book about "a lady with two personalities, and I thought it was so fascinating and I just had to write a song about it. She's a little weird, but . . . I hope you like it because it's brand new." She giggles, turns to the band and says, "And don't play it too fast." The band plays it too fast.[27]

In Jacksonville, "her hair falling in a long, tangled heap of curls . . . sometimes serious . . . almost demonic at times," Nicks announced that she and Buckingham had joined another group.[28] The crowd booed, then cheered a bit when she gave its name. Polydor lacked faith in her, she told the entertainment guide *Birmingham after Dark*. Just as relocating had propelled her father to the top, joining Fleetwood Mac would allow her to skip several steps ahead:

> It would take us years to build up the reputation they have. And Warner Brothers is really into Fleetwood Mac. They're not a monster or a giant act, but they consistently sell more albums than they did the last time. They're going to put us on a long major tour where we'll be playing to everyone. And they are super nice people, so we figured it will be a tremendous learning experience. They can help us and we can help them, so it will be a give and take thing.[29]

That it was.

BDE

What Fleetwood Mac "did not need," Nicks recounted years later, was "another girl."[30] It needed instead her specific "BDE," the bella donna energy she absorbed, and tempered, from the female rock icons preceding her: Janis Joplin and Grace Slick, for certain, but also Bonnie O'Farrell of Delaney & Bonnie and Lydia Pense of Cold Blood.[31] Their voices gave music a bold, fearless, radio-unfriendly edge that the hit parade couldn't countenance.

Joplin and Slick we know, less so O'Farrell (later Bramlett) and Pense. Born in Granite City, Illinois, in 1944, O'Farrell began her career as a blue-eyed blues backup singer, performing with the peripatetic who's who of southern US musicians (the list includes Gregg Allman, Charlie Daniels, Stephen Stills, and Tina Turner). Her childhood was wrecked by violence, and she escaped to Los Angeles. There, at a bowling alley concert in 1967, she met musician Delaney Bramlett, whom she married. The duo cut several records of Nashville-style R&B; the song "Soul Shake" stands out. Prominent tours followed with Eric Clapton and George Harrison, who learned slide guitar with Bramlett. O'Farrell almost had a big break when Mick Jagger asked her to sing (or shrilly *over*sing) on "Gimme Shelter," but her husband loathed the Stones and forced her to decline the offer by claiming a sore throat.[32] The marriage dissolved in a haze of heroin and highballs. O'Farrell never stopped hustling, recording in a broad range of styles: blues, country, funk, and most recently gospel as a born-again Christian. Nicks met her through Olsen, who had enlisted Delaney & Bonnie drummer Jim Keltner for the 1973 *Buckingham Nicks* album. In the early nineties Mick Fleetwood recruited the Bramletts' daughter Bekka, a rockabilly performer, for his spin-off band the Zoo. Bekka also subbed for Nicks on tour in 1993–95 and replaced her as vocalist on the Fleetwood Mac album *Time* (1995).

Pense was born a year before Nicks in San Francisco. She sang brass-driven blues in the late sixties and "East Bay grease" (funk) thereafter. Blond-haired, dark-eyed, and diminutive, she was arguably the mightiest of the mighty "blues belters" of the period, overpowering the saxophones and brasses of her band Cold Blood and compared positively to the Joplin of "Piece of My Heart."[33] Pense's agent ruined her chances by greedily signing her to two labels simultaneously (taboo in the industry). Her career "stalled" and she was forced to keep it real and local—as "living proof that blazing talent is but one part of the formula for artistic success. For every Stevie Nicks, there are singers of endless promise who for a variety of reasons—bad management, weak material or woeful airplay—can't seem to make it to the top."[34]

Nicks most often acknowledges the influence of Joplin, noting an occasion at the start of her career, "a hot summer day in 1970," when her band Fritz opened for Joplin but played much too long. "Being yelled off the stage by Janis Joplin was one of the greatest honors of my life," she joked before her second Rock & Roll Hall of Fame inauguration, in 2019.[35] Joplin gave Fritz a profanity-laden scolding, but Nicks lingered after the rest of Fritz scurried away, captivated by Joplin's sound and look.[36] Although she didn't mention Patti Smith when describing her musical upbringing, a connection has been made by Amanda Petrusich: "Nicks is hyperfeminine, intuitive, and bohemian; Smith is androgynous, cerebral, and gritty. But both are unusually perceptive chroniclers of their time and place."[37]

THE WHITE ALBUM

Fleetwood Mac found new life as an amalgam of the blues, rock, and folk with fresh ideas from Nicks's journals and cassette tapes and borrowings from the Beatles and Beach Boys. Three weeks after the meeting at El Carmen, with Olsen planted behind the console in Sound City's Studio A, Fleetwood Mac began to do what it had not done before— produce different varieties of generically accessible music: anodyne chill-outs (the single released in the United Kingdom, "Warm Ways"), good-time sing-alongs, a meditation on life's seasons, and an ode to a witch. John McVie had the hardest time adapting to Fleetwood Mac's new reality, at one point going up to Olsen and saying, "Keith, you know we used to be a blues band?" "Yeah, I know, John," Olsen retorted. "But it's a lot shorter drive down to this bank."[38]

Nicks contributed "Landslide," "Rhiannon," and the redone "Crystal" to "the white album," as the eponymous 1975 Fleetwood Mac disc is nicknamed. She sang on all the tracks. It's a record of leftovers that is perceived as a successful "convergence" partly because of the arranging, elaborating, and polishing that brought demos to the airwaves.[39] The album was officially recorded in the first three months of 1975 for a release date of July 11, 1975, but the dates don't reflect the protracted genesis of the material before Nicks and Buckingham joined Fleetwood Mac. Olsen took this material and bleached it. *Fleetwood Mac* is Motown's, R&B's, and Blaxploitation's antithesis, suburban rather than downtown, a treatment for the band's former blues that might not have succeeded were it not for Nicks's hard work on the road. "We just played everywhere and we sold that record," she told *Uncut*. "We kicked that album in the ass."[40]

The kicking began well before the album was released. The band rehearsed and tuned-up onstage in San Diego, then opened a two-leg, twelve-month tour with a concert in Edmonton, Alberta, on May 5, 1975, followed by a mid-month show at the County Coliseum in El Paso, a jaunt through southern and central Texas, and a flight from Austin to Detroit for a swing through the Midwest into the Northeast. "The great British-American-male-female-old-new-blues-rock-ballad band" (the ads read) toured for seven months straight on the first leg and then almost five months (April 22 to September 5, 1976) on the second leg.[41] Fleetwood Mac hotfooted it to the Calgary Stampede and straggled into the Trenton War Memorial, traveling in between to one-nighters at fairgrounds, speedways, colleges, and ice rinks. The band would leave for the next gig before the set for the last one was struck. It was a high-and-low affair, marred by a dispute with a deposed Fleetwood Mac manager, Clifford Davis, who, in one of the most audacious cons in rock 'n' roll history, sent a lesser-skilled copy of the band on the road before the real one began touring. In addition, Fleetwood Mac's August 7, 1975, show in Vancouver was hamstrung by aircraft-engine trouble (the band drove three hours from Seattle) and equipment problems. "For two-thirds of the concert, [Nicks] could not be heard, and it seemed she would be relegated to just standing around looking beautiful." Her singing sounded "strained" through Buckingham's monitor.[42]

Nicks pushed the album up the charts and into the music industry's flagship magazine *Rolling Stone,* hurting her voice in the process. She promoted *Fleetwood Mac* in venues as small as Trod Nossel Studios in New Haven, Connecticut, whose owner gave away free tickets—first fifty callers win!—for an up close and personal Fleetwood Mac concert that was also broadcast on local radio. She didn't respect the limits of her range and didn't get enough sleep, so her throat, she told her mother, was perpetually sore. But she toiled heroically, and audiences responded. "Lindsey brings to the band a lyrically powerful guitar style and a strong sense of melody. Stevie's vocals are twangy, with an edge that provides a pleasant contrast to Christine's smoothness," the *Courier News* of Blytheville, Arkansas, let its readers know.[43] Readers of the *Capital Times* in Madison, Wisconsin, were told more:

> During a big, foot-stomping number she will unburden herself with a sort of gritty, raspy, scratchy voice that says, "this mama knows what she's talkin' about." . . . But look at her: she's wearing a delicate black dress bare at the midriff and with a gauzy black veil thrown over her shoulders, and while drummer Mick Fleetwood sets up a wall of authoritative rock behind her, she floats and glides around the stage as though she were listening to a minuet. It looks a little odd at first, as though a glitter-struck young singer had dreamed up a costume and image for herself and then slipped the nearest band over her fantasies like a long black glove.[44]

Nicks's majorette razzle-dazzle, her indigo denim bell-bottoms, all-black top-hatted ensemble, chokers, silken cardigans, patterned skirts, and ankle- and knee-high boots became the focal point of Fleetwood Mac performances, with "Rhiannon" her musical emphasis.

In 2020, *Rolling Stone* gushed about a June 11, 1976, rendition on the television variety show *Midnight Special,* noting that after about four minutes, "there's a hush and you think the song is over." But no, "the music speeds up. [Nicks] stares through the camera and right into your very soul. She's belting now: 'Take me like the wind, baby! Take me with the sky!' Lindsey backs her with a couple of power strums. Total shawl-hair fusion. It's a little scary how intensely Stevie quakes, chanting Rhiannon's name, and you notice how steely she looks under all that black lace. She practically jumps out of her boots for that nine-second final howl, and then—like Rhiannon—she's gone." In the studio version, the earthy groove beneath the singing is a precise loop: four tracks are given to Buckingham's riff and strummed guitars; the overlaid background vocals are impeccably seductive. On *Midnight Special*, Nicks takes the song to another level, performing as Rhiannon instructed, becoming "the coolest thing in the universe."[45]

She presented herself to the public unafraid and unabashed, the inherent passion of a teenager cultivated and embraced rather than repressed in her twenties, thirties, and beyond. Nicks entered Rhiannon's space and stayed in a world of powers unrecognized by her bandmates. Over time, she made those powers known, first by transforming Fleetwood Mac into her own star vehicle, and later as an independent artist. Imported into the mystique were gestures and poses taken from ballet, which she must have studied in childhood (later, she would claim she'd taken lessons with a Russian ballet teacher, and she put a ballet studio in her Phoenix house). Photographs suggest she was relatively flexible stretching at the barre, despite bending her standing leg.[46] Her feet are weakly pointed in the tendu and sus-sous poses. However imperfect, her balletic onstage movements, mixed with steps taken from other genres, set her apart from all other rock 'n' rollers.

In counterpoint to Nicks's "sinuous dancing and raw, gutsy vocal," Christine McVie sat behind a keyboard, unflamboyant and staid, her dreaming confined to sentimental ballads about Harlequin romance–type love.[47] The contrast between them caught reviewers' attention. Yin and yang, they didn't seem to notice each other onstage; their voices, however, blended perfectly. Between shows they stuck together, and it was McVie, rather than Nicks, who learned to put Buckingham in his place when his bossiness rankled John McVie and Mick Fleetwood, the band's ancien régime. Nicks deferred to Buckingham in the studio, though never on the road. The deference lessened as the Welsh witch's powers grew.

There were bad reviews, nights spent sleeping on top of equipment, horrible meals, and long stretches between showers—the typical experiences of rock bands. Conditions immensely improved as ticket and record sales increased, with the high life glimpsed and then, at the end of 1975, realized. Nicks and Buckingham and their Alabama backing band had begun the year modestly, receiving a flat fee of $2,750 and free wine for a sixty-minute appearance on January 31 in Birmingham.[48] Recording *Fleetwood Mac* in the early spring and learning Peter Green's most popular songs for her new band's tour, Nicks earned $200 a week and was able to settle old debts.[49] By the time Fleetwood Mac reached Diamond Head on Oahu for a tour-ending New Year's Eve appearance at "Hawaii's Woodstock," she no longer needed to ask how much something—anything—cost before buying it.

RUMOURS

Fleetwood Mac was still rising up the charts as the second record was begun, and the problem of improving on the formula—should the new record repeat, reject, or revise?—weighed on the band. The pressure was also felt, acutely, by a new producer, Ken Caillat, who had befriended Richard Dashut in Los Angeles at Wally Heider Recording and joined forces with him on the project after Olsen exited in a dispute over profits.[50] The *Fleetwood Mac* compendium took mere months to produce and package up. *Rumours* stretched out over a year of combat, love, and loss. Recording began in Sausalito at the Power Plant and ended, after Fleetwood Mac toured and took a much-needed break from one another, in Los Angeles.

Meanwhile, singer-songwriter Walter Egan, a transplanted New Yorker, was working on demos at Sound City in Van Nuys. He had been hoping for Brian Wilson or Todd Rundgren to produce his first album, *Fundamental Roll*, but Wilson was struggling with addiction, and Rundgren was seriously overbooked. In May 1976, Duane Scott, an engineer at Sound City, gave Egan the first solo disc by Buckingham and Nicks; he loved it. He met with Buckingham and watched him overdub harmonies on a track of his own. For a few days in June, in between their Fleetwood Mac commitments, Nicks and Buckingham produced and performed for *Fundamental Roll* and contributed as well to the record that followed. Nicks's contribution on the salacious song "Tunnel o' Love," taped in the pre-dawn hours with the studio lights dimmed, stoked Egan's romantic interest in her. He dropped her off at her apartment at Olympic and La Cienega utterly besotted.[51] Pressing his feelings forward complicated his relationship with Buckingham, though Egan insists that Nicks and Buckingham were estranged during this time. (Egan also had a girlfriend.) The matter ended with the writing and recording of Egan's second-album single "Magnet and Steel," which less describes mutual attraction than infatuation. "Stevie's a chapter in my life," Egan began his description of the making of the massive hit, "but I'm just a footnote in hers."[52]

Egan recalls leaving the studio at three in the morning, driving to Pomona behind a "pimped-out" Lincoln Continental painted in metal-flake deep blue with twinkling lights around the windows. The license plate, "NOT SHY," provided the ironic title of the shy musician's second album.[53] Egan conceived "Magnet and Steel" in a retro doo-wop style with soothing vocals, golden harmonization, and a laid-back 6/8 tempo. "I wanted to write a 'stroll' which was influenced by a dance shown on American Bandstand when I was young," he commented. "It had a cadence I'd always loved."[54] Buckingham suggested the toy piano heard behind the chorus. He, Nicks, and a member of the *Fundamental Roll* touring band, Annie McLoone, sang backing vocals that were recorded a cappella before being added to the guitar, bass, and drum tracks. The snare of the intro represents the magnetic pull while the toy piano supplies metallic twinkle. Egan sings "Magnet and Steel" at a sock hop in the pre-MTV-era video, and there are photographs of him with Nicks dressed as a cheerleader and Buckingham in a letter sweater from Egan's high school.[55] (The disheveled, squint-eyed photographer Moshe Brakha gave Nicks the creeps.) "Magnet and Steel" has been used in movies: Paul Thomas Anderson gave it pride of place in his R-rated tribute to Burt Reynolds and the seventies, *Boogie Nights,* as did Jason Bloom in the rom-com *Overnight Delivery.* Egan took *Not Shy* on the road in 1978, and Buckingham and Nicks joined him onstage for "Magnet and Steel" and other audience pleasers. Comedian John Belushi heard the penultimate show of the tour on Thanksgiving eve at the Roxy Theatre in Los Angeles. Near the end he convinced Egan to allow him up onstage with his band, Nicks and Buckingham included, for an impromptu performance of Elvis Presley's "Jailhouse Rock."[56] Egan didn't see Nicks much more after that, but for him her magnetism never waned.[57]

Rumours was released before Egan's album, on February 4, 1977. It was Fleetwood Mac's eleventh record, but just the second with Nicks and Buckingham energizing the lineup. No more pretense, no more meandering improvisations that failed to chart: the new Fleetwood Mac followed the three-minute, radio-friendly songwriting formula. "By the time [*Rumours*] was made," journalist Jessica Hopper eulogizes, "the personal freedoms endowed by the social upheaval of the sixties had unspooled into unfettered hedonism. As such, it plays like a reaping: a finely polished post-hippie fallout, unaware that the twilight hour of the free love era was fixing and there would be no going back." Nicks's Rhiannon was in, the magical housewives of the sixties sitcom *Bewitched* out. In 1976, Hopper continues, "There was no knowledge of AIDS, Reagan had just left the governor's manse, and people still thought of cocaine as non-addictive and strictly recreational. *Rumours* is a product of that moment and it serves as a yardstick by which we measure just how 70s the 70s were."[58] Once the measure was taken, Mick Fleetwood got mercilessly trolled in the press for becoming fiendishly addicted and leading his bandmates down the same path.[59]

Cocaine is extracted from the paste of the leaves of the *Erythroxylum coca* shrub that grows in the Andes Mountains, and its use goes back over a millennium to Incan spiritual practices. Spanish colonialists permitted enslaved Indigenous peoples to chew the leaves while laboring. When feeling blue, Pope Leo XIII, Queen Victoria, and Ulysses S. Grant enjoyed a coca wine drink called Vin Tonique Mariani (à la Coca du Pérou). Refined by botanists and chemists, in the 1890s cocaine became an indispensable medical additive and supplement. It put American babies to sleep; salespeople hawked it door to door along with detergents and cosmetics; it enriched soda fountains and helped, its promoters promised, with alcoholism. Coca-Cola is still sold in cans of red and white, the colors of the flag of Peru, the country that once supplied its happy-making ingredient. Southern politicians blamed African Americans' "sniffing" for increases in crime—"Negro Cocaine 'Fiends' Are a New Southern Menace," the *New York Times* blared—and so for deeply racist reasons the 1914 Harrison Act curtailed its distribution.[60] Prohibition followed for liquor.

Historian Robert Sabbag adds that cocaine entered the illicit trade "in the twenties and thirties as the drug of choice among musicians and film people, *à la recherche du temps perdu*. [It] was effectively absent during World War II, not to emerge again until the rock years, when musicians picked it up once more."[61] Cocaine became the "life in the fast lane" drug. The 1972 Blaxploitation film *Superfly* associated it with "ambivalence" and "high fashion and sex versus addiction and crime."[62] Traffickers from the city of Medellín, Colombia, routed it through the expat neighborhoods of Los Angeles for distribution, overrunning the Westside "drug princes," whose supplies came from Miami.[63] Before the cartels replaced the locals and the scene turned lethal, the "champagne drug" defined the celebrity high life and those aspiring to it. Fog and dementia rolled in; the dealers and groupies ringing the pool were exposed as "leeches."[64] The 1976 Eagles hit "Hotel California" tells of the dark side: "desperation, panic and imprisonment amid the fountains of champagne, medieval gluttony, sexual deviants and lines of cocaine on the mirror."[65]

Nicks befriended cocaine during the making of *Rumours*. It was nowhere near as dangerous as heroin, everyone believed. She became addicted during the making of *Tusk* and did not extract herself from the "Peruvian flake," to cite one of its nicknames, until the Reagan era. She put her life at risk and could have become another tragic victim of stardom. The premature deaths of hooked artists gave rise to the morbidly fetishistic "27 Club," a listing of those who died at or around that age, then joined "the great gig in the sky."[66] Like Fleetwood, Nicks has been honest about the risk she took—"I was the worst drug addict"—and about how long it took her to check out of the hotel. Clonazepam dependency followed cocaine (she will never forgive "Doctor Fuckhead" for getting her hooked on the anticonvulsant). At the same time, she also "suffered long bouts of chronic fatigue syndrome" after an elective medical procedure.[67]

Before the angst, before the good old days turned bad, *Rumours* topped the *Billboard* chart for thirty-one weeks. In 2003, *Rolling Stone* assigned it the number twenty-six spot on its "500 Greatest Albums of All Time" list because of the symbolism it had accrued: it spoke more to the crackup of the US psyche than to sleeping around.[68] Rob Sheffield marked its February 3, 2017, anniversary by declaring it "an album that has eerie soothing powers when you hear it in the midst of a crisis, which might be why it hits home right now, with our minute-by-minute deluge of apocalyptic news, the rottenest month to be an American since FDR died." The final track is therapeutic: "After all the tantrums and breakdowns and crying fits, the album ends with Stevie Nicks asking you point blank: 'Is it over now? Do you know how to pick up the pieces and go home?' If the answers are 'no' and 'no,' you flip the record and play it again."[69]

The changes in personnel and differences in musical backgrounds make the seamlessness and cohesiveness of the record no less remarkable than the subject matter: the tangled tales about the band's intimate lives.[70] A dissolute Mick Fleetwood came up with the life-as-art concept: "Hey guys, why don't we chill out here and do some *transcending* and just write music about all this hassle?"[71] There is a "desert hearts" vibe to the slower tracks amid the fuck you of "Go Your Own Way," and the subjects of divorce and abjection find their weird antecedent in the testicular fantasy of screwing whatever lover comes your way in a

cornfield. The front cover, a dream image made into best-selling merchandise, has Nicks twirling in black as Rhiannon and Fleetwood in
Renaissance Faire garb—the patriarch with a foot on a stool and a pair
of wooden balls hanging from his belt (good-luck charms, he said,
nicked from a toilet in a bar).[72] She raises and bends her left leg atop his;
he holds a crystal (recycled from the previous Fleetwood Mac album)
into which she might be gazing. The outtakes—the photographs that
didn't make the cover—are more relaxed, even playful.

In the words of *Uncut* magazine's Nigel Williamson, Fleetwood Mac
was "rock's greatest living soap opera" but also a group of musicians
with a contractual obligation who had to turn up at the studio at two
o'clock for a twelve-hour music-making shift.[73] The gossip, the proto–
Melrose Place sordidness, the Bacchic revelries, and the nostalgie de la
boue inspired the album's name while also providing convenient expla-
nations of the lyrics and musical content.[74] These don't quite add up:
Nicks and Buckingham raged at each other while recording "You Make
Loving Fun"—and "I don't want to live with you, either!"—but nailed
the blissfully happy chorus.[75] On "Songbird" Christine McVie sings "I
love you like never before," in her silky alto voice, either in reference to
a hypothetical relationship or to her love for John increasing despite
their marriage ending. The album is framed in popular culture by the
novel *Fear of Flying* and the film *An Unmarried Woman*. Hippies
became swingers hosting key parties. *Rumours* is the seventies, to be
sure, but also a grown-up sixties. It reckons with the consequences of
free love and gazes into a void of pleasure pursued for its own sake.

Nicks changed. *Rumours* taxed her; Buckingham taxed her. "She
loved to laugh," Ken Caillat recalls. "She was so great back then, really
down to earth. What a change she would go through."[76] The same
could be said of the era, which *Rumours*—the good, bad, and forsaken
of it—emblematizes. Her journals from the making of the album and
the long, long tour that followed document the change: "August 24,
1977. One more time, on the plane. As usual Lindsey is his usual ass-
hole self. I am slowly coming to the conclusion that Lindsey and I are at
an end. So good to see good love go bad." Later: "Seattle. Worried
about Christine. Wishing some spiritual guidance would come from
somewhere. Where are the crystal visions when I need them?" Even
later: "As I'm writing prose, I'm also writing songs. 'Gather the cur-
tains, gather the darkness, gather me if only for a moment, gather the
seconds for soon it could be going, gather the blessings, for the years are
showing.'"[77]

Fleetwood Mac cognoscenti prefer the grittier opening and closing tracks of side B of *Rumours* over the pop of side A. "The Chain" pulls together fragments from demo tracks that all the musicians had a hand in fashioning. It opens with modal Dobro resonator guitar, together with a plodding kick drum and lyrics of murk and storm. The little guitar riff at the start is recycled from "Lola (My Love)," a 1973 Buckingham Nicks song especially popular on the duo's Alabama stops. The lyrics for "The Chain" came in at the end, from Nicks's inspired pen, and rescued the assemblage of outtakes from becoming an outtake itself. The close harmonization of the three singers on "listen to the wind blow" gets its mystique from Nicks's alter ego as "Rhiannon." The atmosphere is thick, the pacing expert, leading to the most memorable musical moment on the album: a brief crash cymbal abruptly muted on the upbeat of the second beat of the measure ending the first chorus. It's the equivalent of a sneer or something spit out in disgust. The group sings in lockstep throughout, musically countering their fractious personal affairs. The lyric "Chain, keep us together" sounds like a plea. The coda gives a taste of what a Fleetwood Mac live jam sounds like, as the gritted-teeth tension of the body of the song is released. John McVie's transitional ten-note bass line (taken from Christine McVie's discarded song "Keep Me There") is arguably the iconic album's greatest moment. The unison vocals of the ending suggest, falsely, adamantine commitment.[78]

The final track of side B, "Gold Dust Woman," captures an imagined California as at once the Wild West and an eastern Shangri-La. The ending is raw and primal—the opposite of the polished sensuousness of the other tracks. "The definitive magical Stevie Nicks vocal would have to be 'Gold Dust Woman,'" Caillat marvels. "She was possibly possessed at the end of that song."[79] He's also said that he can't listen to the album, having devoted "at least 3,000 hours" to it. "I spent everything on that, you know, there's nothing left of me ... and I just, really, almost wish I could enjoy it like everybody else. But I ... every time I listen to it, I can remember every part, every issue, every fight, everything. So it's not as much fun for me."[80] The ending of "Gold Dust Woman" did not require as much devotion from the martyred producer. The jamboree was spontaneous.

In a 1976 interview, Nicks described "Gold Dust Woman" in terms that most girls at a high-school party could understand. "It's about groupie-type ladies," she claimed, "about women who stand around and give me and Christine dirty looks but as soon as a guy comes in the room are overcome with smiles."[81] She has also said it's about success and as such reveals some of the secret of her success: the blend of "rock" singing, associated with the masculine, and the full-bodied whispered huskiness and breaks into a thin high register that connote the feminine.[82] Then there is the related price-of-success reading that makes the song about the "black widow" of cocaine, which creates a heightened response to touch, sound, and sight, along with irritation and paranoia. Buckingham offers exotic sitar-like effects on the main guitar line and bays at the moon. Fleetwood plays cowbell and shatters glass.

In a book about gender and rock, Mary Kearney offers both micro and macro perspectives on the song as a "tale of a heartless, drug-addicted woman who preys on a man's affections only to leave him broken and disheartened" and as an example of a "demeaning" representation of a female by a female songwriter. Most such representations, Kearney clarifies, come from men, about whom Nicks rarely sings on her own.[83] Still, most covers of "Gold Dust Woman," fifty and counting, are by women, and one can hear in both the original and the variations the rueful passion that defines Nicks's aesthetic.

Christine McVie's warm, reverberant "Songbird" provides the ambiance the rest of the album suppresses. As Tim Sommer noted, "One of the defining aspects of *Rumours* is claustrophobia. Sonic claustrophobia, that is," such that the listener feels trapped inside Fleetwood's tightly closed hi-hat.[84] To increase the feeling of liberation and openness, "Songbird" was not recorded in Sausalito at the Power Plant but at Zellerbach Hall at UC Berkeley. The choice of location was Caillat's; he had been smitten with the song since he first heard her try it out and wanted to give it a distinct aura. "As a surprise for Christine, I had requested that a bouquet of roses be placed on her piano with three colored spotlights to illuminate them from above. I really wanted to set the mood! . . . When Christine arrived, we dimmed the house lights so that all she could see were the flowers and the piano with the spotlight shining down from the heavens. She nearly broke into tears. Then she started to play."[85] The piano sound is huge on the recording, enriched only by intentionally understated acoustic guitar accompaniment.

The harmonization on the album, as "The Chain" demonstrates, is tight and close, as the Power Plant's acoustics prescribe. The electric guitars and keyboards share wah pedals, and the acoustic guitar lines are equalized to pick up the higher frequencies. The glossiness is comparable but not identical to Brian Wilson's aural watercolors. Layers of overdubs are nonetheless spacious enough for the ear to isolate each line, the album premised on the addition of discrete sounds across bridges and between verses and choruses. Christine McVie's "Don't Stop" is perhaps the strongest example of one voice part grafted onto another, but it is also the bluntest, least nuanced song on the album, so precisely calibrated for the baby-boomer hit parade that it became fodder for Bill Clinton's 1992 political campaign. McVie had kicked it around before the *Rumours* recording sessions, and it belongs, contra the lyrics, to the jangle piano past. McVie and Buckingham share duties, singing in tandem in the verses, finishing each other's phrases in the chorus, such that her voice cannot be distinguished from his. Each seems to forget what the other had done. Nicks is much less audible; the other two band members grind along, stopping at the base of the crescendos, starting again to fill them out. "Yesterday's Gone" was going to be the title of the album. *Rumours* (with the English spelling as a nod to the band's history) won out.

"DREAMS"

Nicks played tambourine and other instruments during the sessions for the foundational tracks, but she wasn't mic'ed, and the band would rerecord all her percussion contributions later.[86] Her singing defined this iteration of Fleetwood Mac, but because she did not contribute any instrumental tracks, she was left with little to do for hours at a time. The original Sausalito Power Plant had two studios along with a Jacuzzi, basketball court, speedboat, and kitchen with a dedicated chef. Studio A had a sunburst pattern on one of the walls; Studio B was decorated with multicolored giant-sized petals. Producer and musician Sly Stone designed and decorated a sunken den with giant red lips as an entrance and synthetic red fur on the walls. Nicks sat on the canopied four-poster bed (which Stone had wired up to a console, allowing him to record while prone), writing in her journal, doing macramé, and noodling on the keyboard.

In this semi-sleazy setting, she came up with a number-one hit, "Dreams," fitting the tune and lyrics atop three chords. She brought the song out to Studio B and recorded "a rough take, just me singing solo and playing piano." Nicks recalls Buckingham being mad at her at the time (when was he not?) but listening with a smile. "What was going on between us was sad—we were couples who couldn't make it through," Nicks recalled. "But, as musicians, we still respected each other."[87] That smile admitted the song's potential, once the original ascending harmonic pattern (Fmaj7, G, A minor) was elaborated into an introduction and three-part form. The first verse cedes to a pre-chorus and an expression of regret—"what you lost/what you had"—that is made poignant with the addition of a ninth to the chord on F and seventh to the chord on G. It is followed by the "thunder" chorus, the second verse, the pre-chorus again, and two concluding iterations of the chorus. It registers different emotions, warmer and cooler, like a musical mood ring.

The demo is moodier than the polished release, as Caillat acknowledges in his account of the arranging and recording. The breaks in Nicks's voice suggest feelings playing on thought, and the worrying of the pitches betrays a folk influence that the studio scrubbed. The tune relies on just five such pitches and doesn't like to end in sync with the accompaniment. D needs to resolve to C but hesitates, giving the song its "hypnotic" aspect.[88] In the studio the hypnosis increased, becoming more akin to the trance referenced in the text through the looping of sounds, including the bass drum and hi-hat sound at the start. The tape track was played through in search of the "most perfect" sample, Caillat relates:

> Believe it or not, we couldn't find eight perfect bars, so we had to have Mick play about a minute of the verse to get them perfectly steady. Eight bars took about sixteen seconds to play. At fifteen inches per second, this meant that about twenty feet of tape would need to be cut out of the drum take and spliced together, front to back, to make a continuous loop. Our tape loop would be a twenty-foot-long circle. . . .
>
> She sang the song eight or nine times, but something was off. She couldn't find the same mood she had had the first time she had sung it. But she was a trouper and didn't give up. Lindsey played an acoustic guitar for her to sing to. Nope. She tried smoking a joint. Better. The big guns came out—Courvoisier. Interesting. She tried a magic bump [a small spoonful of the white stuff]. Nothing had the feel of her original vocal.[89]

Ultimately, something of that original vocal was retrieved, and preserved, along with the Sly Stone–inspired reveries. In a review of the album, John Rockwell dismissed the "trippy" lyrics but praised Nicks's "husky, nasal, sensuously confident soprano" and flower child image as a match for Christine's fuss-free alto "earthiness."[90]

Nicks often gives her "kids" (songs) mystical single-word titles. "Dreams" is the first in a long list. The opening guitar swells create a certain vibe (much as the Mellotron does in the Beatles' "Strawberry Fields Forever"), and the word "thunder" receives a cymbal crash. The lyric "Now here you go again/You say you want your freedom" is a message to Lindsey Buckingham but also a timeless sentiment for anyone in the midst of a breakup. After much discussion, "Dreams" was placed on the album between Buckingham's "Second Hand News" and "Never Going Back Again," such that his harsh goodbyes frame her "you'll regret this."[91] In an early take of "Go Your Own Way," he sings "You can go your own way / You can roll like thunder, yeah yeah," but the final version has the line "You can call it another lonely day."[92] She stole his thunder.

"Dreams" incorporates smooth R&B textures and the moodiness, much in vogue in the mid-seventies, of Steely Dan's *Aja,* released the same year as *Rumours.*[93] To enhance the song's intimacy, or "proximity," Caillat "put a rubber band around a wind-screen and [placed] that on the microphone, making sure the wind-screen was about a half-inch from the front of the mic. I'd say, 'Keep your lips up against that wind-screen,' and that way I got a lot of bottom, to which I'd then add top if I wanted to."[94] He softened the edges of the attack in the guitar with swell pedal and rotating (Leslie) speaker. The bass throbs in a syncopated two-note pattern in tandem with the bass-drum pedal. The background singing imitates the Beach Boys, and the phaser on the hi-hat suggests something aquatic to Caillat, a "slightly squishy and swirling" sound, something sharing the frequency of the theremin-infused megahit "Good Vibrations." The Spinners' track "I'll Be Around" includes vibraphone and perhaps prompted Caillat to add the crystal-clear tone of that instrument to the second pre-chorus. Using a Wurlitzer in the transition from verse to chorus and a Fender Rhodes in the chorus gave the song the "classy" quality (at least by the twenty-fourth take) Caillat wanted for it.[95] But "Dreams" remained Nicks's song. She is "on the mic, bringing both the thunder and the rain, her unguarded, open-veined rasp painting every one of her crystal visions in such rich, vibrant color that they actually sound like they're causing Buckingham's guitars to openly weep."[96]

For all the anguish in the band, this song, like the others on *Rumours,* affirms that bad lovers can make good music. Nicks speaks of what Buckingham had and what he lost, urging him to "listen carefully to the sound of . . . loneliness." Here and in the gorgeous, forsaken "Silver Springs," Nicks cautions her bad lover that her voice will always echo in his head. He won't escape it, and indeed Buckingham never has. Haunting—as a crossing of here and now with then and there—remains a theme.

MARYLAND

The tale of the making and abandoning of this now-iconic song attests to Nicks's precarious second-tier status in Fleetwood Mac at the time; it also foreshadows the first of her exits from the band. The best guess is that Nicks conceived it while on the first leg of the 1975–76 Fleetwood Mac tour, her relationship with Buckingham on the rocks. The band would have passed Silver Springs, Maryland, en route to a gig in DC. She picked the town's name for the song and recorded a draft on cassette.[97] The words speak of her faithfulness despite his faithlessness: "You'll never get away from the sound of the woman that loved you." Buckingham detested it but saw its potential, perhaps including the potential to excise its stabbing lyrics. He and Caillat began to arrange it.

Sections resemble Peter Green's "Albatross," released by Fleetwood Mac as a single in 1968. "Silver Springs" also has country intonations and so perhaps echoes Nicks's grandfather—the music sung by Aaron Jess Nicks Sr. The opening is cast in a silvery translucent C/F major heard high in the keyboard; the chorus drops to A minor before building to a spell-binding, then shattering, climax. In the words and music, the sylph becomes the sorceress, enacting revenge on her former suitor. She just might tear his heart to pieces like he did hers. The drama is enacted in several of Nicks's power ballads, this one the most powerful of all, owing to the patient co-opting of the listener's attention and the upward push of the chorus, an act of sheer will that pulls minor back to major. The atmosphere changes from deceptive calm (keyboard) to resignation (Nicks's iterated "I don't want to know"), after which there is the click track–aided breakthrough of the chorus, and the provocation of Buckingham's solo that sparks Nicks's fury in the outro. "Was I just a fool?" The question isn't answered; it's never been answered.

The song moves from halcyon lull and rather flat affect into a cri de coeur that pushes the pitches of the tune away, along with all of the happy arrogance of Buckingham's guitarwork. At the low point Nicks gets up off the mat, as represented by the alignment and assemblage of the tracks into loud unison declarations. (The melodic line ascends in the chorus, but the harmonization sinks, first-inversion A minor falling to first-inversion G and F major.) Caillat remembers plane-crash simulations in the studio:

> We had cut "Silver Springs" with the Fender Rhodes keyboard, electric guitar, bass, and drums and Stevie's vocal work on Wednesday, so that's where we started. We needed to get the basic track just right; ultimately, we'd use a grand piano on it, but for now the Rhodes was fine as a placeholder for the grand piano later. Laying out a song this way often meant that we'd have to use our imaginations to fill in the sounds until we added the other parts.

We got about nineteen takes, some all the way through, others just par-
tials. Yet none of them were right, and, finally, we just ran out of steam.
Perhaps relying on our imaginations just wasn't good enough. Richard
[Dashut] and Mick did a couple of skits to break up the work. One of their
favorites was reenacting a plane crash, as odd as that sounds.

That was in Sausalito. In Los Angeles, Caillat and the band listened to
the work they had done and concluded that the song needed much more
work; it still sounded "thin" and "empty" and had to go.[98]

Rolling Stone cites a 1991 BBC radio interview in which Nicks said
Fleetwood met with her in the Record Plant parking lot to break the
news, as the band's manager, that "Silver Springs" had been excised
because it was too long. Twenty-two minutes was the maximum length
for the side of an LP before sound quality diminished, he explained.
"Second Hand News" could have been dropped to give "Silver Springs"
a place on *Rumours,* but no. There were "a lot of [other] reasons" to
cut it.[99] These included Buckingham's inability to get over the lyrics and
the need for equal representation of the other songwriters on the album.
"Silver Springs" would have been the third Nicks ballad, after "Dreams"
and "Gold Dust Woman." All wasn't lost—Caillat wanted to preserve
the song and continue working on it in Los Angeles—but Nicks was
inconsolable. She launched into a profane tirade at Fleetwood in the
parking lot and stormed off. He wondered if she'd return. Nicks had
dedicated the song to her mother, which added to her anger and humil-
iation: "When I first recorded 'Silver Springs,' I gave it to my mother
as a present," she reminisced. "My mother would never take a penny
from me"—in truth, she didn't have to, given her husband's success in
business—"so I figured the only way I could actually give her some
money was to give her a song to put away for a rainy day. She got the
whole thing—publishing, royalties, everything. . . . She'd even opened
an antique store and called it Silver Spring Emporium. Then they took
it off the record, so it was very much a dud gift. It was like, 'Well Mom,
guess what? It's not going on the record, and I'm really sorry.'"[100]

"Silver Springs" ended up on the B-side of the "Go Your Own Way"
single and in greatest-hits packages. The hurt lasted, and the band and
Warner Brothers exploited it on the impassioned performance that
serves as the official music video. Buckingham's gaze sends daggers
across the stage as Nicks sings the line "Really, I don't wanna know,"
changing the lyric from the original "Baby, I don't wanna know." She
retorts with "But you won't forget me." The rest of the 1997 performance is a staring match, expertly filmed, the two of them making space

for each other on the stage. The entreaties of the opening verses are negated as the sound builds to remarkable emotional intensity before artificially dissipating.[101] "When we're [onstage] there singing songs to each other, we probably say more to each other than we ever would in real life," Nicks explains. She despised "Go Your Own Way" as much as he despised "Silver Springs," especially the third verse. "Every time those words ['packin' up, shackin' up is all you want to do'] would come onstage," she added, "I wanted to go over and kill him. He knew it. He really pushed my buttons through that. It was like 'I'll make you suffer for leaving me.' And I did."[102] Other performances of "Silver Springs" mirror the standoff; it became, for the two of them, an obsession, a publicly repeated what-could-have-been catharsis. At a 2004 show in Madison, Wisconsin, Nicks walks away from her microphone with the back of her hand on her mouth, in what looks like an emotional moment, but then flips into dancing, twirling, and air drumming, facing Fleetwood and with her back to the audience. She then picks up her mic stand and turns it to face Buckingham as they engage in another set-to.[103]

The version that ended up on Nicks's 2001 solo album *Crystal Visions* features rerecorded guitar lines, delays, swells, and harmonics.[104] This version has a much harder, faster feel and fades out on the chorus, as opposed to returning, resigned, to the intro.

"I DON'T WANT TO KNOW"

"Silver Springs" was replaced on *Rumours* by "I Don't Want to Know," also by Nicks. It harkens back to the Buckingham Nicks days and an earlier popular-music syntax, with a I-V-IV-V chord progression, handclaps, and bright McCartney-style bass line bouncing from the root of one chord to another. The other throwback on the album is "Never Going Back Again," which highlights Buckingham's picking style. Evidently on Caillat's advice, he changed his strings every twenty minutes while tracking the song. "I wanted to get the best sound on every one of his picking parts," Caillat claims. "I'm sure the roadies wanted to kill me. Restringing the guitar three times every hour was a bitch. But Lindsey had lots of parts on the song, and each one sounded magnificent."[105] The song's style is rustic, recalling the San Francisco folk scene of the late sixties. To hear "I Don't Want to Know" and "Never Going Back Again" alongside "Dreams" is to hear the changes in popular music across the decade.

Keyboards and a thick bass sound over crisp beats are the gin of blue-eyed soul and the tonic of seventies light rock, with maracas, tambourine, and vibraphone included. The original Fleetwood Mac appropriated African American music, as did the SoCal recording business. Songs took time to find their identities. "Dreams" was originally called "Spinners," according to an August 21, 1976, track sheet.[106] The groove recalled the R&B group of that name, specifically the track "I'll Be Around."

LOVE AND HATE

Buckingham increased his role in the production of *Rumours* midway through the twelve-month process. In May 1976 the rest of the band took a break from one another and the project. Buckingham went back to work before the others, redeveloping several of the songs in Los Angeles.[107] Stephen Davis recounts the final phase of recording, and the fact that the time spent in Sausalito almost went to waste:

> March 1976. Fleetwood Mac was leaving the Record Plant after several tormented months, returning to their homes in Los Angeles to finish the new album. . . . They played their tapes, which didn't sound right in a different studio. There was panic until someone found Producer's Workshop, a mixing room tucked amidst the sleazy porn theaters along Hollywood Boulevard, and their tapes at least sounded good enough to work on. Now, while Stevie took her friends off to a holiday in Acapulco, Lindsey and the two producers basically discarded almost everything they'd done so far except the drum tracks, and Fleetwood Mac began to dub in new instrumental parts and all the vocals. Once more the subsonic vibrations of the group heartache filled the atmosphere as the three writers—Stevie, Chris, and Lindsey—kept telegraphing punches via their new lyrics.
>
> The studio had a pretty young receptionist, Carol Ann Harris. She was in her mid-twenties, smart and blond, with blue eyes and a great smile. Lindsey took up with her, and she began to hang around the studio to be with him after her working hours.[108]

Harris was Buckingham's on-again, off-again girlfriend from the time of *Rumours* through to 1984 and his second solo album, *Go Insane*. Her guileless fantasies of the rock 'n' roll high life crashed into the nightmare of physical assault that she avenges in her memoir. She describes Buckingham's hands squeezing her neck, his eyes bulging with anger; the dismissal of Mick Fleetwood as manager; burglaries; an eviction; a car accident; and the "cutthroat competitive battle" with Nicks that became "all-out-war" with the success of Nicks's first solo album.[109]

As to the "subsonic vibrations of the group heartache," Fleetwood Mac profited from and then became a prisoner of its own melodrama. The musicians have never really escaped the love-hate songs of their twenties and thirties.

The problem with the tapes began in Sausalito, where the twenty-four-track machine at the Record Plant proved inadequate for the intricate vocal and instrumental texture expected for the sequel to *Fleetwood Mac*. On *Rumours* more groups of tracks than typical had to be "bounced—mixed down to a single track—to save space," and "over 60 tracks" ended up getting printed on a "single [master] reel of tape," the technicians told Richard Buskin of webzine *Sound on Sound*. Another challenge was posed by the dead acoustics of the padded, smoke-filled studios and control room and the thin, dull sound running through the lines. Caillat and Dashut twirled knobs and adjusted feeds in an anxious effort to enrich the sound. The wear and tear on the deck and the leaching of oxide from the oft-rewound multitrack tape dulled the sound further.[110] The high frequencies of the percussion were especially impacted.

The band relocated to Los Angeles after the two months in Sausalito, some songs still unfinished or, like "Silver Springs," needing cuts. Caillat and Dashut returned to their regular employer, Wally Heider Recording on Sunset and Cahuenga Boulevard, in hopes of salvaging the *Rumours* master tape, which sounded worse and worse. The solution was found in another studio, ABC Dunhill, on Beverly Boulevard, and a technician named Bob Bullock, who invented a method for transferring tracks between the second-generation backup, or "safety" master, and the original first-generation master.[111] Bullock went back to the original multitrack of the drums and tried to mix it with the current master (the one with all the tracks) to bring the drums back to life. In doing so, he had to account for the variable speeds of different tape machines by hand, a mind-boggling task. He also had to go back through the bounce history to recover the better-quality original tracks. Caillat adds that "when it came time to mix *Rumours* (five months later), we found a pristine little mix room that specialized in super clean electronics, called Producers Workshop (where Lindsey met Carol). Me, Dashut, and the entire band spent two weeks and mixed the final version of *Rumours* over Christmas 1976."[112]

Meanwhile, Buckingham tinkered with the guitar parts on the most commercial songs and the percussion on "Second Hand News." The background is an unpretentious shuffle behind locomotive strumming.

Bright acoustic guitar (with Nashville tuning) decorates the end of each phrase of the verse, as if in response to Buckingham's singing, and a distorted second electric guitar injects energy midway through before bursting into an affirmative lead part in the coda and fade-out. Hearing the initial mix, Buckingham balked at Fleetwood's drum pattern, and while the rest of the band was on hiatus in May 1976, he recorded an additional percussion part apparently inspired by the Bee Gees' "Jive Talkin'"—the sixteenth-note popping sound—played on the back of an office chair.[113] The tapping enhances the hook of a song that is basically all hook, with syncopated "bow ba dow" scatting and the titular line of the chorus repeated over and over, as is Buckingham's "Lay me down in the tall grass and let me do my stuff."

The personal disputes intensified, but the band remained together despite Buckingham announcing the opposite in "Go Your Own Way," whose lyrics are incidental to the hook and propulsion of the music. The song is richer than it sounds at first, owing to the inclusion of a doubled six-string acoustic guitar on the back end of phrases as counterrhythm to the straight-ahead chugging of the electric guitar. Fleetwood, a generally unintrusive drummer, opts for sparse tom-tom interjections in the verses before powering the "four on the floor" chorus with a thudding bass drum. Buckingham had calculated randomness in mind for Fleetwood's part before the first chorus, and Fleetwood tried to accommodate it. ("Street Fighting Man," by the Rolling Stones, probably provided inspiration.) The drums go their own way before locking in for the words "go your own way," a paradox Fleetwood attributed to ineptitude and dyslexia.[114] Decorum and restraint end in the chorus; spitefulness is exposed. Caillat reports that Fleetwood got "distracted" when he played hi-hat, so he would more often keep time with the kick drum instead.[115] The drumming in the song's outro is curiously restrained. Fleetwood refrains from cymbal crashes and protracted fills.

Christine McVie sings earnestly and (given the circumstances) ironically about making "Lovin' Fun," using a Fender Rhodes keyboard and Clavinet (one of Sly Stone's) at the start.[116] The verses alternate between g-minor (vi) and F-major chords (V) before opening up to the tonic of Bb in the chorus (the key relationship could be flipped, depending on the listener's perception). The chimes that respond to "ways of magic" in the chorus are something of a pop-rock cliché, but the lush background vocals and drums that stutter in the chorus are more imaginative, despite the overarching influence of the Byrds.[117] The angelic song is countered by the power ballad "Oh Daddy," about marriage (if not love) on the rocks. John McVie's melodic bass dialogues with his soon-to-be ex-wife's Hammond organ playing, adding earnestness to the bittersweet sound—and how galling it must have been for him to play on a song narrating his departed lover's erotic fantasies. The strong accents in the lower range of the piano and the milder guitar beats over a crisp snare denote the rock 'n' roll urban outlaw song. (Bruce Springsteen's "Lost in the Flood" provides an example, Bon Jovi's "Wanted Dead or Alive" another.) The castanet flourish during the bridge ensures the listener catches the allusion. Buckingham adds harmonics; his strumming is mic'ed and equalized to emphasize the metallic sound of the strings, filling out the higher range.

The line between the twin turn-ons of love and hate is thin, and it's crossed again and again on the album, as it was in the marketing of the *amours impropre* and on the global ninety-six-stop tour that followed from February 24, 1977, to August 30, 1978. Legions heard the band live in ten- to fifteen-thousand-seat arenas, and even greater numbers bought the original vinyl edition of *Rumours* or listened ad infinitum to the singles on the radio. Nicks bid farewell to the old authentic days of station wagons and motels but brought along her childhood friend Robin Snyder for company and occasional dog sitting. Fleetwood Mac traveled by private jet and stayed in five-star hotels and presidential suites painted pink and equipped with white grand pianos, fabulously rich, living a life of debauched decadence with personal caterers, masseuses, and security guards, swilling fine wine, ingesting cocaine from Heineken caps, and delivering inarticulate interviews. Travel breaks were occasions for loony fun, including, for Nicks, a martial arts photo shoot with a massively red-haired Australian bodyguard named Bob Jones.[118]

The UK dates were a homecoming of sorts for Fleetwood and the McVies, and the dates in the Southeast US brought out devotees of *Buckingham Nicks*. Girls all over showed up dressed like Nicks, having waited all night in line for tickets. Reviewers praised the ninety-minute set for its overall excellence and the pleasure-sustaining Nicks-McVie dialectic. John Rockwell attributed the women's "highflying harmonies" to a Mamas & Papas imprint—shades of Changing Times—and spotlighted the band's "illusion" of "supportive community."[119] Nicks was both siren and angel in his assessment, her "sexy, mysterious ballads" involving "seraphic posturing." He found her manner "compelling and endearing" but also "a little stagey" (not untypical for stage shows).[120] "We're not God's gifts as technicians," Fleetwood told Rockwell, when asked about his skill set. "We make more mistakes than some bands," Nicks agreed. "But there is a very loving thing up there, and it comes across."[121] Showing the love once again shredded her voice. Sleeplessness, self-medication, and brutal travel took its toll on intonation; in some of the footage Nicks is radically out of tune, and the Syracuse gig had to be scuttled to give her throat some rest. A speech therapist wanted her to sing in a higher range. Fleetwood suspected the band's sound would have to change but didn't seem bothered by the prospect. Genealogy never mattered to his group, nor consistent affect.

The band performed at Nassau Coliseum on Long Island after Buckingham had his wisdom teeth extracted. Nicks compensated for his onstage listlessness, which taxed her voice even more and provided fodder for deeply horrible comments in the press about her "shaggy-haired love object . . . mystique," "drunken sailor" gracelessness, and "valiant" but failed effort to hit the right notes.[122] Thus Peter Herbst, the author of these insults, said goodbye to his backstage pass.

Nicks didn't read the reviews, privileging instead her own perspective on the long, bruising tour: she and the other musicians "basically" liked each other. "The problems, fights, arguments, disagreements" vanished onstage. No one wanted to call it quits. Touring was lucrative and usually fun. When it wasn't, "It was just, grit your teeth and bear it."[123]

Buckingham grit his teeth too, then spat. "By the time we finish this tour," he said to a backstage camera crew, "we will have done ninety-eight shows since the end of March, or, the beginning of, when was it? The beginning of March, the end of February. Ninety-eight shows and I'm sick of playing! Finished!" He grunted, "I hate it, I hate it."[124]

TUSK

The follow-up to *Rumours, Tusk,* said goodbye to the seventies by fundamentally rethinking everything Fleetwood Mac had recorded since the two Californians had joined—Christine McVie's "Warm Ways" and "Over My Head" and all the major-key songs on *Rumours* and the "white album."[125] Stagflation arrived; the take-it-easy vibe lost favor. Embracing the role of Fleetwood Mac's creative director with his bandmates' general agreement, Buckingham sensed the shift in the zeitgeist and responded to it, albeit idiosyncratically. After the *Rumours* tour ended he lavished funds on a double album that enraged Warner Brothers management and delighted cultists. Liberating himself from the pressure to create an overtly commercial sequel to *Rumours,* Buckingham started from scratch on *Tusk,* messing around at home and at Village Studios (housed in a former Masonic temple on the edge of Santa Monica) for month after month with bits and pieces of material that refused to coalesce. Lore has him shouting himself hoarse lying on the floor and installing a four-track recorder in a bathroom; there's footage of him singing in a push-up position into a microphone taped to the resonant brown tiles.[126]

Track 15 of *Tusk,* "I Know I'm Not Wrong," abolishes its own hook, a little cadential motif played by Christine McVie on accordion before being overlaid by a guitar solo. A song before that, the bluesy "Brown Eyes," is sha-la-la apotheosis. The title track expresses a primitivist preference for the tom-tom over the synthesizer. The University of Southern California Spirit of Troy marching band enters Dodger Stadium and someone moans "We are savage-like" as the brasses cascade and the batons twirl. The beer-drenched arranging and recording session happened on a Monday afternoon, June 4, 1979, when the Dodgers were out of town.[127] The album's master tapes include random cymbal crashes, guitars tuned down to the bass range, and the sound of a tissue box and slabs of meat being thumped, and yet the final cost of production for such weird, cheap effects far exceeded $1 million. Buckingham blamed others: "One of the reasons why *Tusk* cost so much is that we happened to be at a studio that was charging a fuck of a lot of money. During the making of *Tusk,* we were in the studio for about 10 months and we got 20 songs out of it. *Rumours* took the same amount of time. It didn't cost so much because we were in a cheaper studio. There's no denying what it cost, but I think it's been taken out of context."[128]

Nonsense. The band members renovated Village Studio D to their taste. Tina Morris, the current manager, showed me around the building, a rabbit warren of interconnected recording spaces for large and small ensembles.[129] On the wall facing the parking lot is a sun-blasted mural called *Isle of California* (1972) depicting a torn-up Arizona-California border after the "big one," the mega-earthquake predicted to eventually strike the West Coast. In Studio D, the generous space in the middle of the first floor, Nicks installed a bathroom of blue, bronze, and Indian mosaic tiles for her private use—still a hit, Morris told me, when the facility hosts parties. I asked her about Nicks's preferred dynamic microphone—a Sennheiser 441—and whether or not Buckingham and Nicks still regard the studio as a kind of home. They do, and present-day superstars still book Studio D and the more up-to-date B for long stretches. (The Red Hot Chili Peppers were in session when I visited.)

Mick Fleetwood, ostensibly the band's manager, occupied an over-sized chair as a throne in the lounge that led to the console room and the live room beyond it. The chair is still there, next to the band's black leather couch. Buckingham paneled a side room with imported quarter-sawn zebrawood to create the darker, fuller acoustic he desired for the record (most of *Tusk* has the same claustrophobic intimacy of *Rumours*). The lamps, mirrors, live-room carpets, and soundboard remain as well; alas, the band's exotic tchotchkes—the voodoo trinkets hung on the walls for the *Tusk* sessions—do not. The superrich superstars ate, drank, and inhaled before getting down to musical business. The recording-session footage (presumably shot by the album's second producer, Richard Dashut) shows just how young they were in 1978.

There was the cost of furniture, paneling, and plumbing, and the cost of doing and undoing take after take of the twenty songs on *Tusk*. The two discs, with their elaborate inner and outer sleeves (the intentionally unattractive cover shows Ken Caillat's dog Scooter attacking his leg), went on sale for $15.98 in 1979 before falling off the charts and into the bargain bins. *Tusk* actually sold an impressive four million copies in its first year, going quadruple platinum in the twilight of the LP era, but given the label's expectations and the much greater success of *Rumours*, it seemed a flop. Sales were slightly dampened by the Westwood One radio network, which played *Tusk* in its entirety on the day of its release, October 12, 1979, allowing fans to tape-record it for free. Now the album gets intellectualized as Fleetwood Mac's deconstruction and easy listening's too.

Such is Sam Anderson's convincing and compellingly written assessment of the album, with an added ironic paean to the digestible sounds of the seventies and the fictions that the FM dial promoted with impunity. *Tusk* is a referendum on the power of sha-la-la to persuade. "The Crystal Palace of Soft Rock will save no one," he writes, with reference to *Rumours* and Eagles records like *The Long Run*.

> It is a beautiful but fragile structure, unfit to shelter us from even life's most minor assaults, let alone the really serious dirt clods and cannonballs and stinger missiles associated with marriage, parenthood, age and death. The Crystal Palace of Soft Rock will crumble. It is good for nothing. Do not trust it. What makes *Tusk* a great album—not just a pop relic of the late '70s but an artwork that continues to speak to contemporary, sentient humans—is how quickly and ruthlessly it exposes this lie.[130]

Anderson rests his claim on the first and second tracks, "Over & Over" and "The Ledge," describing them as a kind of thesis and antithesis of the mauve-and-orange Malibu sunset against a rude florescent-bulb awakening. Everything is in its right place on the former, no pitch out of tune, no wrinkle in the fabric or dent in the shape. But no sooner have the essential oils clouded your senses than the album crosses the threshold from the seventies into the eighties. "The Ledge" is grunge avant la lettre: half skiffle, half punk, with a lick or two drawn from the Beatles' "Wild Honey Pie." Buckingham recorded "The Ledge" at home using a drum machine and sped up his voice to sound like Nicks in the background. The lyrics are nursery rhyme drivel—"counting on my fingers, counting on my toes"—with a mean twist. The line "slipping through your fingers" becomes "flipping you the finger." Consider that in the context of the album's title, Fleetwood Mac slang for "dick." Looking over the ledge at the ruined relationships below, Buckingham is telling us to go screw ourselves.

Anderson elaborates the antithesis: "The defining tension of *Tusk* is perfection versus destruction, gloss versus mess—the lure of soft rock versus the barb of art rock. It is where obsessive artistic control circles around into raggedness, where chaos and order dance together in a cloud of whirling scarves. The album probably has five too many songs, and a handful of tracks are two minutes too long, but that's the cost of this kind of genius: excess, bombast, hubris, getting carried away."[131] Fleetwood Mac's founder, Peter Green, enriched the twelve-bar, three-chord blues format, grasping for sounds in music that he had "experienced" though mescaline and LSD imbibement, and Buckingham enriched the enrichment.[132]

Tusk toggles back and forth like this, the dials in Village Studio D turned 180 degrees between tracks.[133] It's brilliant insofar as it anticipates its own failure. Credit (or blame) has always been assigned to Buckingham, with the four other musicians in the group mere foils for his psychodrama. There was no step down. He stepped off the ledge.

The reviews were all over the place, and the album (remastered and marketed in deluxe editions with outtakes and alternates) continues to be reviewed, as Anderson's 2015 "Letter of Recommendation" attests. At the time of its release, Stephen Holden panned *Tusk* in the pages of *Rolling Stone* in semi-inspired prose: "If the band has an image, it's one of wealthy, talented, bohemian cosmopolites futilely toying with shopworn romantic notions in the face of the void." Of Nicks, he added, "There's a fine line between the exotic and the bizarre."[134] She was neither, and there is no fine line, but the void of which he speaks is part of the album's legacy. Reviewing it three and a half decades after the fact,

Amanda Petrusich leaves us to wonder if all that positive-minded studio footage and happy twirling in the sun in Dodger Stadium was a put-on:

> By the time *Tusk* was released, the two primary relationships sustaining the band (Christine and John's marriage, and Lindsey and Stevie's long-standing romance) had fully dissolved, which seemed to qualify Fleetwood Mac, in some perverse way, to go on to become one of our best and bravest chroniclers of love's horrifying tumult. Being tasked with singing backing vocals for a song written by your ex-lover, about you, months (and eventually years) after the relationship ruptured? Hold that in mind—just how excruciating that must've been.[135]

Despite the pain, the five musicians stayed together for a long, long time, their label, their promoters and producers, the hundreds of employees in their entourage, shareholders and boards of trustees—an entire sector of commercial entertainment—reminding them, lawyers and dealers in tow, that there were hundreds of millions of dollars at stake. We can hold that, too, in mind—how much pressure that must've been, before, during, and after the avant-garde crackup called *Tusk,* and how matters private, intimate, and discreet continue to be given shameful public exposure for profit's sake.

Hernan Rojas, assistant to producer and engineer Ken Caillat, added to the excruciation by falling in love with Nicks—a topic addressed in their book about the album—and Christine McVie had a dalliance with Dennis Wilson of the Beach Boys.[136] (A side note: Brian Wilson was much more of a musical point of reference for Fleetwood Mac than his brother Dennis, but the band did record a cover version of Dennis's "Farmer's Daughter" from 1963. It ended up not on *Tusk* but on the *Fleetwood Mac Live* album of 1980, despite being recorded in the studio.)[137] Fleetwood lost his father while working on *Tusk,* as had Buckingham just before, and both had serious health scares. Fleetwood checked out, and Buckingham checked in, obsessively. He made several versions of "I Know I'm Not Wrong" at home, for example, with the first no worse or better than the last. Coarsening the sound after polishing it, alternately barking and cooing into the mic, un- and retuning the instruments, he captured the contradictions of the text in music: "The dreams of a lifetime/A year gone bad." Nicks was prepared to work, but her ex-partner assumed total control of the project and created a deliberately uneven record that lures listeners in with "Over & Over" and escorts everyone out with "Never Forget." These bookends, by Christine McVie, are polite. The rest is not.

The excesses of *Tusk* have frequently been noted, less so its response to popular-music history. It answers the bric-a-brac and longueurs of the Beatles' *White Album,* the imitative polyphony of the Beach Boys, the Talking Heads, and whatever Buckingham appreciated about punk as well as Cowell- and Cage-type ultramodernism. It is a corrective of sorts to the anodyne musical culture of Los Angeles's Laurel Canyon, which, with fewer people than eucalyptus trees in its heyday, offered sanctuary to folk and rock musicians, their hangers-on, and their pot-headed pop progeny. The neighborhood lacked the cohesion of an actual "scene" but produced (or was given credit with producing) a floaty, squishy sound and a hazy vibe critics love to hate.

Nicks supplied five of the songs on *Tusk,* and these complicate the narrative of dissolute, out-of-it self-demolition, because each is so sophisticated. She contributed "Angel," a reimagining of an "old-time dance hall girl" track; the luxurious, immersive "Sara"; the devastating ballad "Storms"; the astral anthem "Sisters of the Moon," whose lyrics remain puzzling even to their author; and "Beautiful Child," which attests to the deepening and enriching of Nicks's voice.[138] None of the songs concerned Buckingham, either as person or artist. She went her way and, on the framing tracks, he went his.

"ANGEL"

The recorded version of "Angel" is slower than how the band played it on tour in 1979, where it came alive thanks to Nicks's fancy footwork and vamping extension of the outro. Buckingham laid down the rhythm with overdrive on a custom-made Turner guitar that he used on the road, not in the studio to record *Tusk.* There he relied on custom-made Les Paul guitars and Stratocasters. The song has a rollicking boogie-woogie underpinning (root and sixth alternating against an eighth-note baseline). Buckingham's fills float over that pattern and follow the lyrics in a distinctive manner. A less imaginative and sensitive guitarist would probably strut more and perhaps default to blues tropes. Throughout *Tusk,* however, Buckingham avoids showiness, instead staying true to a filigreed fingerpicking technique that is pianistic insofar as the right-hand thumb plays bass parts (like the left hand of the piano), and the fingers play chordal arpeggiations, melodies, and fills.

In the studio, Buckingham and Nicks had a hard time mastering the two-part harmonization of the song's chorus, according to footage of one of the recording sessions. Nicks tries earnestly to compare the har-monies to those of the Mills Brothers, the African American jazz quartet first famous during the Great Depression which continued to enjoy considerable success in the fifties. No one listens. Nicks finally throws up her hands. "Nobody understands what I'm even saying," she laments, shaking her head as the men banter on.[139] After they resume, Buckingham sits at the piano tracking Nicks in thirds underneath her line, holding to that pattern until he makes an oblique shift with a passing fourth and a couple of sixths. The entire song is, in a sense, an elaboration of that loose shift.

The chorus is forgotten less than halfway through, rendering the form unconventional: v1 chorus v2 chorus v3 v2 v4 and outro. Perhaps verse 2 is the real chorus, or perhaps the song is meant to seem like an improv, rolled out on the spot in a Badlands saloon. The interaction and synthesis of rhythm and rhyme fascinate atop the steady beat and busy bass. Like the harmonic underpinning—three block chords, the dominant, subdominant, and tonic of G major—the lyrics are pithy and the language inscrutably clipped.

The upbeat tune sets a text about profound love that has degenerated into coldness between newfound strangers. Each speaks, or seems to:

> You feel good
> I said it's funny that you understood
> I knew you would
> When you were good, you were very, very good.

These chorus lines are followed in verse 2 by a mystical reference back to the tale of Rhiannon and the figure of Arawn, "the great lord of darkness," whose touch causes eternal sleep.[140] "So I close my eyes softly/Til I become that part of the wind." The wind is breath, psyche, and inspiration, and the song, Nicks tells us, is about the bliss of painless sleep and the gift of death. "And in that nonexistence of pain there will be happiness. Because it was only given with great love. And this was in a haunted song, and a charmed hour, and this was the angel . . . of my dreams."[141] The music matches the lyrics about shape-shifting.

Producer and engineer Ken Caillat has recounted the band's addled conversations from four decades ago with implausible precision and clarity in the book *Get Tusked*. Perhaps Caillat and his coauthor, Hernan Rojas, took detailed notes throughout their time with Fleetwood Mac, or secretly recorded the studio banter. It is stressful in Studio D, Caillat relates at the start of the book; the band, or what's left of it after the *Rumours* tour, can't get its act together or even show up on time, but Caillat's worries are fleeting. He drives his Ferrari up the Pacific Coast Highway from Santa Monica to Malibu. Planes glide into LAX.

Chilled wine and a discarded leotard await him in his rented dream house on Big Rock Mesa. He is in his mid-thirties; his twenty-one-year-old girlfriend, Cheryl, waits for him in the pool. A soft-porn scene ensues.[142]

"SARA"

Caillat also writes about microphones, amplifiers, and the specifics of songs like "Sara," the second single from *Tusk*. Nicks recorded a first draft on a cassette player with help from musician and producer Tom "Tommy Rude" Moncrieff, then added a second layer of singing to the playback. The demo was made at the Bel Air home studio of Fritz founding member Bob Aguirre. On December 9, 1978, she brought the song into Studio D, some six months into the fifteen (June 21, 1978, to September 30, 1979) it took to record and master the album.[143] Rojas worked up the piano-vocal original into a simple arrangement using a Roland TR-77 drum machine. Moncrieff provided a bass line (on a Fender Precision bass, imitating John McVie's style), and Annie McLoone contributed background vocals. (McLoone performed with Nicks and Buckingham on Walter Egan's "Magnet and Steel.") Acoustic guitar came next, along with richer vocal harmonies. Fleetwood replaced the beatbox line with his own, inspiring McVie's remodeling of the bass line. The kit was tuned down, the bass-drum and floor-tom thuds emphasized. There followed the familiar ritual of abbreviating and tightening up the structure, but Nicks balked at the production team's cuts, lamenting the disappearance of verse after verse: "I was to the point where I went, 'Is the word *Sara* even going to be left in the song?'" Caillat confirms that "the buck stopped with me" when it came to the cuts. "Early on Lindsey would guide me in the initial cuts, but later I would work with Stevie, cutting the lyrics, removing the fat, usually while she cried. Of course, the fact that Hernan was secretly having an affair with her didn't help!"[144]

The original version of "Sara" was sixteen minutes long, which Rojas reduced to thirteen and then eleven minutes. Later, on Caillat's command, the song was cut to 8:49—this edit begins with Nicks uttering, "I wanna be a star/I don't want to be a cleaning lady"—before additional pruning to 6:22 for the release. (The single is even shorter, at a roughly edited 4:41.) Rojas rightly feared ruining the master by cutting it in the wrong place, ahead of rather than behind a downbeat. The edits were manual, the tape marked with white pencil and "rocked" to

the right spot between the tape reels for the excision. Once the operation was accomplished, error-free, Rojas pitched the song to Caillat and
the album's second producer, Dashut, after which it was presented to
Buckingham, who acknowledged its potential and began to work on it.
His guitar playing, the final layer of polish added to the song, was
recorded by Caillat on three microphones. One of them took the sound
through a "fat box" into the console; another brought it through a
Mesa/Boogie California Tweed amplifier nowadays associated with
classic overdriven sounds.[145] The third microphone, a Sony EMC50
lavalier, was "taped under the strings between the pickups to capture
the subtle string work," a highly unusual thing to do in search of a new
tone. (Caillat first deployed the lavalier in this fashion on Joni Mitchell's
1974 *Miles of Aisles* live album.)[146] Buckingham sought to build a fragile and delicate latticework of strumming, jangling, and off-kilter,
slightly out-of-tune syncopated plinking buried deep in the mix. The
guitar part absorbed five or six tracks in stereo with the piano lines.
Buckingham's sounds are interwoven or (as the lyrics signal) interlaced
above McVie's circular bass pattern and Fleetwood's brushstrokes.

The familiar interpretations of the lyrics do not entirely convince:
Fleetwood as the "great dark wing"; Don Henley or another boyfriend,
John David Souther, "undoing the laces" of a chemise; Sara as the singer's
alter ego or a child Nicks never had.[147] Such analyses suggest the blurbs
on the cover of a bodice ripper: "forbidden passion," "an intrigue of a
darker nature," "fortunes change and reputations—even lives—are
imperiled."[148] Either Nicks imagined herself as a character in such a novel,
or something more's afoot. She has occasionally tempered the specula-
tions about the autobiographical elements, informing *Entertainment
Weekly* in 2009 that the song was definitely not about model and singer
Sara Recor, "who was one of my best friends—even though everybody
thinks it is."[149] Recor, for her part, remembers sitting with Nicks when she
was working on the song, and believes that it references events in her life
as well as in Nicks's—chiefly their almost intertwined romantic relationships with Fleetwood.[150] Recor has further contended that Nicks "changes
her thoughts" about its contents and meaning, "depending on how she
feels about me, and the others involved."[151] In 2009 Nicks's thoughts
about Recor were decidedly mixed—so much had happened in their lives.

> I used her name because I love the name so much, but it was really about
> what was going on with all of us at that time. It was about Mick's and
> my relationship, and it was about one I went into after Mick. Some songs

are about a lot of things, some songs only have one or two lines that are that main thing, and then the rest of it, you're just making a movie, writing a story around this one paragraph, that little kernel of life. "When you build your house" was about when you get your act together, then let me know, because until you get your act together, I really can't be around you.[152]

The ambiguities perhaps explain the changes of tense in the lyrics. The narrator addresses her paramour in the first person in verse 1 and the third person in verse 2, with Sara becoming another addressee in chorus 2. Then the oscillations: the lover is gone but remains, or the love remains; the song affirms closure, then denies it; "call me home" defines a seam in the form as a double entendre. If the lyrics had an actual basis in Nicks's life, is "drowning in the sea of love" the best description of the shambolic partner swapping? The demos and archived performed versions don't add much clarity, excluding the 1979 St. Louis performance, where she emphasizes the emotional significance of the outro line "There's a heartbeat that never really dies" by repeating it.[153] Her roaming between microphones and instruments is striking as a visual acknowledgment of the song's discursiveness, even in its final pared-to-the-bone manifestation.

The opening features tack piano, also known as jangle piano, a regular piano that has been modified with tacks or nails to give it the old-time, out-of-tune sound of a saloon upright. It's a miraculously sophisticated stylization of the piano playing on the tape-recorded rough draft, which Nicks replicated on an unreleased VH1 Storytellers episode. Midway through a minute of limited-skilled honky-tonk, she reclaims authorship from Buckingham and the producers: "I did write it."[154] Two tack-piano tracks are panned on opposite sides, producing guitar- or dulcimer-like arpeggios, though with a more percussive attack than those instruments provide. McVie's and Fleetwood's groove kicks in. The words maintain their mistiness even as they advance a melodic hook.[155] Much of the magic lies in the smooth-as-silk, breath-filled production and the exquisite textural response to the tug of the words, from the half-minute protraction of "And undoing/and undoing . . . the laces." Sensuousness is placed in service of forfeited innocence and emotional betrayal. The three background vocal lines represent the lacework as well as its undoing, swirling around each other before drifting down and apart. The lines coalesce at the end with exhaled iterations of the title word, "Sa-ra." There are anticlimaxes throughout, including Nicks singing "home" far back in the mix after the line "But when you build your house / Then call me."

Crucial, I think, is the phrase "And the starling flew for days" in the third verse. It's a paradox: starlings congregate, cling to telephone lines in bunches, and alight in thick, dark flocks. Perhaps their murmuration is a "great dark wing," or perhaps it is a more traditional metaphor for melancholia. Starlings have long inspired composers (like Mozart) as well as poets. The starling might not look interesting from a distance, but up close, Mary Oliver writes, one sees "stars in their black feathers." Together the birds form remarkable patterns in bleak skies, a celestial dance that has been likened to cloud and vapor, plumes of smoke against the uncertainty of *nuages gris*. The swirling, unguessable logic to the movement has long been related to the flitting of thoughts and emotions as well as the rhythms of the world. Brendan Kennelly produced gritty verses about this phenomenon:

> I expect him any minute now although
> He's dead. I know he has been talking
> All night to his own dead and now
> In the first heart-breaking light of morning
> He is struggling into his clothes,
> Sipping a cup of tea, fingering a bit of bread,
> Eating a small photograph with his eyes.
>
> . . . .
>
> The door opening to let him in
> To what looks like release from what feels like pain.
> And over his shoulder a glimpse of starlings
> Suddenly lifted over field, road and river
> Like a fist of black dust pitched in the wind.[156]

That is Nicks's voice on this track: a starling—just one—pitched in the wind. Likewise the name "Sara" is a congeries within the experience of an artist committed to finding the stars in the dark feathers, the beautiful passage in the sad sequence.

Such are the labyrinths into which the song pulls its listeners, many of whom hold the song dear. As for Nicks herself, consider this anecdote from 2014. Roy Tannenbaum of *Billboard* interviewed her in her residence in Pacific Palisades. Before the conversation began the singer "peered out the window and saw black angel wings. The wings were so pretty, she thought about taking a photo. But after several minutes, she heard ambulance sirens and realized that a boat had caught fire: The angel wings were in fact black smoke."[157] Shape-shifting again.

"STORMS"

The melancholic honky-tonk of "Sara" finds its companion in "Storms," another song pinned to bad breakups and crudely derided by Buckingham on first pass as "crap, but maybe salvageable," according to the author of *Gold Dust Woman*.[158] ("No one told Lindsey his [songs] were crap," Caillat told me in response, "because Dashut was always sucking up to him.")[159] "Storms" is the indie track on the album, anticipating Cowboy Junkies and Mazzy Star in its probing of dark emotional recesses. The guitar hovers in a folksy pentatonic, gapped scale behind the vocal line, while the counterpoint between instruments (acoustic, though the 2015 remix adds an electronic twang) weaves a pattern as delicate as lace. The voice falters in the middle, and the lyrics are barely audible by the end. Some of the sparseness of Nicks's future melodic writing is captured on the pre-1973 demos she made with Buckingham on a four-track Ampex tape recorder—arguably as important an artifact in twentieth-century music as Jimi Hendrix's and Janis Joplin's outtakes.

The song has the quality of a lullaby, the hook nothing more than C#-D with the introduction of B minor chords on last syllables of the vocal lines, after the presentation of the sturdier triads of D major. The A major dominant, when heard in the intro, comes with sus4, anticipating the C#-D toggle in the voice, which quivers, runs out of breath, cracks, comes close to breaking. Some words on the lyric sheet cannot be heard. The song is about becoming the "brokenhearted" one rather than "truly" winning, and self-blame pushes toward self-annihilation. "Storms" is richly harmonized in the background vocals, a sound meant to soothe but which, for the protagonist, cannot. As Nicks describes stark solitude, the accompaniment proposes comfort, but it doesn't work, as the sudden introduction of muted bass drum in the demo makes clear. The effect is crude and anesthetizing. Meanwhile, the tambourine jingles; the guitar lines float away on the pentatonic. "This is just another test," a line about love's labors, is uttered with the conviction of someone who has had enough tests.

The recording was also a series of tests in the form of myriad takes, and the exhaustion of tussling with Buckingham might be built into the texture. The song, one of Fleetwood Mac's most affecting, leaves the listener gutted because it is itself gutted, the tragicomedy of *Rumours* now firmly pushed to the side of the tragic. The tune is thin, a threadbare cant, trapped in an overproduced haze that reminds us of the power of music to lie. The singer declares herself the "storm," but the ambience is "blue calm sea," corrupt and innocent at the same time. Madison Bloom finds that "the Stevie singing 'Storms' is exhausted by her own power, and what it is capable of when left unchecked."[160] The song is the seventh track on an album representing self-aware narcissists (it follows a track called "What Makes You Think You're the One?"). "Storms" is the reckoning. It's not suitable for lovemaking because it invokes the memory of desire, and that's what makes Nicks so moving: she doesn't describe passion in the moment, except insofar as the song itself is the passion, a deeply immersive listening experience.

Fleetwood Mac's record label did not want this song's iridescence but the opposite: chart-topping incandescence. No one was happy, perhaps because only Nicks recognized that the recollection of the experience can be more interesting than the experience itself. The distance paradoxically brings one closer to the reality of the situation.

LUNA

"Sisters of the Moon" is darker, harder, faster. The title might refer to nocturnal goddesses of pagan ritual, but no one knows (least of all Nicks) if she had that in mind. Stylist Margi Kent fashioned a necklace for Nicks with a triangle pendant representing "sisterhood & continuity," the unbroken existence of goddesses, and I assumed this was the song's message.[161] I consulted a practicing witch, Kristen Sollée, for clarification, and she shared that "the title is certainly evocative of the mythological connections between the moon and the witch, the divine feminine. Ancient Greece and Roman lunar goddesses like Hecate and Diana were incorporated into late medieval and early modern witchcraft lore, which was revived and reframed by occultists and feminists in the nineteenth and twentieth centuries for their own political and spiritual purposes, so the serpentine path of witch history comes to mind when I listen to that song."[162]

Spiritual references pervade the lyrics. Performing "Sisters," Nicks is a twirling, serenading being of higher calling; she embodies the "spirit of sexual *espièglerie*" (to quote cultural historian Perry Anderson).[163] The song recalls "Rhiannon," but the texture at the start is from "Gold Dust Woman," so perhaps the psychotropic is at work along with the paranormal. "Sisters" references thresholds, doppelgangers, metamorphosis, and the "dark at the top of the stairs," suggesting travel into the realm of the dead and back again. Like "Tusk," "Sisters" was developed by Fleetwood Mac on the road, and the second verse might reference the demands of fans: "The people, they love her / And still they are the most cruel."

The title emerges in the fourth line, as opposed to being worked up through the verses and giving the listener satisfaction when it arrives. Fleetwood provides a mesmeric pulse on kick drum and clamped hi-hat; Nicks offers mysterious "oohs" in the background. The layered background vocals and Nicks's line "and she called, to me" move out of sync with each other. This song and "Sara," Stephen Holden wrote in *Rolling Stone*, "weave personal symbolism and offbeat mythology into a near-impenetrable murk."[164] This put-down puzzlingly convinced Stephen Davis, in his book about Nicks, to call "Sisters" "more of a mood than an actual song." He likened it to "a famous series of watercolors from the 1930s" by the English-born Mexican artist Leonora Carrington, which featured "idealized magical heroines and spiritual intermediaries such as Diana the Huntress, Fantasia, Iris, the goddess Rumor," and, Davis derogatorily and redundantly adds, "the Gypsy queen Indovina Zingara."[165]

Fleetwood Mac performed the song on the 1979–80 *Tusk* tour in supernatural mode. Footage of "Sisters" begins with preshow glimpses of each member prepping backstage. Buckingham fixes his hair in the mirror, Christine McVie sits cross-legged smoking a cigarette, Nicks also touches up her mane, and Fleetwood gasps for air and even dons an oxygen mask. The song begins with Nicks in a black stole battering a cowbell with a drumstick. Past the verses and choruses, Nicks bellows the line "Know my name, yeah!" as Buckingham enters the aggressive phases of his solo. The lights go out, then explode in bright whites and yellows. Nicks sings with her hand raised as the crowd becomes rowdier. She grasps the mic stand, reaching out to the audience and mouthing something inaudible, before kneeling to the ground as the lights fade out.[166] Her vocal power is embellished on this occasion by Buckingham's guitar.

"Sisters" runs through A minor, F major 7, G major, and A minor for the verses and A minor, G major, E minor, F major, G major, and A minor for the power-chord riff. Led Zeppelin's "Stairway to Heaven" (1971) might have put this progression to rest, but it returned throughout rock music's Season of the Witch. The song has a meandering intro, two verses punctuated by the riff, a bridge, and the riff and a blistering guitar solo as an outro. The solo fades out on the album but abruptly and raggedly cuts off on the 2002 remaster.

The band built up the song through thirty-six takes in a congenial atmosphere, Caillat claims, but he excludes the rather inconvenient detail that Walter Egan had been playing a differently harmonized version of the song on the road under the title "Sister," with Nicks's permission, and had intended to record it on his second album.[167] Buckingham blocked him from doing so "out of disdain" for Egan "connecting with his former partner."[168]

Hearing it now, it's hard to imagine it as a song intended for Egan: the production is so characteristic of Fleetwood Mac, with multiple guitars blending into a whole greater than the sum of the parts. Egan's music, in comparison, is riff-driven; Fleetwood Mac's is much less so, with Caillat striving for filigreed textures. He turned "Sisters" into a brilliant example of stereo imagining, which somewhat makes up for the pithiness of the syntax. One guitar begins on the right playing light fills; another in the center strums; then another enters on the right with more processing and a touch of chorus. Finally, a guitar enters on the left, the most assertive, yet it is destined to become the overdriven solo line. Different degrees of reverb create a sense of depth in the stereo field. The solo on the left is echoed and panned to the right, blurring the sound. The song begins in barrenness and ends with a primal scream.

DISAPPEARED YEARS

"Beautiful Child" comes as well from an "astral plane," but it is stripped down rather than built up, rightly sized for its subject.[169] Like "Sara," it perhaps speaks to the mother Nicks never was, surely a commentary not so much (or not only) on her reproductive choices but on her creative energies—her ability to birth and raise her own inspiration to maturity.

Nicks has recently claimed that "Beautiful Child" concerned the Beatles' press officer Derek Taylor, with whom she had a fling. (Add that to the long list of Fleetwood Mac romantic intrigues, in this instance admitted long after the fact and in a detached manner, as though the affair and the song involved someone else—the artist of four decades prior.)[170] Taylor was sixteen years older than her and married; their liaisons at the Beverly Hills Hotel had to be discreet and ended in nothing.

The lyrics also address dealing with life and death and father-daughter issues, being treated like a child in emotionally and psychologically abusive situations, getting older and wising up as a matter of course, not of will. The lines "Too trusting? Yes/But then women usually are" are the acute nexus. The song is a berceuse, rocking in the piano between two pitches in the right hand, and three in the left at the start, and it twinkles like the stars. The form is opaque but reduces to three interrelated chords—F major 7, G major 6, and A minor—that drift apart in the arrangement, the emptiness between them growing.[171] The astral element reveals *Tusk* to be a labor of love with a hole in its heart, as the production makes plain. The snare-drum track is reversed such that the attack's resonance precedes the attack itself on its first entry; the bass-guitar part is replicated by synthesizer an octave below.[172] The texture opens up as it is hollowed out. Nicks, Buckingham, and Christine McVie sing in the background, their tracks recorded separately in an exceptionally reverberant live room. The ending of the song brings them together in faint, shrouded eeriness.

Some hear the influence of Brian Wilson's as yet unreleased album *Smile,* but it's frankly less audible here than on Buckingham's ballads "That's All for Everyone" and "Walk a Thin Line."[173] Both are master-pieces of dovetailed, overlapping vocal harmonization, capping a lineage stretching back through the Beach Boys, Beatles, and Four Freshmen to jazz and the blues.[174] The surround-sound experience of "Beautiful Child" reveals slight differences in the seeming assimilation of the voices. It's a Derridean trick: the unspoken, like the unheard, cannot be reduced to the same.[175] Indeed, after Nicks sings the line "Your hands, held mine so few hours," McVie inserts an unrelated phrase over a cadence: "I fell into love." Thereafter, from 3:33 of the original version, the background singers assume the lyrics that Nicks had sung before. She says she "will do as I'm told," but the voices in the distance, along with the voices in her head, iterate that she will not. She is no longer a child.

The concluding track on *Tusk,* Christine McVie's "Never Forget," is a Malibu sunrise after the final pool party of the era. The mood she sought to create is undone by "ennui."[176] Caillat's extended version includes electronic treatments that are unceremoniously snuffed out. The needle lifts on a beguiling double record created by an inebriated, dissolute, checked-out ensemble. The result is comic, tragic, profound, wacky, ground-down, built-up, perforated, and luxuriously padded. Then there's the marching band, marching in place for the sake of the mics. Nicks was offended enough by the name *Tusk* to threaten to quit the band. She had threatened to do so once before, over "Silver Springs." Soon she would.

THE KINGSTON TRIO

Both Nicks and Buckingham were in demand outside of Fleetwood Mac, she for her voice, he for his production skills. Consider the tale of their collaboration with John Stewart on "Gold," Stewart's biggest single, inescapable on the 1979 radio dial. Stewart, largely unknown outside of the US folk circuit, recorded ten albums with the second incarnation of the Kingston Trio. Politically uncontroversial, the Kingston Trio avoided investigation by the House Un-American Activities Committee (HUAC), which had earlier gone after the Weavers and Pete Seeger for communist allegiances. The Weavers were a group of left-wing idealists who hoped their music might expose white American middle-class audiences to "other" peoples. The effort was seen as dangerous and seditious by McCarthyites, leading to Seeger's August 1955 appearance before HUAC and his First Amendment defense.[177] Their inclusion of the music of oppressed groups was an unapologetic cultural appropriation, as two nuanced accounts of the "roots" of American folk festivals and their politics—Robert Cantwell's *When We Were Good* and Benjamin Filene's *Romancing the Folk*—illuminate.[178]

The Kingston Trio was studiously and stereotypically clean-cut, blond, blue-eyed, WASP, and all-American. The group rehabilitated folk fare, including the ancient bluegrass gambling song "Little Maggie," for the general public. Stewart toured nonstop and lived respectably, if not lavishly, having proffered the Monkees their massive hit "Daydream Believer" in 1967. He hailed from San Diego, the son of a horse trainer (he credits his rhythms to hoofbeats), and had played guitar as well as banjo since childhood.[179] Johnny Cash enjoyed pride of place in his record collection. He sang rock 'n' roll in the shower but stuck to ballads about the elements (wind and fire, especially) on tour. After the Kingston Trio initially disbanded in 1967, he and singer Buffy Ford toured the country in support of Robert Kennedy's presidential campaign, playing in school gyms, from the backs of trains, and on truck beds. Kennedy was assassinated on June 5, 1968, at the Ambassador Hotel in Los Angeles; Stewart responded with the cult album *California Bloodlines,* a gathering of autobiographical reflections and days-of-yore tunes influenced by John Steinbeck and Jack Kerouac.[180]

The Kingston Trio provided the soundtrack of Nicks and Buckingham's first years together. As Nicks exclaimed to Stewart when they first met, "If you knew how many hundreds of hours Lindsey made me sit and listen to your albums!," referencing the fact that Buckingham had developed his guitar-playing approach under the Kingston Trio's influence.[181] In 1979 the musical beneficiary had a chance to repay the benefactor. Stewart had signed with the RSO label and was dreaming of gold. Maybe he'd find a hit. He dropped in on the *Tusk* recording sessions and heard in the toe-tapper "That's Enough for Me" a distant Kingston Trio–like imprint in the banjo-style playing of the guitar. RSO had doubts about Stewart's ability to make a winning record on his own and rejected drafts of several songs; no hits here, RSO head Al Coury declared. Buckingham stepped in, but the $100,000 production budget had been absorbed. Heeding Stewart's plea, Buckingham donated his time and money to the project.[182] He earned coproducer credit on the album, titled *Bombs Away Dream Babies,* which included "Gold," a song about trying to write a hit song that became a hit song, as well as two other singles: "Midnight Wind" and "Lost Her in the Sun." "Gold" is close to being a twin of one of Walter Egan's finest songs, "Hot Summer Nights," which he wrote as a replacement for "Sisters of the Moon" after Buckingham confiscated it (obviously with Nicks's say-so) for *Tusk.* Stewart and Egan knew each other, and Stewart even told Egan, at the Local 47 musicians' union in Los Angeles, that he wanted to write a song just like "Hot Summer Nights."[183] That he certainly did. Egan might have had a copyright infringement case, but he didn't pursue it and "Gold" reached number five on the *Billboard* charts.

It was Stewart's second hit-making effort. The first, as he told an interviewer in London in 1979, was "Midnight Wind." Buckingham "and [keyboardist] Joey Carbone and [drummer] Russ Kunkel came down and played for free on 'Midnight Wind.' . . . It was the best birthday I ever had, yeah, it was great. Got drunk out of our brains."[184] It wasn't a hit, and Nicks told him he needed to up his game for "Gold." Stewart recalled their conversation differently, in terms that reduce her musical acuity to serving his fantasies. "John," he claims she told him, "make it so it turns you on. Because if it doesn't turn you on, it won't turn them on. Because they are no different than you are." The gold in "Gold" is a shuffle Stewart invented backstage between shows, paired with the internal rhymes of a children's song: down/town, car/guitar.[185] The turn-on is threefold: "California girls," "each one a song in the making"; the feeling of driving along the Pacific Coast Highway just before dawn, well over the alcohol limit, everything becoming fuzzy; and the pursuit of fame. Stewart lived in Malibu, and he references the "California town" of Agoura Hills, as well as Kanan Road, which crosses Ventura Freeway between Thousand Oaks and Malibu.

Stewart had enlisted Nicks as a backup singer on "Midnight Wind" but didn't have the budget to add her to "Gold." Fortunately for him, Nicks brought her girlfriend Mary Torrey to the studio:

So when [Nicks] came down that night to do "Midnight Wind," I had "Gold" out . . . and pretended I was mixing it or whatever. I could tell when she walked in by the look on her face that she was not going to sing that night. She just had that "I ain't singing" look on her face. So I said, "Stevie, I'm gonna do the tag on this song—let's you and Mary and I go out [to the live room] and sing the end." Well, Mary began to cry and I went, "Oh, my God, what did I say?" Stevie said, "John, this is Mary's dream to sing on a record." I said, "We've got to go out and do it." So we went out and did the tag and Mary was singing and crying.

I had the lyrics to "Gold" written out on enormous cue cards because Stevie really can't see too well. Mary went back in the booth, and I grabbed Stevie and said, "Stevie, come on, let's just do the verses on this song. It's not going to take long." I said, "Turn the tape on," so they turned the tape on and held the cue cards out, and I put my hand over Stevie's mouth when she wasn't supposed to sing and hit her in the back when she was, and she did it in one take, and I got her on the song.[186]

Stewart takes pride in his abuse precisely because, he deludes himself, Nicks tolerated it. She might not have had the power or will at the time to end his career, but she could have walked out of the studio. Instead, she sings without conviction and falls further and further behind the beat, for all to hear.

The prodigal son, having left folk music's Eden for rock's badlands, made his prodigal song. Stewart reached his apex lip-synching it on the music show *Solid Gold,* just before performances by Blondie and Supertramp.[187] RSO contracted him for another album, *Dream Babies Go Hollywood,* which flopped. The fancier places stopped inviting him to play. He never saw what Nicks saw: entire seas of upturned, fawning faces. Stewart renounced "Gold" and began making folk records again on his own imprint, Homecoming, and playing small venues in front of his die-hard fans. He and Buffy Ford married, each the muse of the other as songs in the making. Stewart died of Alzheimer's in 2008, but not before another awful remark at Nicks's expense: "A lot of people think Stevie Nicks is really nuts. She isn't, she has just found or created a lifestyle for herself so she can function in the right lobe." Then, too late, he says something truthful, born out of resentment rather than admiration: "She's one of the most underrated songwriters in America."[188]

"THE GOLDFISH AND THE LADYBUG"

Fleetwood Mac broke up after the *Tusk* tour, disappointed that they had played most everywhere except the Soviet Union.[189] John McVie, a student of politics, expressed enthusiasm for going to the USSR, and Mick Fleetwood and the others were intrigued. The contract rider for the high-maintenance band would have been a challenge for the Soviets to accommodate, yet the idea of a show in Moscow had been mooted since 1977, with support from the White House, the US State Department, and the Russian Embassy in Washington, DC. Embassy staffers had received comps to see the band play in Landover, Maryland, and an invitation to an after-party organized by the United Nations and Warner Brothers. "Anyone who saw those Russians clutching their Fleetwood Mac albums to be autographed, clustered around sexy lead singer Stevie Nicks like bees to honeysuckle, could sense there was hope for the future of détente," the Associated Press reported on July 15, 1977. The Soviets liked the band's "cleanliness," according to lawyer Mickey Shapiro, and the embassy's loquacious press counselor, Valentin Kamenev, endorsed the idea of a television broadcast of Fleetwood Mac playing at Red Square, with proceeds from the licensing going to UNESCO.[190] As sweetener for the bureaucrats back home, Kamenev asked for a crate of copies of *Rumours*. Shapiro remembers traveling to Moscow in the dead of winter for three days of discussions with chain-smoking, tea-swilling officials, after which he toured television facilities and received a letter of intent for a performance in the concert hall of the massive Rossiya Hotel, adjacent to Red Square. The matter, however, was punted. Geopolitical tensions and the band's volume both needed to be lowered first. The Soviet invasion of Afghanistan and US withdrawal from the 1980 Moscow Olympics killed the idea for good.[191]

Nicks's post-*Tusk* plans pointed in multiple directions: a musical, ballet, film, and collection of stories, including her fairytale "The Golden Fox of the Last Fox Hunt."[192] Drummer Don Henley of the Eagles brought her into contact with manager, producer, and entertainment guru Irving Azoff, a brilliantly quick-witted, sometimes intemperate dealmaker. "To get his clients top dollar, he'll rip up a contract, yell, scream, terrorize, stomp, pound and destroy inanimate objects . . . gleefully. He is the American Dream taken by the balls"—so Cameron Crowe fumed about him in 1978, after relating an incident in which Azoff took out his ire on the walls of a hotel room with a chainsaw.[193] Azoff agreed to serve as Nicks's manager after she enlisted Paul Fishkin and Danny Goldberg to create an independent label for her solo work to be distributed through Atlantic instead of Warner Brothers. Fishkin had worked with Todd Rundgren and Warner's Bearsville Records label, and Goldberg with Led Zeppelin and Atlantic's Swan Song. Both were in Nicks's circle of friends and confidants: she and Fishkin started a romance after meeting at a record industry convention; they agreed that she had not been credited properly by Fleetwood Mac. Nicks increasingly resented Mick's pushing her around in business matters. Looking for an exit, she consulted with Margi Kent, Robin Snyder, and photographer Herbert Worthington, who did the "white album" and *Rumours* covers. It was a high-stakes moment in her career, personally, creatively, and financially, in which she was caught in the middle of negotiations among Fleetwood Mac, Mick's interest in working out a solo deal for her that he could control, and her own team.

Goldberg met Nicks "in '77 or '78," becoming friends and staying in touch "even after she and Fishkin broke up." He recalls "running a PR firm, and Bearsville, which Fishkin was president of, was a client." Goldberg had "aspirations to do other things in the business," as did Nicks, who "initially asked me for some PR advice about how to get Margi Kent, who designed her clothes, into *Vogue* (I was unable to deliver); then I worked with her to try to get a movie made based on Rhiannon—a film that was never made but on the development of which we worked for more than a year."[194] Goldberg has pleasant memories of eating tacos in Nicks's kitchen and listening to her working on possible songs for the movie on her Bösendorfer piano. He was "mesmerized by her intuitive writing process. She would sit at the piano and zone out for hours and come out with a song. Stevie's mysticism was entirely self-taught. Not for her were studies of Rimbaud, Blake, or Ginsberg, nor even the Bible. She was an autodidactic mystic who viewed the universe through the eyes of a middle American."[195] Later he joined her on a trip to Tucson to meet Evangeline Walton. Goldberg pitched the Rhiannon project to various studios. Alas, it made no headway. "There was a deal with United Artists films—I was a 'producer' and then 'coproducer' with someone who had actually produced movies, named Rob Cohen," he explained. "A screenwriter named Paul Mayersberg (responsible for *The Man Who Fell to Earth*) was hired to write a draft, which did not excite the studio, and that was that."[196]

Another idea was floated, "an animated TV special based on an unreleased song Stevie had written called 'The Goldfish and the Ladybug,'" which didn't get past a "development deal at ABC TV."[197] The discussion looped back to her plans for a creative separation from Fleetwood Mac and an independent recording, production, and distribution arrangement. Goldberg created a label for her: Modern Records. Nicks dreaded breaking the news to Mick Fleetwood, but word of his romance with her friend Sara Recor made doing so much easier.[198]

CHAPTER 3

Bella Donna

Irving Azoff had the Eagles, Steely Dan, and other chart-topping groups in his profitable corner of the market. With Stevie Nicks on Modern Records he had a star for the eighties—although getting her into the new decade would mean, she recognized, changing her sound and look and moving musically out of California and into the white working-class heartland. Experimentation, suaveness, and an aesthetic that "bespeaks not roots but a lack of them" all needed to go.[1] Her first solo album essentially asks Fleetwood Mac fans to change their listening habits. Fewer dreams, more recognition of life's cheats.

She initially called it *Belladonna,* in reference to deadly nightshade, a plant long associated with magic and spiritual practices, but changed it to *Bella Donna.* Goldberg notes that he advised Nicks of "possible backlash about naming her album after a [highly toxic] psychedelic, and she changed it to *Bella Donna,* which she said was what she always had in mind because it meant 'beautiful dancer.'"[2] The cover is an homage that also denotes a fresh start. She stares bright-eyed into the camera, in white gown and extremely high heels, gold bracelet glinting in the flash of the bulb. Her brother's cockatoo, Maxwellington, perches on her raised, awkwardly folded right hand. White roses, a translucent tambourine, and a crystal ball form a shrine at her feet.

Nicks recorded it with Jimmy Iovine, who worked as a sound engineer and producer before becoming an all-powerful record executive.[3] Iovine did three records with John Lennon, then assisted Bruce Springsteen,

Patti Smith (on the epic song she adopted from Springsteen, "Because the Night"), U2, Eminem, and, crucially for Nicks, Tom Petty, who would join the ranks of the extras in her career, an occasional influencer whose hustle, prematurely grizzled voice, and torn-up sound she dug. Lennon's December 8, 1980, murder shocked and horrified Iovine, as it did Nicks. When interviewed for stories about corporate movers and shakers, Iovine preached humility—not believing one's own BS—but he has frankly led an alpha-male existence, pouncing on great ideas, overcoming obstacles, stepping on people.[4] Introduced to Nicks by Paul Fishkin and Goldberg, he toughened Nicks's sound and abetted her long-anticipated departure from Fleetwood Mac.[5] Her manager, Azoff, and his partner, Howard Kaufman, approved the move.[6] In an excellent account of the making of *Bella Donna* and its deluxe rerelease in 2016, Annie Zaleski describes the sessions with Nicks and two Fleetwood Mac backup singers. They came together "in the living room of a rented oceanside home, working out harmonies and singing together while the album's musical director, Benmont Tench (keyboardist with Tom Petty and the Heartbreakers), added accompaniment." Then Iovine commenced his work. He recruited "a gaggle of hotshot male musicians for the studio sessions, including members of the Heartbreakers, the E Street Band and Eagles. Waddy Wachtel (and, on occasion, Mike Campbell) tosse[d] off searing guitar licks, while Russ Kunkel's reassuring drums, Tench's lush organ and Roy Bittan's introspective piano add[ed] depth."[7]

In her songs Nicks laments a loss of resolve and weighs the price of unleashed passion. The process is intentionally indiscernible; frailness of form and line becomes an expressive strength. Some lyrics seem surely autobiographical, but vaguely so; memory plays its tricks. Petty sings more generically of false promises, luck running out, pride becoming pain. The sentiments endeared him to Johnny Cash, who wrote a letter to Petty calling him "a good man to ride the river with."[8] His music is efficient and focused, fond of sequences, brighter than Nicks's (though, as a person, he was a morose, truculent type), plus populated by southerners and sassy girls. The guitar playing ranges from begrimed to neatly clean. His videos, once MTV emerged, indulged the subversive and surreal. Nicks was slower to embrace the medium.

"She came into my life like a rocket, just refusing to go away," Petty said of Nicks, conveniently covering up the fact that when she expressed an interest in ditching Fleetwood Mac for his band in the late seventies, the head of Atlantic Records, Doug Morris, told her that Petty didn't allow women in the Heartbreakers.[9] Their first meeting was a bust;

Petty wasn't comfortable with Nicks's "sisterhood" of "hangers-on." He claimed that "we never had guests in the studio. I wasn't used to it."[10] Still, he liked her voice because it blended well with his fragile-forceful country-rock timbre.

Iovine was his producer, and Iovine became hers too—a consternating development for Petty after Iovine and Nicks briefly became romantically involved. Petty feared Iovine would focus more on Nicks's music than his own. Nicks moved into Iovine's house for a while after he stayed with her, keeping out of sight when Petty came over to test out material for his album *Hard Promises* (1981). Petty was in top form, and the album came together quickly. Partly and wholly worked-up songs that other musicians would have killed for didn't make the final cut.

"STOP DRAGGIN' MY HEART AROUND"

Nicks's album began slowly (demos date from before the *Tusk* years), but Iovine brought it to rapid completion, recording, mixing, and mastering it between the fall of 1980 and spring of 1981. She felt (or was told) that the album needed a big ballad, a Fleetwood Mac emancipation song, but also a tune that made a statement against synth pop—pro Booker T, contra the Cars. She hoped Petty would get involved and lobbied Iovine to entreat Petty to write a song for her. Petty eventually did, a bittersweet ballad called "Insider." She accompanies Petty quietly, just behind him in the mix. Iovine loved it, as did Petty, who sat Nicks down to say that he couldn't let it go; he wanted it for *Hard Promises*. Acting either out of guilt or pressure from Iovine, Petty allowed Nicks to rummage through his outtakes for a replacement. Her ear was drawn to a song he had recorded with Heartbreakers' guitarist Mike Campbell: "Stop Draggin' My Heart Around." Petty sang the vocals on the track by himself before Iovine brought Nicks into the studio and transformed it as a duet. When he heard the final version, Petty felt he'd been duped: "He plays me *Stop Draggin' My Heart Around,* the same track, with her singing. I go: 'Jimmy, you just took the song . . . ' His comeback was like: 'This is gonna buy you a house.' But it pissed me off because it came out at the same time as our single ["A Woman in Love"], and I think ours suffered."[11] Although "Insider" is arguably the better song, it didn't chart at all. "Stop Draggin' My Heart Around" ascended to number three on the *Billboard* Hot 100 after the July 27, 1981, release of *Bella Donna.* Buckingham infuriated Nicks by deriding her hit, calling it "Stop Draggin' My Career Around."[12]

Bella Donna was engineered at Sound City by Iovine's longtime side-kick Shelly Yakus, whose assistant, Brian Hart, spilled the beans as to exactly how Petty was duped. Hart reports that at seven each evening, Iovine would tell him and Yakus what still needed to be recorded or repaired. Hart's job was to load the tape and keep a record of the changes made to it. Petty's version of "Stop Draggin'" had been ringing in his head for five days. Hart was sick of it but considered it finished, hence his surprise when he saw Nicks in the studio and Iovine asked him to find an empty track for her vocals. She sang the song, and then Yakus integrated her voice with Petty's, manufacturing a duet out of it that Hart considered "both funny and horrible, but I didn't say anything because I didn't want to lose my job."

> About a month later, I was driving when I heard a familiar song on the radio. "Holy smokes, this is 'Stop Dragging My Heart Around!'" I recognized that organ riff at the start, along with a specific guitar part. However, as the vocal started, instead of hearing Petty's distinctive voice, I heard Stevie Nicks'. Then, as the song progressed, I heard a blend of Tom and Stevie. It sounded like they were in the same room and had sung a duet together. This was definitely not one of the mixes that engineer Shelly Yakus made back in the studio that night, but a completely new one.
>
> Turns out Iovine had taken the tape with the tracks we had recorded, brought it into a different studio and had Yakus mix it and press it to vinyl, as was done with records back in those days. It had been released as a Stevie Nicks record.

Petty's irritation softened slightly when he learned that the decision to reassign "Stop Draggin'" to Nicks and press it to vinyl came from management.[13]

AGE OF SEVENTEEN

Petty indirectly inspired another *Bella Donna* hit, "Edge of Seventeen." To get on his good side, Nicks made friends with his wife, Jane Benyo. She asked Benyo how she and Petty had met. Both of them grew up in Gainesville, Florida, Benyo replied, and became friends at the "age of seventeen"—which sounded like "edge of seventeen" in what Nicks snobbishly (she was the first to admit) called Benyo's "Florida swamp accent."[14] Nicks kept the ring of the phrase in mind for a song. Benyo was flattered. Nicks also kept in mind Benyo's "swamp accent," parroting it on "Stop Draggin' My Heart Around."

"Edge of Seventeen" isn't actually about turning seventeen, despite the unnerving teenage defiance in Nicks's voice, which social critic Camille Paglia cleverly likened to a "druid seer showering her maternal passion on youthful romantic trauma."[15] The song addresses Nicks's own woes too: poor health; getting sued, absurdly, for copyright infringement over the lyrics of "Sara"; the shellacking she received in the press when her voice gave out or her personal life changed course; and bouts of imposter syndrome.[16] She grieved the death of John Lennon and the loss of her uncle Bill, Jonathan William Nicks (1923–81), who died of colorectal cancer at just fifty-seven, soon after she began recording *Bella Donna*.[17] The opening lines came from—or, as Jeva Lange prefers, were "plagiarized from"—something Nicks read on a flight back to Phoenix from Los Angeles in 1980. "I was handed a menu that said, 'The white wing dove sings a song that sounds like she's singing ooh, ooh, ooh. She makes her home here in the great Saguaro cactus that provides shelter and protection for her.'"[18]

Nicks explained the rest of the text in *Rolling Stone:*

"And the days go by like a strand in the wind"—that's how fast those days were going by during my uncle's illness, and it was so upsetting to me. The part that says "I went today . . . maybe I will go again . . . tomorrow" refers to seeing him the day before he died. He was home and my aunt had some music softly playing, and it was a perfect place for the spirit to go away. The white-winged dove in the song is a spirit that is leaving a body, and I felt a great loss at how both Johns were taken. "I hear the call of the nightbird singing . . . come away . . . come away."[19]

Wachtel's guitar riff on "Edge of Seventeen" severely tests a musician's stamina: two measures of palm-muted, rapidly picked sixteenths on the root of E minor precede a measure on C and a measure on D, over and over. A song by the Police, "Bring on the Night," provided inspiration.[20] The special feature, the bristle Wachtel added to the sound, is the dotted eighth note delay and the slow-moving modulation effect using chorus. (Police guitarist Andy Summers here prefers phaser.) The four-measure ostinato runs through the 5:28 song, fully up front in the mix with the tightly closed hi-hat at the start, pulled back for the vocal, drum, and piano entrances.[21] At the break before the final chorus, 3:11, Iovine pushes the ostinato forward again—exposing, or laying bare, the song's primal element. The piano imitates the guitar in the bridge, dribbling on E and C, and cycles through the same trio of chords in different inversions. Nicks assaults the span from i to V of E minor at the opening of the first verse. The "ooh ooh ooh" consequent to this antecedent relieves the pressure, drifting down from G through F# to the tonic. The pattern repeats, with the drums entering and the pressure building up again. It's a fiercely compelling song, with powerful unison backup singing (a real departure from Fleetwood Mac); offbeat, Stewart Copeland–inspired "bombs" in the bass drum and cymbal; fluttering piano fills; and the powerful vocal interjection "everything sucks" behind Nicks's "nothing else matters."

The result mattered to Petty, who told her she was "one of the premiere songwriters of our time" owing to her authenticity.[22] Danny Goldberg seconds Petty's claim in his memoir. The "Edge of Seventeen," however, is a painful memory for him. Though untrained in videography, he had proposed directing the video himself, believing that "Stevie's own environment, filled with cosmic drawings and knickknacks, and her own private flamboyance would be a great visual accompaniment to the song." The result was "unflattering" and had to be "scrapped" in favor of footage from her performance of the song for HBO. Goldberg was humbled; Nicks forgave him and the song took off.[23]

"AFTER THE GLITTER FADES"

Nicks dedicated *Bella Donna* to her grandfather A.J. "I can't believe that the next life couldn't be better than this," she mused in *Rolling Stone* a month after its release. "If it isn't, I don't want to know about it. I think that if you're reincarnated, you're probably reincarnated as many times as you want to come back—once you've cleaned up your karma, your office. I think my grandfather is very close right now; I don't think I would have put country songs on my album if he wasn't. I try not to analyze it too much, but I think that for me, in the next life, it will be easier."[24]

The country fare on the album is an imagined reminiscence of A.J.'s gin-mill gigs. Michael Little lampooned it so lovingly that Nicks could hardly be offended, even if he misses the point about the specific female audience she's addressing in her words, amid the odes to imposter syndrome and, for A.J., the feeling that you'll never make it. Little writes that

> "After the Glitter Fades" has such a "Rhinestone Cowboy" vibe to it Glen Campbell saw fit to cover it, and for good reason; it's pure El Lay Country Glam right down to Nicks's "Well I never thought I'd make it here in Hol-

lywood." And Nicks drapes country lament "The Highwayman" in fairy lights with a lot of witchy "Haute Couture and Western" lyrics along the lines of "Her horse is like a dragonfly / She is just a fool." I can hear Hank Williams Jr. singing the song but I sure as hell can't hear him singing the words, if you know what I mean.[25]

True, Campbell covered "After the Glitter Fades," but back in the seventies Nicks imagined Dolly Parton singing it. "It got sent to her, and I don't think Dolly ever really got it. I think if she'd ever got the song, she would have wanted to do it."[26] Parton could neither confirm nor deny this anecdote.[27]

"BELLA DONNA"

In terms of pitch selection and structure, the title song is the opposite of an exercise in transcendence. It never tries to overcome its limitations and indeed narrows in focus and range as verse becomes chorus. The refrain, sung to the words "my bella donna," sits atop two seventh chords related at root by semitone, D minor and Eb major. These are drawn from the home key (Bb) and its relative minor (G), one being the shadow of the other.

The beginning is also an ending. The opening features a typical cadential formula of ascending thirds—Eb-G, F-A, G-Bb, A-C, and Bb-D—which crack open a door to a mixture of resignation and resolve. The lyrics seem to be the melancholy reminiscence of a woman looking back at her younger self. She's still beautiful, Nicks insists, and needs to "come in out of the darkness." Nicks also, however, sings about hubris and, in her allusion to circus tricks, something larger: don't look down, so you won't fall; live fearlessly, eyes forward. Wachtel's guitar playing takes several forms: acoustic doublings of the keyboard; gnarled, grinding rhythmic fillers; and hovering, lingering melodic fragments and echoes that emerge as the song's strongest element. The extensive use of swells, aided by a volume pedal, resembles Larry Carlton's playing on Joni Mitchell's records of the seventies and, together with the bends and sliding framing the vocals, provides the song's ambiance.

Nicks's reversal of sentiment is magical. To age is to witness a halo becoming a shroud, but in "Bella Donna" the halo remains, increasing in brightness. The song's coda drops all pretense; it is just Nicks and her backup singers, a flourish on the piano, and strummed chords.

FACE TO FACE

Then there's "Leather and Lace," which Nicks, unusually, wrote for someone else. Back in 1975, "Outlaw" country singer, balladeer, and *Dukes of Hazzard* narrator Waylon Jennings had commissioned it from her for a collection of duets with his wife, Jessi Colter. It bounced back to Nicks after Jennings and Colter separated in 1976, owing to his dependencies and infidelities as well as her "return to faith."[28] Jennings doesn't mention the commission in his coarsely plainspoken autobiography, nor does Colter in her more atmospheric memoir of their troubled times together. Nicks recorded a demo with Don Henley shortly after they began dating. She plays guitar, more capably than she's ever given credit for, and sings with an affecting break in her voice. Henley rushes through it, but sweetly.[29] Another demo, from 1980, contains several false starts.[30] Henley was pursuing another project, so Sharon Celani, a singer with a dark, rich middle range, took his place. The demo is beautiful—all of it, even the errors—and could have been, had it been released, an anthem for women through the ages. Benmont Tench quietly counts beats in the background on a couple of the takes. Nicks pauses to correct the tempo and remind herself of the return of the opening guitar pattern. Her hands perspire; she needs to dry them off. Her nails catch one of the strings; she curses. The second-to-last take breaks down at the end of the first verse as she sings, in a voice that evokes the best of Dolly Parton, "I am stronger than you know."

Iovine brought Nicks and Henley into the studio to record the duet. He captured their voices on separate days, and so the finished product lacks the intimacy that makes the girl-boy, girl-girl demos special. Meantime, Jennings and Colter reconciled, separated again, and rereconciled. In 1981, the same year as *Bella Donna,* they released an album called *Leather and Lace.* The song of that name is excluded, because it remained in possession of its author. Nicks and Henley broke up as well, without prospect of another go-around but on generally good terms. When Henley decided, in his other life as an environmentalist, to organize an auction and concert of golden oldies in support of the Walden Woods Project, "dedicated to protecting the historic woods in Massachusetts where author/philosopher Henry David Thoreau first championed the concept of land conservation," Nicks agreed to perform.[31] She sang "At Last," a 1941 song from the Great American Songbook, dazzling the celebrity crowd at Los Angeles's Wiltern Theatre.[32]

SHARON AND LORI

Besides Celani, whom Nicks had "adopted" back in 1978, *Bella Donna* features her sister-in-law Lori Perry Nicks (Loretta Ann Psaltis, b. 1951) as backup singer. Both women hailed from Los Angeles County, and both joined Nicks's musical family by chance. Celani's tale is the simpler one. Born in 1957 and raised Catholic, she attended Villa Cabrini Academy in Burbank before enrolling in Ulysses S. Grant High School in Van Nuys. She sang, danced, played piano, and, inspired by jazz legend Gene Krupa and his performance on "Sing, Sing, Sing," took to drums.[33] In 1972 the gifted all-around entertainer joined Renaissance Women, "five Valley coeds" from three schools who played rock and R&B covers and some of their own songs.[34] From SoCal Celani relocated to Maui, where Bobby Lozoff, another California transplant, had turned a relaxed Ka'anapali Beach bistro named Bluemax into a nightclub sensation, booking acts like Elton John and Linda Ronstadt.[35] Celani joined a band that performed at the club. Nicks was in Hawaii in 1978, taking stock. (During her stay, she casually "dropped in" on George Harrison, helped him out with a song, and talked with him about the perils of celebrity.)[36] One night, Nicks went to Bluemax for a show. Impressed by Celani's singing—perhaps her free-form dancing too—Nicks picked up a tambourine and joined her on the other mic. A thrilled audience took pictures; one or both of them sang Warren Zevon's "Poor, Poor Pitiful Me" in Ronstadt's gender-altered version.[37] Celani stayed in touch during Nicks's time on Maui and obtained a piano for her to use in her tropical getaway. Nicks invited her over to record a demo and established a relationship that has lasted to the present. For a few years, in 1979–84, they lived together.

Lori Perry Nicks grew up in the San Fernando Valley, sang throughout middle and high school, and then, interested in joining the music industry, attended business college.[38] She worked as a legal secretary and recorded commercial jingles. In 1979 she married Gordon Perry (Edward Gordon Perry III), a music producer from a socially prominent family who had collaborated with Keith Olsen in the seventies. She met Nicks briefly in 1973 and then again, six years later, in her husband's recording studio in Dallas, Goodnight Audio, housed in a former Baptist church. Nicks was in Dallas on July 23, 1978, on the *Rumours* tour and booked the studio to work on the songs "Beauty and the Beast" and "Sara." Nicks asked Perry to sing with her and then signed her to sing on the solo records released between 1981 *(Bella Donna)* and 2001

(Trouble in Shangri-La). She had superb range, pitch, and power and considerable coolness to boot. Like Sharon, Lori joined Nicks on several tours and appeared on *Saturday Night Live* with her in 1983—a career high point. After divorcing Perry in 1985, she married Nicks's brother, Christopher, who did design and merchandising work for his sister. The couple had a daughter, Jessica, and lived in the Paradise Valley suburb of Phoenix in the estate Nicks built there in 1981, not far from her parents' house. (Nicks sold it in 2006 for $3 million.) Both Sharon and Lori take pride in their longtime relationship with Nicks, never speaking ill of any aspect of their life and work together. That fact hasn't prevented imaginative "fans" from creating a fake online blog for Perry Nicks—and for other members of the Fleetwood Mac clan—that turns her life in Paradise Valley into hell, focusing on her divorce from Christopher after twenty years of marriage and his severe health challenges (addiction and bladder cancer).[39] The odiousness is part of the business; Nicks ignores it, and so too do her backup singers, the "renaissance women" who caught the attention of reviewers of *Bella Donna*—both the album and the tour that followed: "Nicks, aided by Sharon Celani and Lori Perry, creates a female vocal extravaganza with a touch of 1960s 'woo woo' soul feel."[40]

Bella Donna was hyped by Nicks's new label and management into a huge success and reached platinum in three months. The all-powerful head of Atlantic Records and distributer for Modern Records, Doug Morris, pushed it to number one on the *Billboard* chart. Technically, both Foreigner's and Journey's new albums were outselling *Bella Donna*, but Morris didn't let details get in the way. He contacted Willis (Bill) Wardlow, the controversial, extremely compromised *Billboard* chart director from 1974 to 1983, and brokered a "quid pro quo."[41] Nicks was asked to have dinner with Wardlow, to be obligingly receptive to him.[42] She did. *Bella Donna* soared to number one for a week, despite actually being number three.

Buckingham followed in November 1981 with a solo record of his own, *Law and Order,* which had one hit ("Trouble") compared to Nicks's four: "Stop Draggin' My Heart Around," "Leather and Lace," "Edge of Seventeen," and "After the Glitter Fades." Meantime, Fleetwood had traveled in colonialist garb to Accra, Ghana, where he recorded *The Visitor,* which briefly charted in the United States, rising to number forty-three in 1981. The title of the fifth track, "Don't Be Sorry, Just Be Happy," captures the album's all-around affability and telling absence of cultural awareness. It features Peter Green, George Harrison, drummer

Lord Tiki, the Accra Roman Catholic Choir, Superbrains (a short-lived Ghanaian pop group), and the Adjo Group. It doesn't cohere; it doesn't want to. Christine McVie took a post-*Tusk* solo trip as well. Her polite, lightly synthesized, *Rumours*-esque song "Got a Hold on Me," from a self-titled 1984 album, did modestly well in the United Kingdom. John McVie withdrew from Fleetwood Mac to reconnect with his previous band, John Mayall & the Bluesbreakers, for a tour.

GHOSTS

The *Bella Donna* (White Winged Dove) tour lasted from November 28 to December 13, 1981, just ten shows, five of them in Los Angeles at the Wilshire Fox Theater, after which Nicks sang four songs for a "Peace Sunday Committee" all-star benefit before a massive crowd at the Rose Bowl. She would have preferred to keep the tour going, but Fleetwood Mac pulled her off the road and back into the studio. The band had a contractual obligation and needed to continue work on music that had begun to be recorded in September. By this time, Mick Fleetwood was a resident of the tax haven of Monte Carlo, having bought an apartment there to prevent the Internal Revenue Service from seizing his assets.[43] Insisting that the new album not be recorded in the United States, he booked the band into an iconic residence-studio northwest of Paris in Château d'Hérouville, Val d'Oise. The château was built in the eighteenth century on the ruins of a castle, atop the graves of lords and ladies. Tales of jilted maidens, illegitimate children, secret trysts, and ghosts fill the region's tourist brochures. Before a top-to-bottom renovation, the grounds included an ancient drinking trough, stables, a gnarled garden, and a tennis court. Inside there were thirty rooms in two wings, separated by a hall and staircase, a grand piano, and bohemian bric-a-brac. Film composer Michel Magne purchased the château in 1962, and between 1969 and 1985 it was a popular destination for seclusion-loving pop and rock stars. David Bowie made an album there, as did the Bee Gees, the Grateful Dead, and Elton John. Jerry Garcia dropped acid and thought he saw the ghost of Frédéric Chopin. That Chopin didn't die in the château (he is instead dubiously rumored to have had trysts with George Sand there) didn't prevent Garcia from holding a séance in hopes of having his ghost join his band, gratefully, as keyboardist.[44]

The dark corners of the château didn't spook Nicks at first. She spent several weeks there working with Buckingham and had the appointed "star's bedroom" lined with pink fabric. She took the white horse

Fleetwood had purchased for a gallop around the grounds, cape billow-
ing behind her, just like the hero of Jean Cocteau's surrealist *Beauty and
the Beast*.[45] She loved the film and would write a song about it for her
second solo album. In a *Rolling Stone* profile, she digressed from discuss-
ing the Fleetwood Mac reunion into a description of the night she
encountered the "ghost of the Château." (Her tale is too much in keeping with the gothic style of Henry James's 1898 novella "Turn of the
Screw" and its television adaptation, *The Haunting of Bly Manor*, to be
taken seriously, yet it entertains as intended.) Slipping into sleep in her
gargantuan bedchamber, she heard flapping noises and felt something
brush against her cheek. The light she had just turned out turned itself
back on. She ran in terror to her assistant, who settled her back in bed.
The haunting resumed in the morning, as sunlight crept into the room.
The French doors in her room blew open with such force that furniture
was toppled and her typewriter thrown from its stand. Kitchen staff reas-
sured her that the château's spirits meant no harm; they just wanted to
introduce themselves. "If the ghosts are friendly and willing to talk," she
ended her story, "I'm ready to sit down at any time. I would *love* to."[46]

Music filled the château's studios. The living areas, excluding imagined
bumps in the night, were quiet; the musicians of Fleetwood Mac didn't
socialize. Buckingham brought along Harris, and Nicks invited Iovine.
The musicians remained financially connected to one another and, in
media appearances, maintained the mirage of comfortable togetherness—
hence the title of the music they wrote in the old, dark house: *Mirage*. The
title might also refer to the band's amnesia about the length and dates of
their stay in France: "It's all a bit of a blur—a big beautiful blur," Nicks
commented.[47] The best guess, from communications with the château's
current owners and the musicians' scattered recollections—is a two-
month residency from December 1981 to January 1982, then a return in
May 1982 for an unspecified period. Additional recording and engineering happened in Los Angeles before the June 18, 1982, release. Brian
Wilson, among other music luminaries, attended the listening party that
night at Studio Instrument Rentals on Sunset Boulevard.

"Buckingham tossed off his songs in under two months," Laura
Snapes of *Pitchfork* wrote about the band's efficient labors. "'What can
I say this time/Which card shall I play?' Nicks sings on 'Straight Back,'
sounding like a woman in search of an idea. She pulls out her well-worn
tarot deck—wolf, dream, wind, sun—and whips up an unconvincing
sandstorm about how 'the dream was never over, the dream has just
begun,' while Fleetwood Mac increasingly resembled an inescapable

nightmare."[48] Perhaps; but the band had a job to do and did it well, hence Snapes's adjoining claim about the sunniness of the album's "desperation."[49] No one got killed; no ghosts were added to the ranks.

"DESIGNS OF LOVE"

Besides "Straight Back," a song that is half programmatic (about Fleetwood Mac trying to revive itself) and half autobiographical (about her breakup with Iovine), Nicks brought to the château a demo from the unrealized *Buckingham Nicks* sequel called "Designs of Love" (alternately, "That's Allright"). Dating from 1973–74, it illuminates the "country" or "Appalachian" elements of Nicks's sound. The folk movement of the fifties and sixties referenced, deliberately, earlier hillbilly and blues recordings, and once these stylings entered the commercial realm, musicians who had no exposure to them in their original guise began to imitate them. Nicks's grandfather presumably knew this music before it became commercial and privileged a more traditional form of mountain music. The mountain music and blues echoes on "Designs of Love" include the use of the pentatonic scale for the verse, which is often (but not exclusively) associated with these genres. Nicks sings with a country twang, imitating the "high lonesome" sound of Jimmy Rodgers as well as the timbres of the Carter Family. The groove has the characteristic boom-chuck of country and Appalachian rhythm, and Buckingham's electric guitar is mixed in a manner that evokes a three-finger banjo sound. His playing obviously comes from the Kingston Trio (that is, commercial) side of things. (Another demo of "Designs of Love," however, has more of a sixties pop-rock groove than a country sound, and the version heard on *Mirage* is even further distanced.)[50] The song is in ABC form, with no particular rhyme scheme, and the chorus in AABB imperfect A—not the ABAB or AABB typical of Appalachian balladry and bluegrass songs.[51]

"GYPSY"

For Robin Snyder, the friend she lost to leukemia, Nicks wrote the single "Gypsy," a song about their high school days and what they had promised to be for each other. Buckingham reduced it from 5:30 to 4:24 in the studio. It was one of two hit singles on the album, the other being Christine McVie and Robbie Patton's "Hold Me," and it rankled Buckingham that, once again, the music of his supposedly lesser-skilled former partner generated the hook, and the sentiment, that resonated with the public. The lyrics of "Gypsy" describe a room with some lace and paper flowers and the child still within her, though that child, that gypsy, is dancing away, like an unfulfilled wish. Nicks indirectly references the Roma peoples, who are subject to elaborate caricature and alternately celebrated (in art) and denigrated (in life) for their "uncivilized" freedom. The Roma appropriation in the song is of the "angels with dirty faces" (from places you don't know) type.[52] Carmen and other femmes fatales are invoked as Nicks sings about her friend's unbridled spirit, shared with her own, and its loss. She mentions a business called the Velvet Underground, "a specific hole-in-the-wall store in San Francisco where one of Nicks' artistic influences, Janis Joplin, found most of her unique clothing."[53] And she reminds us that she is the prima donna of her troupe—beautifully fearless and fearlessly beautiful, advancing, swinging her hips, spreading her mantilla, tapping her morocco shoes, planting her fist on the hip, proud to be seen as an exotic Other if that suits your fancy. How different is a rock band's tour from vagabonding around the world? "Gypsy" went through the typical Fleetwood Mac process: the meandering demo settled into a shorter, more conventional form. Nicks's habañera retains the calm, casual playfulness of the rough takes, however, and the backbeat in the remix is bouncier.

The videos were not happy affairs. "Hold Me" was filmed in the broiling Mojave Desert. Inspired by *The Catapult of Desert*, René Magritte's 1926 surrealist portrait, and quoting other famous Magritte images, the video has no explicit relationship to the song, excluding a shot of two hands grasping at the end. Magritte captured the surprises and fragments of experience that consciousness filters out but that the unconscious and imagination allow back in. Surrealism refers to an uncoupling between what one sees and what one thinks one sees. The video shows the band's instruments being pulled out of the sand. Portraits of the band members are painted, mirror reflections of them shattered. Buckingham is there in flesh and blood, properly attired for the climate, at an easel; Nicks is a desert mirage in a ruby gown and heels, reclining in the sand on a chaise lounge. He will try painting her picture; he will give up and walk away.[54]

The video's director, Steve Barron, regretted the commission and painted a grim picture of Fleetwood Mac as "not easy to work with" and uncomfortable together "in the same room for long." The producer, Simon Fields, added a vulgar tirade about the band's fractiousness.[55] He too was no fun to be with; it was a bad fit for all of them there under the hot sun.

The "Gypsy" video places Nicks in a boudoir, then a city during the Depression, then somewhere in the space of *Casablanca*, and finally free in a forest. Film noir–style footage contrasts with rainbow palettes. The crystal ball shown at the beginning represents two things: seeing beyond the real, as fortune-tellers claim to do, and childhood memories. The feathers, dolls, and flowers of the past remain intact, safe and secure. The point of view, however, is that of a male voyeur gazing into the boudoir through mist or fragrances. The camera captures the back of Nicks's head as she sings to herself in the mirror, doing a split on the floor. The camera moves into the room, interrupting her gaze, and suddenly she begins to perform for it, still contemplating the mirror. The scene changes to the Depression, the images disconcerting and unanticipated.

Flash forward to find her fabulously wealthy, in a hat with mesh netting, dancing among potted palms and women in furs caressing long cigarette holders. She spins, her head tilted up in the rain (the cliché of the unbridled feminine), then the video fades to a present-day Nicks moving through a fantasy realm of pastel pinks.

The video was extremely expensive to make, a sumptuous MTV premiere that propelled album sales. Nicks contributed to Russell Mulcahy's storyboard. The tense dance for the camera, in the mirror, is its greatest revelation, along with the curious manner in which the symbolic and semiotic, cinematic realism and fantasy, interlock and collapse into each other. The singer-dancer submits to the gaze, and she controls the gaze.[56] At the end of the video three younger girls join Nicks on a pastel cliff. They step in sync, all in white, suggesting that the hero has endured through decades and generations to stand now in a position of power.

THE WILD HEART

Nicks recorded her second solo album with Iovine at the helm, mindful of the success of the first and not wanting to change the recipe. Several minutes of backstage video footage exist of Nicks getting ready for a *Rolling Stone* photo shoot (for the September 3, 1981, cover story "Out There with Stevie Nicks"). She sings the words to the nascent title track of *The Wild Heart* over the demo of another track by Buckingham, "Can't Go Back," which features on *Mirage*. She or someone else had put the demo on while her makeup was being applied; the result is an unintended Buckingham Nicks song. She moves her hips a little and surprises the makeup artist, who pauses as the camera focuses in. One of Nicks's backup singers joins her in near-perfect harmony. Nicks gives a furtive smile at the end. The singing is free and easy—maybe like Changing Times sounded decades earlier at Arcadia High School. It's a far cry from the way "The Wild Heart" or, for that matter, "Can't Go Back" sounds on record. Judging from the YouTube comments, Nicks's modest, natural, makeup-session singing receives more love from her fans these days than the hyperproduction characteristic of Iovine's work with her in the early eighties.[57]

San Francisco–born, Houston-raised singer Sandy Stewart served as muse for *Wild Heart,* contributing to three of the songs: the thumping "Nothing Ever Changes"; the new wave "If Anyone Falls," based on a Stewart synthesizer track called "The Last American"; and "Nightbird," a memento mori with a steady pulse, elegant arabesque of a tune, and imitative counterpoint in the chorus. Hidden behind the drum machine and offbeat block chords in the keyboard are the strains of "Dreams," but the song is otherwise its own entity. The bridge to the final chorus begins with a piano cascade, birdlike calls, and, in the harmonized line "just like the white-winged dove," a nod to *Bella Donna.*

Stewart was a friend of a friend who had met Nicks in Dallas, where, at Goodnight Audio, two songs on *Wild Heart* came to be. She had been playing in a band called Sirens on the smaller club circuit in Texas and Louisiana. Nicks repaid the songwriting assistance by singing on Stewart's 1984 *Cat Dancer,* an edgy piano- and synth-driven album. Its single "Saddest Victory" was regrettably just that (MTV showed the mopey, Billy Idol–esque video, but it didn't chart). Stewart became a duet singer with Nicks and had modest success as a plugger.

"BEAUTY AND THE BEAST"

Stewart sang in an alto range and so was replaced by another friend, Carolyn Brooks, on the soprano part of "If Anyone Falls." Brooks also sang on "Beauty and the Beast," which became the album's novelty. It was recorded with a small string orchestra: fourteen violins, four violas, and four cellos. Kenneth Whitfield and Paul Buckmaster's arrangement also includes, as fairy-tale sweetener, harp. The musicians were booked for three hours in a church in New York. Champagne and black gowns enhanced the mood.[58]

The song was inspired by Jean Cocteau's 1946 film of the same name, an oneiric treatment of the 1740 story by Gabrielle-Suzanne Barbot de Villeneuve. The visuals draw from seventeenth-century painters. The statue of Diana, guardian of the Beast's treasure trove, is taken from Johannes Vermeer's depiction of Ovid's *Metamorphoses*—a subtle detail that Nicks's song references. The grisly tale of *Bluebeard's Castle* is also alluded to. Cocteau randomized Georges Auric's soundtrack to make it asynchronous with the visuals. Both mulled the paradoxes of filming at twenty-four frames a second, the artifice of the medium, with Cocteau wondering whether there was any difference between reality and fantasy on-screen. Instead of answering, he made that boundary as malleable and permeable as possible.

For Cocteau, the Beast's trauma is linked to lost childhood. During the filming, he saw a photograph of himself and was struck by how old he looked. The Beast was a representation of himself as an old man, what the poet must become if he is to remember and reclaim the past. He also proposed that Beauty's ambivalence toward the Beast is ambivalence toward death, not to sex. He conceived his film as a dreamscape, where the borders between several worlds dissolve. "In dreams," he said, "the course of events is muddled, the Fates tangle their threads, and, freed from our blinkers, we are permitted to live side by side with the dead and in unapprehended circumstances."[59]

The song moves from innocence to experience, with an unbearably sad conclusion that pushes beyond pleasure into pain; the strings transform both the sung line and the lyrics by insisting on Hollywood Romantic ecstasy, whereas Nicks expresses what she called "desperation."[60] Her voice is childlike and hesitant at the start, grows robust, and sinks low at the end like a flickering flame at the base of a wick. Parenthetical whispers take us inward, just as they do in the film. Nicks mentioned Mick Fleetwood as partial inspiration for the Beast but also talked about the passing of his father, and so a specific moment of loss is captured. At its core her song carries the torch for Cocteau's Beast and his enchanted realm. Her lyrics quote a comment attributed variously to Greta Garbo or Marlene Dietrich when they first watched the film, which ends with the transformation of the Beast into a Prince: "Give me back my Beast." The Beast entraps Beauty but symbolically sets her free, liberating her desires.[61] "My aim," Cocteau confirmed, "was to make the Beast so human, so appealing, so superior to men, that his transformation into Prince Charming was a terrible disappointment for Belle, in a sense forcing her to accept a marriage of reason and a future summed up in the last sentence of a fairy story: 'and they had many children.'"[62]

When Beauty enters the dream space of the castle, her white gown turns "into seemingly eternal waves and folds."[63] The Prince and Beauty ascend heavenward at the film's conclusion, and so do the violins in Nicks's song—a song that, judging from the comments on YouTube, taps into deep wells of emotion. Her voice approximates the gown's waves and folds, and the undulating rhythm and chordal progression are like a ghostly barcarole, a slow 6/8 that sinks from F major to D minor to Bb major, over and over. The barcarole is traditionally associated with reverie and escape. It is also associated with death and the image of Charon's barge floating along the waters of the Styx. Beauty is bereft at the end of the song, crumpled on the floor. The Beast is gone; the Prince hasn't appeared.

"STAND BACK"

The other tracks blend rock and country and disco, simultaneously hat-tipping to Janis Joplin and Barbara Mandrell while heating up the dance floor. The album's biggest hit, "Stand Back," surprisingly features Prince on keyboard. It's fiercely infectious, edgier than anything on *Bella Donna,* and a foot-stomping staple of Nicks's solo repertoire.[64] Prince's involvement was luck and kismet combined. Nicks heard his "Little Red Corvette" on the radio just after her wedding. She and Kim Anderson were driving to Santa Barbara for their honeymoon and reimagined the chorus as an imperative: "Stand back." She told the rest of the tale in concert: Nicks asked Anderson, who worked for Warner Brothers, about Prince and "Corvette"; had him fish around in the car's glove compartment for a pen and paper so she could draft lyrics; ducked into a pharmacy for cassette tapes and a boom box; and stayed up all night—ostensibly the start of her honeymoon—ping-ponging "from cassette to cassette to cassette to cassette to cassette to cassette" until her version of the song had replaced Prince's original.[65] Demo in hand, Iovine contacted Prince for her. He lived in Minneapolis but was recording in Los Angeles. "I know that 50 percent of it is yours," she told Prince by phone, "and, what are you doing later? Because we're here at Sunset Sound [actually, they were at A&M Studios]. . . . Do you have any interest in coming down and hearing it?" Prince and his bodyguard went to A&M, where he added bass and keyboard parts using a Roland Jupiter-8 and Oberheim OB-X synthesizer, respectively. Neither Nicks nor Iovine was familiar with drum machines, so Prince added percussion as well. "Takes him an hour; he gives me a little 'I don't really know you' hug, and, uh, he's gone. Like a little spirit."[66] It's a delightful image, meriting inclusion in the Fairy Investigation Society's list of sightings.[67] Prince departed with half of the royalties from Nicks's hit.

The similarities between the two songs include the harmonic structure of the verses: G, A, b, and G in Nicks's case, contra Bb, Ab, bb, then an enriched extension (bb7, Gb7, and Gb). The progression at the start is the same, displaced by semitone. The chords of the two choruses differ (Nicks maintains G, A, b, and B; Prince opts for Gb, Ab, Db, Gb, Ab, and Bbm7), but "Stand Back" can be sung to the tune of "Little Red Corvette" and vice versa. Likewise the message and meaning of the two songs are comparable. Prince had a lascivious, provocative side and built-in references to prophylactics, horse racing, and one-night stands in a song that likens a woman he can't control to a sports car.[68] Nicks chooses paradox over subversion: ordering the man who has left out of the room; turning away from the person she asks not to turn away; and aligning standing back with standing in line. "Corvette" is a dystopian post-disco, post–Top 40 song, almost danceable (though not in platform heels), flirting with polymeter in the overdubs and, like most Prince hits, impatient to escape its own hook since he has other melodic ideas he wants to try out. Nicks locks in the pulse and insists on songwriting's rules because her subject does. Saturday night doesn't make it all right.

There are two official videos for "Stand Back," the first of which Nicks rejected. Director Brian Grant opted for a *Gone with the Wind* theme, relocating "Tara" to Beverly Hills. Despite contributing to the storyboard and allowing the song's romantic conflict to be allegorized as a Civil War scene, she thought the result "insane—it didn't go with the song at all. It was so bad it was almost good." She wears an emerald-green velvet dress while riding a white horse toward a grand white mansion. Props include farm fowl, a quill pen, candles, and a saloon. Goldberg cameos in the battle scene with a bloody towel around his head, and Fishkin congregates with Nicks's backup singers in the bar. On this occasion, equestrian sports didn't suit her; the horse bolted toward a cluster of trees, and she had to jump to save her skin. The video cost a fortune to make, and Azoff called her an "idiot" for snubbing Grant.[69] She stood her ground, however, and commissioned a second video choreographed by Jeffrey Hornaday of *Flashdance*. It has a neutral nightclub setting and features ensemble dancing derived from Jerome Robbins with nods to Michael Jackson's "Thriller." Again tensions erupted, this time between Hornaday, his girlfriend, and Nicks's entourage. Iovine proposed changes, which Hornaday resisted. After an exchange of fuck yous, Iovine slugged Hornaday in the face, knocking him flat.[70]

"Stand Back" is usually included in her set lists, shawl spinning at select points. Performances with Fleetwood Mac include Mick's beloved congas and Buckingham singing backup. In Landover in 1983 Nicks performed it while holding, spinning, and dancing with a five-year-old girl, "Elaine," whose father worked crowd control.[71] Her high-octane performance with Waddy Wachtel at her 2019 Rock & Roll Hall of Fame induction channeled Prince in memoriam.

Part of her sadness at his 2016 passing concerns the death of possibilities. They didn't become friends, their paths merely crossed. After a March 15, 1983, Prince concert, Nicks attended the 2 a.m. after-party he hosted at the Registry Hotel (now the Mall of America Grand Hotel) in Bloomington, Minnesota. She and Prince delivered an impromptu performance of his signature tune "D.M.S.R." She tapped a cowbell with Prince at the drums. (It's not known if she contributed to the four other songs played at the 2 a.m. jam session, or what those songs were.)[72] On July 16, the day after a concert of her own at the Met Center in Bloomington, Nicks visited Prince's Kiowa Trail home studio on Lake Riley. He picked her up in his Trans Am and drove her to his purple house at high speed; they experimented with some tracks in the live room before he whisked her to her tour plane. The day resulted in the rough draft of a never-released song called "I Know What to Say to You," featuring call-and-response singing, synthesizer, and LinnDrum. Nicks invited Prince to join her on tour in 1986, but he declined because he was touring his *Parade* album. Their other interactions were purely social. Nicks claims to have left the premiere of the 1984 movie *Purple Rain,* appalled by the scene in which the character acted by Prince slaps a woman, Apollonia, when she tells him she's leaving to join an all-girl band.[73] A bootleg called "All Over You" has been swapped around on the Internet for decades, and there has been considerable debate as to whether or not it is an actual duet between Nicks and Prince or a fake. Further complicating matters was the accidental inclusion, by Atlantic Records, of "All Over You" on the draft list of songs and demos for Nicks's retrospective box set *Enchanted,* from 1998. Atlantic made another mistake on *Enchanted,* including the wrong mixes of four songs from Nicks's 1994 album *Street Angel* on it, which greatly upset her. In truth, "All Over You" is an unfinished track by David Munday, who wrote songs with Rick Nowels and Sandy Stewart—all fans of Prince.[74]

JOE

While on the road in 1983, Nicks became involved with guitarist and singer-songwriter Joe Walsh, another member of the Eagles. The acoustic guitar opening of "Hotel California" is his, along with the torn-up riff of "Life in the Fast Lane." Walsh's "Rocky Mountain Way" is iconic, and an impeccably goofy self-confessional, "Life's Been Good," remained popular into the grunge age. He had considerably more downs than ups without the Eagles, including a two-decade gap between a pair of self-parodying records no one heard: *Songs for a Dying Planet* (1992) and *Analog Man* (2012). Don Henley thrived in the eighties with the synth-based hits "Dirty Laundry" and the Mike Campbell–donated "Boys of Summer," and even acted in an episode of *Miami Vice*. Walsh didn't thrive, or at least he thinks he didn't. It's all a blank. "I wish I had 1985 to 1994 back," he has lamented of the time he lost.[75]

To Nicks in 1983 he was special, a brand-new key for her roller skates. "There was nothing more important than Joe Walsh—not my music, not my songs, not anything," she eulogized.[76] Later Nicks demoted Walsh to "friend," knocking out the contact sport.[77] He called her his "soul mate" and a "refuge."[78] The relationship began after her separation from Anderson and shortly after the start of the *Wild Heart* tour in Las Vegas on May 27, 1983, for which, beginning with the third show, in Knoxville, Walsh's group opened. The tour lasted almost six months and was confined to the United States (Nicks's only scheduled appearance in Canada—July 19 in Toronto—was canceled to give her a chance to rest). At the first of her two shows in mid-September at Radio City Music Hall in New York, a fan grabbed one of Nicks's bracelets, prompting her to lecture the crowd of 6,000 about stealing.[79]

The tour book includes a photograph of Nicks's parents and the horse she rode in the spurned "Stand Back" video. Nicks dedicated the book to the artist Sulamith Wülfing, who painted the magical creatures (angels, nocturnal butterflies, sirens, mist-bathed maidens and knights) who had come to her in visions. Nicks has long been a fan of Wülfing's art, including the set of tarot cards Wülfing once illustrated, and her clothing for the tour showed its inspiration. Nicks's jewelry, winged heart gold rings and pendants, came from Philadelphia's Henri David, praised for turning "rocks and metals into aphrodisiacs."[80] The softness of her look wasn't to critic Stephen Holden's taste. He took in a show and acerbically called Nicks an "anachronism" for avoiding synthesizers "and a tougher post-punk stance," after having previously praised *Wild Heart* as a "recapitulation and a broadening" of her "musical scope."[81] The *Philadelphia Inquirer* focused less on changing tastes than the way Nicks entertained a crowd. "In her wispy gowns and in the fluttery, flyaway dance steps she executes onstage," the newspaper commented, "Nicks plays up the dreamy aspects of her music. The songs she writes are full of wise, young witches, bold princes and glowering monsters—this is fairy-tale rock 'n' roll, delivered with roiling melodrama."[82]

She and a creature of another sort, the devil-may-care Walsh, had plenty of time to spend together during the tour. Each of them admitted to playing with fire during their "wacked-out years," increasing each other's wackiness. "We were a couple on the way to hell. It took me a long, long time to get over it," Nicks said after the flame went out.[83]

Walsh had come to depend on Nicks's musicianship and so enlisted her to contribute to his 1985 album, *Confessor.* "She rode shotgun with me on that one and gave me some direction, and she's really good at the craft of songwriting. If I'm left to my own devices, I will have eighty-five pieces of paper with a couple of words on each, and people like her and my wife, Marjorie, now will help me get eighty-five words on one piece of paper." There was no talk of a long-term relationship and certainly not marriage; both of them recognized their time together would end on the road, "as rock 'n' roll relationships do."[84] In 1988 Walsh started seeing, and abusing, Kristin Casey, a Texas-born stripper (she is not shy about using the term) turned writer and sexual counselor. Her roller-coaster ride with him and preceding years strutting around in Lucite platform heels—narcotics, alcohol, and BDSM all included—is the subject of a book called *Rock Monster.* Shortly after she met Walsh, she reports, he gave her three items from Nicks's expensive concert wardrobe: "a breathtaking vintage [flapper] blouse of sheer black silk with intricate beadwork," "an antique lace peasant dress and a brown knit tunic with gold-and-orange detail." Casey asked him why Nicks gave him her clothing. He "shrugged."[85] I asked Casey if she still had the three items, and she shared photographs of herself wearing them.[86] Casey also generously provided a 1991 photograph of Walsh and Nicks hugging. His hand is dug into her shoulder like the talons of his beloved parrot, Ralph, shown in the background. Nicks looks uncomfortable.

Love fails, courtesy prevails: few in Nicks's circle have been entirely cut loose. Her inclination is to forgive without forgetting (though with Buckingham it's somewhat the opposite). Reflecting on the do-nothing-yet-up-to-no-good men in her life in concert in 1986, she said, "They are poets, and yet they are the priests of nothing."[87]

"DON'T COME AROUND HERE NO MORE"

Dave Stewart was one of the poets, according to his chronicle of the song "Don't Come Around Here No More." It is credited to Petty, but Nicks was involved in its creation—at least at the start. Stewart and Annie Lennox (together known as the Eurythmics) performed a show at the Wilshire Ebell Theatre in Los Angeles on April 25, 1984. The post-punk duo was best known for a synthesized shudder called "Sweet Dreams (Are Made of This)," and for Lennox's "performed androgyny"—her short dyed hair, conservative business suits, ice-cold gaze, lipstick and mascara.[88] Stewart was the straight man to her straight man, a duller, more predictable musician without a distinct style of his own. He acknowledged men in Lennox's life being dreadful to her without thinking that the charge could be leveled against him as yet another male rock star living it up, libido unleashed. Stewart seems to have respected female musicians to the extent that he could benefit from their skills, and he certainly recognized in Lennox something that did not exist in popular music. Otherwise he could behave deplorably with women.[89]

His memoir provides proof. There he claims that Nicks attended the Eurythmics gig, introduced herself to him backstage, invited him to her Bavarian-style villa in Encino for a party, and asked him to spend the night on the rebound from her breakup with Joe Walsh. He takes advantage of her out of concern: "she seemed vulnerable and fragile as I was leaving that morning." He claims that he spontaneously came up with the line "Don't come around here no more" in the studio. Nicks might have said it to him as he was leaving, or to Walsh, who turned up at her residence uninvited.[90]

Everything's askew in his account: Stewart recalls that he and Lennox played at the Wiltern Theatre on April 25, not the Wilshire, and that he dashed to San Francisco for a concert on April 26, less than twenty-four hours after his unromantic encounter with Nicks at her place in Beverly Hills. He also says that he wrote the song on the fly, using a four-track Tascam Portastudio.[91] In fact, Stewart hung around Los Angeles for three days and appeared at the Grammy Awards on April 28. After that the Eurythmics traveled to San Francisco for an appearance at the Kabuki Theater.

He returned to Los Angeles in May and played the Portastudio tape to Iovine while staying at his house. Iovine and Stewart took it into Sunset Sound in Hollywood, intending to have Nicks work it up. Nicks and Iovine began to fight, as ex-lovers do, so Iovine enlisted Petty's help.

Questions remain. Did she sing the first take in a bizarre approximation of Shakespearean English, as Stewart claims, or did she leave the studio angry that nothing seemed to be coming out right and she was frustrated? All that's known for certain is that "Don't Come Around" ended up with Petty, who turned it into a hit, thus atoning for the injustice of losing "Stop Draggin' My Heart Around."[92]

An alternate, much more plausible history has Stewart, Iovine, Petty, and Nicks working on "Don't Come Around" together. Indeed, she brought in two of her backup singers, Kentucky native Marilyn Martin (recruited from Walsh's 1983 touring band) and Sharon Celani, for the recording. Nicks is faintly audible in the background but isn't credited. She vaguely recalls Petty coming up with lyrics—including the title—and then wanting the song for himself. He convinced Iovine to let his band record it. Either he or Iovine broke the news to her. "Even though I was deeply hurt, I knew it was a great song and that Tom deserved to sing it," she confirmed years later. "He sounded great singing it, and I told him so. I said nothing about feeling wounded. I kept those feelings to myself."[93] The two of them also recorded a lively track called "The Apartment Song," which Petty kept for later.

"Don't Come Around" landed on Petty's album *Southern Accents,* having been recorded in 1984 and released as a single in 1985. An outlier in his output, the song took weeks to produce, involving cello, reggae beats, and gospel elements provided by Stephanie Spruill (then a backup singer with Talking Heads) and a garage-rock ending (a nod to the Ramones). The tune and the song's five-chord backbone sound like Petty's; the Coral electric sitar, drum machine, and synthesizer are Stewart's. Mike Campbell, Petty's longtime bandmate, takes the Prince-like psychedelic solo. The lyrics provide the southern element, part "snarling, angry old man at the door yelling at kids to get off his lawn," part busted-heart lament.[94]

The MTV video of "Don't Come Around" is a rude send-up of *Alice in Wonderland,* with Petty as a smirking Mad Hatter and Stewart smoking a hookah on a toadstool. The tale of the genesis of the song is thus also a rude send-up of Nicks's private life and drug habits. (Hatters supposedly sometimes went mad in nineteenth-century England because the mercury used in making hats seeped into their brains.)[95] Stewart's parting thoughts on his time with her—"I really liked Stevie, and she seemed vulnerable and fragile when I was leaving that morning"—are contemptible.[96]

Nicks's father predicted she would never get married because music mattered too much to her, and indeed her one marriage was basically over as soon as it began. The other relationships—with Walsh, Iovine, Henley, and of course Buckingham—are tabloid fodder and the model for seemingly "every prime-time special about a female celebrity."[97] She ended the relationships and broke the chains as the un-dutiful daughter and un-devoted partner of the longest revolution. Speaking recently to Tracy Smith on CBS television, she critiqued the archaic definition of a woman's happiness as getting married and having children.[98] The clips of her songs heard before and after the short interview reinforced the critique.

ROCK A LITTLE

Had Nicks kept "Don't Come Around," it would have been included on her third studio album *Rock a Little,* released on November 18, 1985. It was a difficult album to make, the protracted creative and logistical challenges exacerbated by cocaine, a major actor in this chapter of Nicks's career. Some tracks went through multiple revisions only to be shelved or made into distant versions of their original selves; others were left unfinished, and still others assembled under extreme time pressure. A song directly inspired by Sulamith Wülfing, "Battle of the Dragon," which Nicks worked on with Petty, didn't go to record, nor did her treatment of the Warren Zevon song "Reconsider Me." By the time *Rock a Little* was completed, Nicks's label had lavished huge sums on studio space in Dallas, Los Angeles, and New York. To management's relief, the album proved a success, yielding four singles, two entering rotation in nightclubs.

The quality of her singing documents the challenges better than anything she said in interviews. She did, however, confess that

> right up to the end of *Rock a Little,* I was fairly horrified that everybody thought there was a bunch of stuff missing on it. . . . I'm going, "What's missing?" You know, like [in] *Amadeus* when he says "What notes do you want me to take out? What's wrong with it?" They can't really tell you. It's just like change for the sake of change, not for the sake of the right thing— just for the sake of them saying . . . "I think it should do this or you should do that," or "If you don't do this on your record it won't make it." That hurts.[99]

Nicks refers to *Amadeus,* Miloš Forman's 1984 movie about Mozart. More fantasy than fact, the movie features Emperor Joseph II's critique of Mozart's 1782 opera *The Abduction from the Seraglio:* "Too many notes, dear Mozart, too many notes," the emperor supposedly told the composer. Mozart replied, "Just as many as necessary, Your Majesty."[100] Iovine or another producer told Nicks to abbreviate and tighten up her songs. She argued that the album still had "a bunch of stuff missing on it."[101] In the end an uneasy compromise was reached between focused dance numbers and slower, meditative songs with fewer layers but richer textures.

Iovine and Nicks's romance was over and his interest in the project dwindled. He began work on the record in Dallas at Goodnight Audio, then left for half a year. In the meantime, Nicks had grown fond of Dallas and invested in a converted warehouse turned nightclub called Starck (named after its industrial modern Parisian designer, Philippe Starck). It attracted a diverse clientele—people in the petroleum business, gay men, and celebrities—as part of the ecstasy-fueled, pre-AIDS licentious rave phenomena.[102] Girls skipped the line if they impressed the bouncers. Nicks and disco queen Grace Jones, one of the club's instigators, played opposite each other on May 12, 1984, opening night. *Rock a Little* drew some of its inspiration from the scene.

At Iovine's suggestion Nicks recorded Bruce Springsteen's song "Janey, Don't You Lose Heart" at Goodnight Audio. Springsteen had sent it to her with final say over its release. In the studio, she changed the chorus to the gender-neutral "Baby, don't you lose heart," which Springsteen rejected. Nicks sent the tapes back to him, and the song was consigned to oblivion.[103] She also recorded the title track and fifth track at Goodnight Audio, both songs with long histories. "Rock a Little" was first demoed in 1981 and "Imperial Hotel" rearranged. The result sounds like Tom Petty and the Heartbreakers minus Petty, because two Heartbreakers—Mike Campbell and Benmont Tench—play on it.

In Iovine's absence, Nicks collaborated back in LA with two other producers. Her longtime acquaintance Keith Olsen came on board in the spring of 1984 to produce the penultimate track, "No Spoken Word," and help write some of the other songs. Iovine's assistant Rick Nowels also worked on the album. Nicks groused about "Iovine dump[ing] me and the record into Rick's lap and sa[ying], 'Goodbye, good luck.'"[104]

A Palo Alto native, Nowels met Nicks through Robin Snyder when Nicks was at San Jose State. He and Robin's brother Scott, Nowels's best friend, had formed a duo to play in San Francisco clubs, singing two-part harmony like Simon and Garfunkel. Nicks and Buckingham came around the house, playing their music. Nowels couldn't help but be awed by Buckingham's fingerpicking and remembers Nicks working on "Crystal" to "folk chords" on her Goya guitar. He admired her "self-assured, direct way of communicating," even though she was "just a kid" (in fact, she was twenty). Nowels and Snyder became good enough to perform set breaks for Fritz. When that band ended, Nowels lost touch with Nicks and Buckingham. Snyder had a bad LSD trip and found himself among the "Jesus freaks," which ended his career writing music for anything other than the gospel.[105]

After dropping out of UC Berkeley, Nowels moved to Los Angeles in 1984. It was too late to form a band—the people he tried to recruit all had actual adult commitments—so a song that he'd started in a rented studio, "I Can't Wait," languished. He managed to get in touch with Glen Parrish, Nicks's personal assistant, and confessed, "I'd love to say hi to Stevie." Parrish invited him to her house. He brought along a cassette with the backing track for "I Can't Wait." She was a perpetual night owl, he remembers, and her manager, Howard Kaufman, was with her until one in the morning. Nowels hung around through the night, "delighted to see her" after all the years. "I had lost Scott, and she had lost Robin," he said, adding that "she acted like a big sister" to him. The sun rose; the birds started singing. Nicks asked him about his music, and he brought out "I Can't Wait." She listened to the cassette a couple of times and asked him to leave it with her.[106]

The next day Parrish called Nowels to tell him that "Stevie has written a track. You should record it." Nowels booked a studio, eager to see what she had done with the music on the cassette. Nicks arrived, swished up to the mic, and sang, "Yes, I know you . . . to be continued . . . it's too much." "It's about you," she told him. The song needed a chorus, and Nowels had one, which Nicks recorded. He asked her backing singers to "build a wall." Iovine listened to it all the next day and called to say, "It's pretty good; you guys should finish it." Nowels rebooked the studio. The song's B section needed words, but Nicks brought along her lyric book, and they found something that connected the pieces.[107]

Iovine "saw that I was a talented guy," Nowels recalled. "Stevie was doing the all-night thing, and Iovine wanted to go home at midnight." He also had a pile-up of commitments with other musicians to attend to. Iovine "sort of let me in to wrap it up." It was Nowels's great privilege to have the album "dumped in his lap," he concluded, because it gave him a career. Nowels would realize most of the songs, bringing in Mick Guzauski as mixer.[108]

Iovine returned to the project in 1985, and completed it at the Power Station studio in New York, where he was living at the time. Nowels remained involved. Iovine worked from his hotel room a few blocks from the studio, deciding what to keep and what to scrap and choosing the lineups for the final stage of recording. For the tracks that mattered (those that had the greatest commercial promise), Iovine enlisted the crème de la crème of expensive session musicians, some for just a few hours. There was no intimacy, the musicians came and went, playing the music they were asked to play, several times in a row, with little contact with Nicks or Iovine. Andy Newmark, who played drums on the eighth and ninth tracks, "Nightmare" and "If I Were You," recalled the experience:

> I only did one 6-hour evening recording session for Stevie Nicks at The Power Station. I recall John Siegler was on bass. We were in Studio A, the big room on the first floor. Aside from saying hello and good bye, I had no inter-action with Nicks except maybe a few comments regarding the track we were playing.
> Iovine wasn't in the recording studio. Shelly Yakus, Jimmy's right hand guy forever, engineered the session. The evening's performances were sent by cassette to Jimmy in his hotel room on Central Park South where he was liv-ing for years. He often always recorded the same song with multiple rhythm sections until he got a version that he liked. Expensive for sure but he got results.[109]

Newmark finished his task not even knowing if his work would end up on the album.

These tracks, unsurprisingly, have an impersonal filler quality. They received less specific attention from Nicks than "Has Anyone Written Anything for You?," which she wrote, with Olsen's contribution, about Walsh's three-year-old daughter, who died in an automobile accident while on the way to nursery school. During the heaviest, most intense phase of their relationship, Walsh took Nicks to see the silver drinking fountain in a park in Boulder, Colorado, that bears his daughter's name in memoriam: "To Emma Kristen, for all those who aren't big enough to get a drink."[110] Her song is a hushed ballad in a slow 4/4 time that uses the same sinking harmonic progression (transposed) as "Beauty and the Beast." Olsen added ambient noises, haunted sounds, to the mix. It fades out with a whispered imprecation: "poet priest of nothing."

Stephen Davis claims that another song, "Talk to Me," also refers to Walsh in the line "You can set your secrets free, baby."[111] It doesn't. The words and music of "Talk to Me" were composed by producer and guitarist Chas Sandford in the ready-for-radio, midtempo, midrange idiom that made it a perfect single for *Rock a Little*. In 1984, Sandford had written a stylistically similar song, "Missing You," with John Waite and Mark Leonard, which became an unexpected hit, getting picked up on regional radio then soaring up the charts—unbeknownst to Sandford, who had decamped to Super Bear Studios in France to put together a cassette of demos. Hearing that Iovine was looking for material for Nicks, he passed along a copy of the tape upon returning home to Los Angeles. Iovine promptly lost it down the side of the front seat of his car, seemingly for good, until he slammed on the brakes to avoid hitting another car as it ran a red light. The cassette popped out from under the seat, and Iovine gave the demo of "Talk to Me" a listen. He knew it could be a hit and called up Sandford in the middle of the night offering him the take-it-or-leave-it chance to record it with Nicks. Sandford was flabbergasted and assumed that one of his friends was pulling a prank by expertly imitating Iovine's voice. But it was Iovine himself, genuinely eager to include the song on *Rock a Little* as the first single ("I Can't Wait" would be the second).

The song was basically done. The drums were automated and would remain so; the doubled-tracked guitar was in place, so too the concluding saxophone solo, having been pieced together in Nice by Sandford using a local bebopper. Nicks only needed to replace his vocal track with one of her own and have Celani and Perry build the wall for the chorus. The sessions at Village Studio B in Santa Monica dragged on for months, however, as they did at the other studios where the album was recorded. Meantime the cost of the album kept rising, crossing the one-and-a-half million mark, to the obvious consternation of management at the label (Modern). A listening session was arranged for a group of executives flying in from New York. Nicks's vocals were not yet added to the master. She had done different takes in different places, the recordings shuffled to post-tape processing on different machines. (A shuffler, used in mid-side processing, takes the left and right signals and mixes them into two separate signals for processing, one being the sum of the left and right signals, the other being the difference between them.) Walsh added guitar to one of the versions, which Sandford rejected as unidiomatic, and Tench some keyboard. The vocals existed everywhere and nowhere, and Sandford was in a panic, scrambling to "fly" the best version into the mix. That version had been recorded in New York a half-step removed from the rest, which meant adjusting the pitch using a Publison Infernal Machine 90, used for pitch-shifting vocals. The tape was run through the IM90 in stages to get the tuning as precise as possible before putting it on the master. Sandford pulled off this improbable feat and ran the reassembled song. Doug Morris, the CEO of Atlantic, loved it, as did Fishkin, Goldberg, and Iovine—at least until the machine started eating the tape and the chorus disappeared. Mercifully, the song that would eventually pay for the rest of the record was recovered from a digital machine onto which it had been bounced.

Sandford remembers the episode with good humor, as an adventure "like nothing else I have ever had in my life." Nicks had no knowledge of the high-pressure scramble to complete "Talk to Me" and to this day thinks that the last take of the vocals was what ended up on the record. She and Sandford remained in touch after the release of the album, and she dedicated the video of the single to Sandford's recently deceased brother Richard. Sandford remembers her turning up for a Halloween party at the "haunted" antebellum mansion he once rented on farmland outside of Nashville. "She looked like Stevie Nicks with glitter on," he recalled, but the other guests mistook her for an impersonator. When she sat down at the piano and started to play, the crowd fell silent.[112]

Rock a Little is defined, at heart, by two songs: "I Sing for the Things" and "Rock a Little (Go Ahead Lily)." The first, concerning the things "money can't buy," evolved from a gentle piano-vocal treatment into a brittle, highly arpeggiated, dulcimer-like arrangement. Synths and steel guitar dialogue in the fadeout. Nicks's singing is frail and raspy yet has less emotional pull than the 1979 demo, which is powerfully unadorned. The tonic, subdominant, and dominant pitches of C major appear in the left hand, the tonic alone (syncopated) in the right. The voice floats above on D and F, shunning the insistently repeated cadential motion in the accompaniment. Nicks sinks E in the direction of Eb for added poignancy in the decidedly unmelodic chorus. "Did the fear inside you/make you turn and run?" is recited, not sung, in mixed rhythmic values on (for the most part) D. Fear is expressed in the tiniest of breaks in elided phrases, small slips in the pitch, and slight quivers. These details come into focus on the voice-alone demo, where the echo of her voice lingers and then folds into a protracted silence after the words "turn and run." The song has been called "postfeminist," although no genders are specified.[113] It's about different kinds of devotion: selfless, distrusted, and desperate. The arranged, recorded version of "I Sing" fills in and enriches the I-IV-V triads (the sixth- and seventh-scale degrees make an appearance), doubles the vocal line at the third and occasional second, and busies the rhythms. It also, as Matthew Hough points out in his analysis, "normalizes" the song: phrase lengths, meter, and tonality are all more clearly defined.[114] Yet Nicks's song is about lack of definition.

"Rock a Little (Go Ahead Lily)" is a song about her father, Jess Nicks, who once prodded her onto the stage when she was sick, using the name of her literary alter ego, Lillian Hellman. (In her poetry of the seventies and eighties, Nicks occasionally referred to herself as Lily and her best friend, Robin, as Julia, in reference to a 1977 film about heroic self-sacrifice called *Julia*.)[115] The gentlest of reggae patterns does a little rocking, not much at all. The title track of her most up-tempo record is a lullaby that hints at dance before becoming a eulogy. The cradle rocks at birth as the rocking chair does before death. Wandering the years in between, we rock from side to side. The idea is captured in a series of photographs by Herbert Worthington showing Nicks in black beside a black cradle and rocking chair. From these, the album's cover, minus the furniture, was extracted.

Like "I Can't Wait," "Rock a Little" took time and friction to complete. Nowels recalls completing a rough monitor mix at six in the morning and taking it to Nicks for her approval. She rejected the version of "Rock a Little" prepared by Mick Guzauski, preferring instead a mix from six months before. She returned to the studio to push the faders herself, resulting in a track that Nowels couldn't make sense of, with "the levels all over the place." Nicks liked what she'd done: "Do you think a 14-year-old kid thinks about that? They listen to the vibe of the record." He never forgot the lesson.[116] The "vibe" is sultry, hot, and humid. Swirling through the heat are the lyrics "funny little dancer" and "rock and roll ballerina," her father's words from when she was little. A maraca shakes out eighths in the foreground, close to the ear, with the title words breathed into the mix at odd intervals by the backup singers. The extended version, adding live drums and additional lyrics, has less ennui and enhances the mild reggae feel of the original.

"Rock a Little" provided the album's title by default. The album was supposed to be called *The Other Side of the Mirror*, based on a song in progress, "Mirror, Mirror." Nicks saved that name for later, however, and the song ignominiously ended up as a B-side to a 1994 cassette single. "I didn't like the way it came out," she commented, before adding a confusing footnote: "'Mirror, Mirror' is the other side of the mirror, and the Gemini personality. The two, you know, the nine or ten personalities that I have, and how I deal with all of them."[117] She spoke like this throughout the mid-eighties, sometimes in circles, round and round, putting into words the feeling of not knowing where she is while gazing at herself—herselves—in a hall of mirrors.

It was a scary feeling, and it informs a scary song, one that was excluded from the album despite having tremendous potential. The demo of "Night Gallery" breaks off after two minutes, but the chorus and two verses were worked out with keyboard and tambourine, which added a frail intensity. Nicks switches pronouns from "I" to "she" and invites her lover to go "deep into the end zone of the moor, where hounds bay and witches fly brooms, and the belief in the supernatural is as natural as breathing, or not breathing." The words are not Nicks's invention but Rod Serling's, from the introduction to the 1970–73 television series *Night Gallery*—hence Nicks's title.[118] The second segment of the first episode of the series ("Eyes," directed by Steven Spielberg) has a blind woman, played by Joan Crawford, regaining her vision during a blackout in New York City. As preserved on cassette, Nicks's song is a congested hothouse in contrast to Serling's and Crawford's "cool dampness."

At the start of the first and second verses, Nicks murmurs (as would Kate Bush in one of her insulated dirges) before entering an expressive abyss that exploits the ambiguity of the ellipsis. She hammers at the nothingness of the word "something" while eliding the endings and beginnings of phrases.

> Well, every day I search to find a new way
> Some new thing to say
> Something to make you stay
> Something that might mean something to you
> Something
>
> Ooh . . .
> In my daily search
> There is no company
> Down the road, I go by myself
> Say you stood in her gallery. . . .

It's a perfect song for *Rock a Little*, but it wasn't finished and couldn't be included, which tilted the album's focus away from the personal and toward more generically up-tempo fare.

The sounds the iconic bands of the eighties privileged, including "carousel keyboards, blocky rhythms, and splashes of controlled guitar anarchy," were antithetical to Nicks's Americana, but she convinced herself to adapt along with the industry.[119] She sang from the heart with neither the notes nor the chords mattering as much as her seasoned country-rock timbre, even while the era focused on delighting the senses with detached major-key hooks. "I Can't Wait" is a tightly wound dance track with, in the final mix, the backing singers' "wall" characteristic of tracks like New Order's "The Price of Love." Nicks's singing is still too edgy, her manner anathema to click tracks. *Rolling Stone*'s

Mark Coleman couldn't get his head around *Rock a Little:* "For a pop album," it "sounds strangely distant, out of touch. Plopped down next to purring synthesizers and the patter of drum machines, Stevie's sugary moans sound harsh and jarring. The attempts to 'contemporize' some of these 4/4 strum-along ditties ruin what would otherwise be an untouched curio, a relic from the forgotten age of the singer/song-writer."[120] Had Coleman confessed that the album bewitched him, he would have written the perfect review.

LIVE AT RED ROCKS

Nicks toured between April 11 and August 28, 1986, opening in Houston, Texas, and closing close to home in Long Beach, California. There were eight additional dates in Australia between September 24 and October 6. Unwell, her voice overtaxed, she experienced vertigo and once fell off the stage.[121] The concert video *Live at Red Rocks* is difficult to watch. It was released as an enhanced CD-ROM in 1987 and reissued on DVD in 2007.[122] The video is embellished with close-ups, overdubbed vocals, and visual effects to conceal blemishes in the performance.

The video opens with a montage accompanied by the first song from the album, "I Can't Wait." Mick Fleetwood, Waddy Wachtel, Peter Frampton, and Nicks are shown arriving at Red Rocks Amphitheatre in Morrison, Colorado, and being greeted by fans. On stage, Nicks sings hoarsely at a flower-draped mic stand. During "Beauty and the Beast," photographs from the seventies are edited into the footage. She is the beauty, Fleetwood the beast. Nicks marches across the stage in pumps, tossing her hands up as though casting a spell on the backing musicians, as the band takes up the intro to "Stand Back." A stagehand passes her a white dove, which holds on to the mic. "Edge of Seventeen" is extended to almost ten minutes (six longer than the single), with the band riffing for three. No longer the bohemian dressed in flowing caftans, Nicks has a more enigmatic, protected persona. She passes behind Wachtel, pausing in an impressive port de bras, her large white sleeves forming the shape of wings. Her performance moves between full throttle singing and abstract, poetic speech: "Well, the sky never expects it when it rains, but the sea changes color." Some two-thirds of the way through, she kneels down to the stage, cradling the mic, and screams as if herself uncaged.[123]

Nicks gave an interview in Los Angeles on May 11, 1985, long in advance of the release of *Rock a Little* and the tour. She still looks twenty, but she's high and speaks both fuzzily and poetically about an album that wasn't right until she had mulled it over for a "few minutes, few days, few lifetimes." At the start she asks to dash to the bathroom, presumably for a bump, but she can't because she's already hooked to a mic. Nicks pulls herself together enough to indulge the interviewer, even smiling and laughing. She gets serious when talking about becoming famous in a male-dominated world. She was "lucky," she explains, "protected" and didn't have "to see too much." Christine took the "hard knocks" in Fleetwood Mac.

> *Interviewer:* How about the tour, are you going to try some different places this time?
>
> *Nicks:* We've played just about every place you could possibly play. I'm gonna go to Europe, of course. I mean I just want to go, like today. I'll probably do the United States. See, I have to wait when the record comes out; then it's like from the day I hand it to them I have about two months, or that's about what it takes until I can really leave this town to go on the road, because if you go too early, you're kind of, I don't know what the word for it is, defeating yourself because it's too early. And so it's better to wait so that means I have to hurry and get this out so that I *can* go and so I have a feeling that maybe I'll go to Europe first. I don't want to go to Europe first. I'd like to go to the United States first before I go there, but it'll depend on the time schedule, and I don't wanna sit around and do nothing for two months after my record comes out. I'll go crazy.
>
> *Interviewer:* You must be dying to get out on the road.
>
> *Nicks:* Yeah, that would be really hard for me. Clubs, clubs.
>
> *Interviewer:* Do you ever get to do that anymore?
>
> *Nicks:* I wish. I would like to.[124]

Nicks is obviously hurting in the interview, which remains available online for all to see.

The hurt lasted, and the albums she released after *Rock a Little* would prove uneven for reasons specific to her and others that reflected changes in the recording industry in general. The music that she wrote before entering the studio finds her speaking her truth—about being dragged around, physically, emotionally, creatively—and seeking to stop it. Freeing herself took years. To become a star, or superstar, requires talent and timing and the right kind of push from profiteers. To become an icon, to find happiness in the afterglow, demands a reckoning. Ultimately, Nicks was able, in her music, to channel the hurt of others.

Buckingham Nicks tour, University of Alabama, January 28, 1975.
The University of Alabama Libraries Special Collections.

The building that once housed Mickie's Tavern in Altadena, where Stephanie Nicks sang with her grandfather. Photograph by Nika Bergman-Morrison.

This is "Fritz," making the good-time sounds ring at last Thursday's College Hour. From l. to r. are: Javier Pacheco, Brian Kane, Bob Aguirre, Stevie Nicks, and Lindsey Buckingham.

Demosthenes Photo

Fritz Does It Up Right

by Jim Keefe

"Fritz Does It Up Right," *The Newspaper*, Cañada College, Redwood City, April 18, 1969.

Last Thursday, Cañada's College Hour presented "Fritz," possibly one of the best, if not the best, bands that has appeared on campus this year.

"Fritz," formerly the "Fritz Raybyne Memorial Band," is not a new band to the Peninsula music scene. They have appeared on a number of occasions at the Santa Clara Fair Grounds, performing in concert with such noted groups as Steve Miller and Deep Purple and appearing with Iron Butterfly at the Expo-69 Teenage Fair, also held at the fair grounds. Recently they appeared on the Ross McGowan Television Show.

"Fritz" started out as a joke, just something to do. They managed to play a couple of places in high school, mainly at their own school, Menlo-Atherton High. The band originally contained Javier, Bob and Lindsey, but with the addition of Brian and Stevie to the group, they really started to play seriously. For the last year and a half the group has played continuously and sees no reason in the future for them to break up.

The group plays quite a variety of music, mainly rock with no definite style. They play all types of rock, including country, folk rock and hard rock. In talking with Bob he said

"when we play we just want everyone to have a good time." He said that some of their material is original, and by the way — it's very good. He said the band enjoyed playing for the people at Cañada and hopes they will be able to play at Cañada again this semester, so make sure that everyone comes.

If anyone wants to see "Fritz" play, they will be appearing with the Youngbloods, Country Weather and Stained Glass at a Rock Concert to be held this Friday night at Aragon High School. Good luck, through hard work and innate talent, seems to be pointing "Fritz" towards a profitable and exciting future.

Recording the "white album" at Sound City Studios in Van Nuys, 1975.

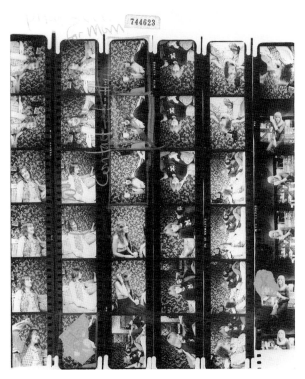

Recording the "white album."

Recording at Trod Nossel Studios, New Haven, October 1975.
Photograph by Fin Costello.

New Haven, October 1975. Photograph by Fin Costello.

Cheerleading in late 1976 with Walter Egan, Duane Scott, and Lindsey Buckingham during the recording of Egan's album *Fundamental Roll*. Photograph taken at 943 N. Beverly Glen Blvd., Los Angeles, by Moshe Brakha.

With Walter Egan, Duane Scott, and Lindsey Buckingham. Photograph by Moshe Brakha.

With Walter Egan. Photograph by Moshe Brakha.

Photo call at Rotterdam. Photograph by Barry Schultz.

◄ Photo call on a cruise ship in the harbor at Rotterdam, the Netherlands, *Rumours* tour, April 1977. Photograph by Barry Schultz.

At Rotterdam. Photograph by Barry Schultz.

Fleetwood Mac headlining Bill Graham's Day on the Green concert, Oakland Coliseum, May 7, 1977. Photograph by Richard McCaffrey.

Bill Graham's Day on the Green concert. Photograph by Richard McCaffrey.

Day on the Green. Photograph by Richard McCaffrey.

Roistering with Rod Stewart at Regine's nightclub in New York, October 21, 1977.
Nicks and Stewart frequently crossed paths in their wilder years and joined forces
on a tour called Heart and Soul in 2011. Photograph by Lynn Goldsmith.

Fleetwood Mac at Ann Arbor press conference, *Tusk* tour, November 1979.
MLive Media Group/The Ann Arbor News.

▲ With Tom Petty at the Cow
Palace, Daly City, June 26, 1981.
Photograph by Larry Hulst.

◀ During the *Mirage* tour in 1982.
Photograph by Lynn Goldsmith.

◄ During the *Wild Heart* tour in 1983. Photograph by Lynn Goldsmith.

With Joe Walsh (and, faintly visible at right in the background,
Walsh's parrot Ralph), 1991. Photograph by Kristin Casey.

A reunited Fleetwood Mac backstage at the inauguration gala for Bill Clinton,
January 19, 1993. Photograph by Lynn Goldsmith.

With Dave Grohl, February 2013, New York City. Grohl
plays drums on "Show Them the Way" and directed the
documentary *Sound City*. Photograph by Danny Clinch.

Rock & Roll Hall of Fame Induction Ceremony, Barclays Center, Brooklyn, March 29, 2019. Harry Styles stands in the background, having introduced Nicks. Photograph by Dimitrios Kambouris.

CHAPTER 4

Sara

In late November 1986, between concert tours, Nicks checked herself into the Betty Ford Center in Rancho Mirage, California, to treat the cocaine addiction that she had been battling for a dozen years (four years beyond the eight she spent in denial). She had tried to break the habit in 1982 but lapsed during the making of the "Gypsy" music video. A doctor friend alerted her to the damage she had done to the inside of her nose (from cocaine as well as the mountain of aspirin she took for withdrawal headaches) and the risk, should she continue using, of a fatal hemorrhage. Friends and family, including her parents, convinced her to get help. She secured her stay at Betty Ford under the name Sara Anderson. It was a brief, monotonous experience of dorm-style living with a middle-aged female alcoholic, chores (mopping, vacuuming, cleaning the grounds), and nine-to-five counseling sessions. It was by no means the "boot camp" she claims. The food was fine, and fans buried her (and the staff) in flowers, plants, and love letters after her presence in the clinic was leaked. Nicks met Ford herself after being discharged and thanked her on bended knee for saving her.[1] She lasted at the clinic for two and a half weeks in 1986, leaving earlier than expected—the prescribed stay is a month—but remained clean.

"WELCOME TO THE ROOM, SARA"

She allegorized her experience, albeit vaguely, in three songs. While detoxing Nicks evidently read Margaret Mitchell's 1936 novel *Gone with the Wind*, or watched the film, since "Welcome to the Room, Sara," which she handed over to Fleetwood Mac to produce, references the melodrama's sentiments about love, including loving something imagined. "Sara" rhymes with "Tara," the name of Scarlett O'Hara's plantation as well as an ancient word for stars, "soul's light." Buckingham takes the part of Rhett Butler, sparring with his soul mate and alter ego Scarlett. The song is also self-referential: the line "welcome to the choir, sir" echoes the lyrics of "Silver Springs" and "Beautiful Child" as well as "Sara." The words "When you hang up that phone / Well, you cease to exist" are something anyone who has been in treatment can understand. It's also a complement to Scarlett's famous line, "Wherever shall I go?"

Buckingham added programmed bongo drums to integrate the song into the rest of the album, and Fleetwood busied up an inert recitation—the chorus sits on a single major chord embellished with a second and sixth—with snare and tom-tom fills. Buckingham doubles Nicks's voice on the chorus, but awkwardly and unmusically. It's a tic on the album, so too the jangling guitar, which lends brightness to a song composed in defiance of anything approaching a hook. The Fairlight CMI is overprescribed, and "Welcome to the Room" anesthetized.

"When I See You Again," which Nicks also assigned to Fleetwood Mac, is fragmentary and barely articulate. Nicks's voice is scratchy and dry sounding. The song is a country ballad with unintentionally wayward tuning. Nicks makes it through a couple of verses and the chorus only in stitched-together segments, judging by the unevenness of Buckingham's production. The instrumentation includes nylon-stringed guitar, gentle tambourine and shaker sounds, distant keyboard flutters in the chorus, and a synthesized string line that fills the holes in the tune. Suspended seconds and fourths lend poignancy: Asus2 and Esus4 define the verses, Bsus4 and Asus2 frame a painful C-sharp minor seventh in the chorus. The second verse describes aimless wandering down halls, staring at stairs; the music captures the sense of confusion. Buckingham takes over for Nicks as singer in the final section, dragging the song across the finish line while making the effort obvious for all to hear.

"Doing the Best That I Can" dates from two years later than the other songs. Its subtitle, "Escape from Berlin," references the fall of the Berlin Wall as well as the Berlin-based movie *Julia* (1977). Exploring the experience of being locked away, the film obviously resonated with Nicks. Rupert Hine's production is lavishly clean and clear; the studio musicians selected for the song (which appears on her fourth solo album, 1989's *The Other Side of the Mirror*) are excellent but uncommitted, their comings and goings as audible here as on *Rock a Little* from four years prior. The shifts between chords (Eb major and minor, Bb minor, Ab major, G minor, and Bb major) are discreet, with a Halloweenish hint of Mike Oldfield's "Tubular Bells" in the rhythm guitar. The texture flatly elides verse and chorus, while the power-rock sound overcompensates for the fragilities in the confessional words, a detail that sinks the track but buoys the album.

"Rather than rock's Shirley MacLaine, this time she's more Sylvia Plath," Steve Hochman mused in the *Los Angeles Times* about this phase in her output, "though Nicks has apparently crawled out from under her unspecified bell jar. There are images of brooding solitude and hard lessons learned abound: besides the angels there's lots of falling rain and disillusioned fairy-tale princesses, all sung about in an appropriately weary but wizened voice."[2] His reductive approach to female artistry—and suffering—rankles. Nicks became famous through the mainstreaming of feminism; the opposition she faced was not monolithic but porous enough to allow her to propel a solo career through it and thus to be credited, in part, with the success of the movement. Nicks compromised to survive until she reached a place where, having climbed above all of her tormentors, she could casually and confidently leave disillusionment behind.

TANGO IN THE NIGHT

Buckingham assembled the Fleetwood Mac album *Tango in the Night* in peripatetic fits and starts between November 1985 and March 1987. It was released a month later, with cover art by Brett-Livingstone Strong: his 1987 painting *Homage à Henri Rousseau,* which Buckingham acquired for his home.[3] The homage is to Rousseau's *La charmeuse de serpents (The Snake Charmer,* 1907). The snake charmer plays seductive music through her pipe, causing serpents to dance in a fantastical, moonlit jungle-scape. It's deeply seductive as a profane Garden of Eden, and Sylvia Plath based a poem on the subject titled "Snake Charmer" (1960). Her eight stanzas drift dazzlingly from a description of an artist's creative powers to the ideations of the imagination. (Rousseau never visited the India his famed image references.) The snakes are the charmer's audience but also her invention. The artist makes something out of nothing, nothing out of something. The demo becomes a song becomes a demo.

Nicks sent in the demos of "Welcome to the Room" and "Doing the Best I Can" but, her health compromised, spent less than two weeks in the studio. The album was produced by Buckingham and Dashut and engineered by Greg Dorman, an Ohio transplant affiliated with Joe Walsh. He worked at Rumbo Studio in Canoga Park, which had been built by Daryl Dragon, the husband of light-rock husband-and-wife duo Captain & Tennille. The building was a slab of gray cement, nondescript but for a pair of elephant statues and a blue awning over the entrance. It operated at "a time when the Valley lingered somewhere between Frank Zappa's ramblings and a real-life version of Paul Thomas Anderson's *Boogie Nights*," an article in *LA Weekly* elaborates. "A mix of agriculture, dust, white wagon wheels, diners, car dealerships, suburban sprawl, new housing developments, and swimming pools, it was held together by all those long streets and lazy vowels."[4] In the eighties Rumbo's slacker vibe made it popular with hair bands like Guns N' Roses. Dorman and Dashut met there while recording Christine McVie's cover of "Can't Help Falling in Love" for the soundtrack to the 1986 Blake Edwards slapstick *A Fine Mess*. Buckingham booked a studio at Rumbo for a solo project while working, in a different studio, on *Tango in the Night*. As with *Tusk*, he also recorded at his house in Bel Air.[5] Mick Fleetwood and the McVies lounged in an RV parked in the driveway while waiting to be brought into Buckingham's laboratory—the studio across the hall from his bedroom—for overdubbing. Work was businesslike and budget conscious.

Tango is a paradox, a pastiche that's part fake orgy, part fake after-orgy. "There's a phenomenal wholeness to the recordings on *Tango* that seems like a superficial compensation for how deeply fragmented the band was at the time," critic Brad Nelson argues.[6] Certain tracks, like "Family Man," are highly processed amalgams of analog and digital sounds; others, including "Seven Wonders," are fragile structures heavily padded with reverb. The song barely holds together, and precision rescues the tango from kitsch. In "Big Love" the ostinato grunting that forms the hook, a throwback to the "heavy breathing" of seventies pop-rock pornophony, is precisely timed to the drum machine.[7]

As ever, Buckingham experimented, listening to tracks at different speeds to refine the mixes (a form of torture for the production team) but also recording at half- and quarter-pace so that the higher end would have a richer sound when brought up to speed. The result is a seamless and spacious analog-digital blend, especially on the album's first three singles: "Big Love," "Seven Wonders," and "Little Lies." Each was recorded on forty-six tracks. Buckingham drew from Kate Bush's hybrid electroacoustic sound world, according to a *Salon* magazine exploration of the making of the album.[8] Digital tapes were cut and spliced and refrigerated to prevent deterioration. Dorman had panic attacks whenever the fickle, prickly Buckingham changed his mind or expressed disappointment or decided he needed to do everything at home by himself.

In one of the few photographs from the recording sessions, Nicks wears thick reading glasses and a loose white skirt and sweater. Buckingham and Christine McVie are beside her, also dressed down, seemingly recording the vocals of "Seven Wonders." Nicks is co-credited as songwriter with Sandy Stewart, who has a big presence on *The Wild Heart* album. Internet lore—which Stewart told me was "false and inaccurate"—has Nicks singing the wrong words in the studio and becoming cowriter by default.[9] The text did change, but not by accident. On the demo "all the way down you held the line" became "all the way down to Emmaline"; and "rainbow's end" turned into "rainbow's edge," an alteration similar to "age/edge of seventeen." "Seven Wonders" describes true love, or true *lost* love, as something greater than the pyramids and the Hanging Gardens of Babylon, simple enough except for the inclusion of "Aaron" in the post-chorus. Nicks isn't referencing her grandfather here but playing with phonemes to make language more musical. The verses and chorus are framed by an intro and outro that explore the Fairlight's wonders and offer up commodified exotica: eerie synth hooks, parallel fifths, a hazy, lazy beat, sponginess, squishiness. *Tango in the Night* makes *Rumours* seem authentic; everything is a simulacrum.

"JOAN OF ARC"

The B-side of the "Seven Wonders" single is an instrumental called "Book of Miracles," which became "Juliet" on Nicks's *Other Side of the Mirror*. "Ooh My Love" also ended up on the solo record, having been excised from *Tango*. Another rough draft, "Joan of Arc," is an unreleased outtake reconstructed from reel tape. Its absence is a loss. The track isn't completely produced, but it deserves to be given the foreground-background echoes of the lap harp, eerie guitar wails in the far back of the mix, clamped tinging of the tambourine, and huskily frail singing of the line "turn it to the wall . . . up against the wall." It fades out inconclusively, which suits the inscrutability of the lyrics. The bend bar on the electric guitar (used beautifully toward the end of the cut) might have evolved from an attempt to imitate the dobro. The other-worldly background sounds are evenly paced, but not the distressed sing-ing. The lyrics are free-form (Nicks generally avoids the ABAB or AABB forms of balladry) and attached to the first five notes of the major (or Mixolydian, missing the sixth and seventh) scale. The obsessive repeti-tions of "turn it to the wall . . . up against the wall" change in attack, detail, amplitude, color. The alterations in dynamics, the unevenness, the way the notes are stretched out or sped up or enlarged or reined in, the flexibility in the shape and texture of the three phrases—all are acts of processing. "Joan" is an enigmatic love song that combines references to ancient legend with talk of limousines and something that happened in the singer's own life. It describes betrayal and bad faith and expresses anguish. The hero is doomed, mounting the scaffold, over the pyre, above the tongues of flame. Putting people up against the wall is what shooting squads do.

In the Joan of Arc legends, some built on rumors, she is the heaven-sent savior of France during the Hundred Years' War (1337–1453), captured by French allies of the English invaders and burned at the stake as a witch.[10] In Voltaire's version, which Nicks seems to have consulted, Joan takes the soldier Jean de Dunois as a lover. The illegitimate son of the Duke of Orléans (thus known as the Bastard of Orléans), Dunois holds back English invaders for several exhausting months during the war. Joan arrives, an armored teenager, foretelling the enemy's defeat. Dunois is skeptical of Joan's power to help, and the song begins from his perspective:

> They wanted images
> When images were unspoken
> They depended upon illusion . . .
> Calling illusion gold and glitter
> And they came in tired
> And they said tired was the end of the line

Joan hears angelic voices summoning her to action, but Dunois evalu-ates them as mere "gold and glitter"—this is the metallic sheen, the brittle, reverberating harp sound that echoes the voice. He concludes, "Well, no there's really nothing that you can do for me." A turning point in the recitation comes at "Go like the wind," referencing the miracle Joan performs at Orléans by changing the direction of the wind to permit troops to cross the Loire River. The perspective changes to the third person:

She saw it all. . . . It was a tiresome ending,
He stormed out hearing the door slamming . . .
Behind him
Ooh, she didn't even know why he left her

Dunois resists Joan's plan, betraying her. She is left outside the protective walls of Orléans and taken captive. Historical accounts suggest her capture, at Compiègne rather than Orléans, was a trap.

Nicks goes for the jugular in the song, denouncing Joan's abandonment, highlighting that she wasn't taken seriously, wasn't listened to, wasn't heard—like the song itself, which Buckingham excluded from the album. "Joan of Arc" was a bad fit for the flirty, raunchy, hyperproduced, hypermasculine songs he contributed to *Tango in the Night*. Boys and girls do terrible things to each other, but none of the terrible things the boys and girls of Fleetwood Mac did to one another will this album admit. Nicks's outtake outs the truth.

Buckingham refused to tour the record, which precipitated a fight with the rest of Fleetwood Mac and his exit from the band. At Christine McVie's home, a gathering of musicians and managers tried to mend fences, but Buckingham decried them all as a "bunch of selfish bastards":

> They tried to twist my arm to play the tour. Four against one. Being the one who picked the raw material and fashioned it in the studio for what they call "the Fleetwood Mac sound," I think they felt a little fear of losing that whole element. So I don't blame them for any tactics they might have used. It was natural. I was trying to be a nice guy but I really didn't want to do the tour. I said no, then I said, Oh, OK. They said, Good, let's all go out to dinner and have fun. I didn't even show up at the restaurant—that's how close I was to not doing it even though I'd said OK.[11]

Mick Fleetwood, in a book cowritten with Stephen Davis, describes another gathering on August 7, 1987, at Christine McVie's house in Los Angeles. Buckingham and Nicks had a terrible fight. "Get this bitch out of my way. And fuck the lot of you!" Buckingham supposedly said, though "fuck the lot of you" is English profanity, not American. He then slapped Nicks and pushed her onto the hood of his car. Others intervened and he disappeared.[12] Buckingham firmly denied the incident in a 1992 interview with the British music magazine *Q*.[13] Fleetwood, however, claimed, that he'd "done it [been hostile] before"—perhaps out of accumulated frustration, or temporary loss of sanity, or excessive libations, or any of the other excuses abusers use to absolve themselves of responsibility for destructive impulses.[14]

Despite this horror, Nicks still wanted to tour, both to earn income and to compensate for her spectral presence on *Tango*. Fleetwood Mac was her band too. She had reservations about her limited role in the project, knowing she had been preoccupied with the promotion of *Rock a Little* and her fragile health, and insisted on recording her backing vocals at the last minute to replace what Buckingham had cut. Because contracts were already signed, the tour had to happen, so Billy Burnette and Rick Vito subbed for Buckingham, with Dan Garfield providing additional offstage synthesizer sounds and Isaac Asanté on percussion. Lori Perry Nicks, Elisecia Wright, and Sharon Celani filled in the backing vocals. The US leg began on September 30, 1987, in Kansas City and ended in Seattle on December 17. The European tour (May–June 1988) was bookended by concerts in the United Kingdom, the most leisurely and rewarding shows, with performances in Sweden, Germany, and Holland in between. The set list excluded the sexual grunts of "Big Love" and all but one of Buckingham's songs, "Go Your Own Way."

In highly scripted public comments the band stressed health consciousness, newfound energy, and a desire to "shake the cage," as the tour was dubbed. The official videos confirm the transformation of the band into a solidly eighties act of prefab polish. Nicks appears in a mere handful of second-long snippets, pale-faced and with her hair teased into a fluff ball, tambourine in hand.

Nicks's stay at Betty Ford was noted in the reviews, as was her fuller figure and the all-age friendliness of the pop-a-thons she and the other seasoned musicians put on. Nicks had to cancel dates to nurse her throat, and a planned Pacific leg was jettisoned owing to fatigue. In an interview with Dee Ann Rexroat from her Florida hotel suite, Nicks spoke ironically about needing to protect her vocal cords by avoiding interviews. The low mezzo huskiness was not, she stressed, caused by lesions or nodes or a tightening of the tendons in the throat. Even if polyps or cysts were to develop, she would never go under the knife to have them removed, she insisted, since such drastic action would spell the end of her career. Post-surgery, "that voice that some people hate and some people love would be clear as a bell," Nicks noted, "and would sound like a million other people." She was asked about Buckingham's absence from the tour. "In my heart he's been gone for a long time," she said. "He's searching for a dream he hasn't found yet."[15] So perhaps was she.

RUPERT

In 1988, Nicks dreamily recounts, she fell for Rupert Hine, who produced her fourth solo record.

> The night I met Rupert Hine was a dangerous one. He was different from anyone else I had ever known. He was older, and he was smarter, and we both knew it. I hired him to do the album before we even started talking about music. It seemed that we had made a spiritual agreement to do a magic album in a fabulous Dutch castle, at the top of the mountain.
>
> It always seemed to me that whenever Rupert walked into one of these old, dark castle rooms, that the rooms were on fire. We all lived at the castle for about four-and-a-half months. I went home with him to England to mix the album at his studio. He left in December. I joined him there in London in January. We left immediately for his studio, Farmyard Studios, somewhere outside London [northwest of London in the village of Little Chalfont, Buckinghamshire]. It was like being in a cottage in Wales, it was a little spooky—the atmosphere was like nothing I had ever experienced. Then something happened to him that simply made it impossible for us to ever be together again. I came back to Los Angeles, a very changed woman.[16]

Hine was born on September 21, 1947, in Wimbledon, London, just eight months before the woman he changed. His father sold lumber for a living; his mother was a nurse. He showed an interest in architecture before taking to music and teaching himself piano.[17] Hine played with a series of bands and made several records before moving into production as an "accomplished synth player and rhythm programmer."[18] He told an interviewer that he "never wanted to be a rock star," seeking instead to be, like his first wife Natasha Barrault, an interdisciplinary artist.[19] (Barrault has been a songwriter, filmmaker, interior designer, and sustainable-materials seamstress.) Hine's musical activities shifted from folk to jazz to art rock; he composed for film, produced, and, more recently, developed music-making apps. He loved Mahler's symphonies, the organ, and the harpsichord. Hine pioneered sound effects that became eighties clichés and then, in the nineties, deconstructed them, angry at the apathy of the industry. He churned out electronic and acoustic hits for diverse singers, including Tina Turner, Howard Jones, Duncan Sheik, and Suzanne Vega. Then he unplugged, exploring the natural acoustics of a hotel lobby in the French Pyrenees to produce an album for the fractious French ensemble Les Négresses Vertes.[20]

Nicks met Hine at Doug Morris's urging, and they joined forces to record her fourth studio album, *The Other Side of the Mirror*. Both sought a Beauty and the Beast setting for the project, settling on a faux castle built in Beverly Hills in 1974. The semi-fortified pile at 1366 Angelo Drive had previously been featured in movies (porn was shot in its over-draped rooms), and Nicks's people (aka Iovine's people) converted it into a functional studio. Davis reports that Nicks rented "Castle Studios" for half a year at $25,000 a month. Nicks and Hine worked and lived there along with her brother, his wife, Lori Perry Nicks, and Nicks's assistant Karen Johnston.[21] She held the May 18, 1989, release party for *The Other Side of the Mirror* on the premises, hosting rock hellions Billy Idol and Gene Simmons in all their campy black leather finery.

Nicks and Hine worked well together, but their romance, as she reports, ended abruptly in Buckinghamshire. The obvious explanation is the pregnancy of his semi-estranged wife. Barrault gave birth to a son in May 1989 in London. That same month, eight time zones away, the album Nicks had made with her courtly lover dropped. Hine did not finish the project; as a replacement, Nicks enlisted Chris Lord-Alge, whose recording technique occupied the eighties space between "hard-hitting and hit-parade friendly" rock—just what Nicks, Modern, and Atlantic wanted.[22] Lord-Alge completed production and engineered *The Other Side* at his Los Angeles studio on a Sony 3348 forty-eight-track digital machine, top of the line in 1989. Chris's brother Tom also had a hand in the album, remixing the fourth single, "Whole Lotta Trouble," one of three songs on the album involving Tom Petty's guitarist Mike Campbell as coauthor.

Back in England, Hine resented being shut out of the process and not having his calls answered.[23] Nicks erased him from her personal life. Business being business, however, he received due and generous credit for his creative and technical contributions to an album that sounded less eclectic at the end than it did at the beginning.

The Other Side was initially inspired by Lewis Carroll's *Alice's Adventures in Wonderland* and its sequel, *Through the Looking-Glass*, but it's a rather diverse offering that also absorbs other children's tales, from the story of Red Riding Hood to the entire cosmos of legends about maidens trapped (or protected) in castles. Nicks dedicated it to her grandmother in memoriam.

In keeping with Carroll's tale, the album's lyrics are consistently disorienting. Plural and singular blur together, while the same things are made to seem different. Several songwriters are credited, some of them strangers, others friends and colleagues. Nicks wrote two of the tracks with Rick Nowels, including the single "Rooms on Fire," which is about the heat generated by her affair with Hine. "Well, maybe I'm just thinking that the rooms are all on fire," Nicks sings, "Every time that you walk in the room." The first line metrically aligns with the music, but the second does not; the words "every time" are distorted and mangled at the start of the phrase. The official video for this song briefly shows Nicks holding a beautiful blond baby, which of course evokes the context of her split with Hine.[24] Clad in flowing white silk, her character hands the child back to a man in black after presumably choosing to spend her life alone. (Nicks decided against wearing old-age makeup for the video.) The "magic" and "fire" in the lyrics are mirrored in the music with chimes and flamenco-style guitar breaks that attempt to enliven the predictability of the chorus.

Hine, Nicks, and Nowels all contributed to "Two Kinds of Love." Nicks sings it with Bruce Hornsby, but a demo of Hine singing the song alone with his own lyrics floats around online, placing the song's origins with him. The produced song, which relies on Nicks's lyrics, dispassionately references a third figure, a "famous friend"—namely Petty. We're looking through the looking glass, seeing relationships inside relationships.

"Cry Wolf" is by Celtic folk and jazz singer Jude Johnstone, who describes herself as the author of "the saddest song on everyone's album." A plugger named Michael Solomon pitched the song to Nicks, who decided to record it and invited Johnstone to the sessions. Johnstone had met Nicks once before, in the late seventies, at the Sunset Marquis Hotel in Los Angeles, when Fleetwood Mac was at the peak of fame. Nicks was "effing gorgeous," she recalls, "at the pool, coked out, because, you know, none of them ever slept." Nicks was an entirely different person by the late eighties: smarter, tougher, and wiser. Johnstone admired her brilliant wit, "the cat's [Nicks's] sharp humor," and the fact that she was past the "whole rock star thing," rolling her eyes and drawling, "oh yeah," about it all: "She's hipper than anyone knows." She and Hine "had something going on," Johnstone remembers, but "he didn't get how great she was" and made her do take after take of "Cry Wolf" without reason or rhyme. Nicks just "laid it out" like a pro, but Hine's production "mucked it up," ruining the groove. Nicks and Johnstone met to see about writing a song together, but it didn't work out, since it got "too precious." When asked why she decided to record "Cry Wolf," a song "about a guy who ran off," Nicks said, "because I wished I'd written it."[25]

Two other songs on the record are *Tango in the Night* outtakes: "Juliet" and "Ooh My Love." Nicks accidentally stole the tune of the latter from a cassette tape belonging to Petty. She thought the tape had been made for her by Mike Campbell and that she was at liberty to listen to its contents—demos that Petty had decided against putting on his next album—to see if anything struck her fancy. But she picked up the wrong tape, grabbing one that contained music Petty actually wanted to keep, not discard. He went ballistic over the mix-up. Petty's schedule didn't allow him to play on *The Other Side,* so Hine enlisted Fixx guitarist Jamie West-Oram for "Ooh My Love" and several other tracks.[26]

Another song, "Alice," has the extra-weird effect of surrealizing Lewis Carroll's surrealism. English literature scholar Michael Wood has written about Carroll's affection for puns and portmanteaus, especially those that expose the "secret life" of repressed behaviors.[27] Carroll's penchant for satire was counterbalanced by a serious love of the madcap, and Nicks's lyrics are likewise knowingly nonsensical yet rich in possible meanings. She casts spells with words, enchanting through her allusions. A "solid piece of armor" is a "steel-plated vest," yet Nicks uses "or" in place of "is." The text aligns unrelated metaphors. Reviewers generally throw their hands up trying to sort through Nicks's language, puzzled by the absence of narrative threads. But sense can be made of "Alice," as a recollection of her frontierswoman grandmother Alice reading Carroll's books to her. The real Alice, not the fictional one, passed through a town in the southwest called Mountain City (mentioned in the first verse) and wore a garter with a stiletto (mentioned in the third).

There are doublings of doublings, and Nicks refers to the real and fictional Alices' amnesia throughout the song:

> Oh call my name
> Like Alice through the Looking Glass
> She used to know who she was
> Call out my name like Alice through the Looking Glass

In Carroll's book, however, she does say she knows her name (and "that's *some* comfort"), but the author builds all sorts of wonderful nonsense about the difference between what something is called and what it is. A lot of literary characters are uncertain about their identities. Nicks must have spotted this great line: "I never should try to remember my name in the middle of an accident."[28] Alice's sister knows her name too and wakes her from her "curious" dream by calling her name: "Why, what a long sleep you've had!"[29]

Alice wants to grow up to read the book about her that will be written when she's grown up, the book she herself must write.[30] "One very natural peculiarity of 'Looking-glass House' is that most things in it are exactly reversed," an 1871 review of Carroll's work reads. "Accordingly if you want to go anywhere you have to turn round and walk the other way. People live backwards too, and their memory consequently works forward."[31] Nicks makes a similar remark about herself: "For Alice to run back and forth between the looking glass is kind of what I perceive my whole life to be, running back and forth between two places—which is obviously my career with Fleetwood Mac and my career by myself. And then of course, there's the other part of my life, which is my own life, which there isn't very much of. But I always seem to be running to one place or the other."[32]

The song doesn't have much of a tune. In places, "Alice" seems to want to break out into "Gypsy," and the mention of "gypsy" in the words explains why. The slower, duller, programmed beat and lack of melodic interest arguably suggest that Alice is simply lost. Her roaming is not as magical as it might have been. The unfortunate saxophone solo, by Kenny G, sounds like, well, Kenny G—mocked by Pat Metheny as "musical necrophilia," with a certain anodyne "charm" but no sense of danger or desperation. If Alice flees anything, it's his "unironic uncoolness."[33]

Those places on the album where Nicks seems to be repeating herself, reverting back to formulas from the past, might be interpreted, generously, as Carollesque. Imagine dreaming that you are having the same dream as before, then telling someone (quite unempathetic) all about it: that's what's happening here. Hine's synths are bizarrely deployed, replacing the guitar and piano on the demos while trafficking in a kind of cheapness that makes the tracks sound like demos recorded using Casio keyboards. Nicks gave the game away in her public comments about the album. She said that *The Other Side* "started out with Rupert Hine, who is an amazing keyboard player, so that whole album sort of went the way of the airy, surreal keyboard and synthesizer thing." He was her spiritual guide into an artificial realm. The "most important" thing for her, she claimed,

was that my songs came through. I have archives of demos, and I have many, many friends who prefer the demos—who have them and listen to them, and that's kind of really hard to take when it costs you nothing to do a demo and it costs you $500,000 or $1 million to do a record, and people come to you and say, "Can I have a cassette of the song when it was just a demo?" . . . It's very important to me that what I'm saying comes through. I'm not a musician. More than musically, it's very important that what I have to say comes through and so on this record, he did what I asked. He let me put my demo feeling through.[34]

At the end of the record, Hine gives a country song a reggae rhythm, for which he deserves a tip of the mad hat. It's a cover of "I Still Miss Someone (Blue Eyes)," by Johnny Cash and Roy Cash Jr., which had been covered before, by Linda Ronstadt and others, confirming that, beneath the polish, the album is layers upon layers of memories: Nicks's own, but other musicians' too.

THE NADIR

Fleetwood summoned Nicks to the studio once more with the McVies but without Buckingham, who took a pass on a Fleetwood Mac reboot. The resulting album, *Behind the Mask* (1990), did not sell as well as *Tango in the Night,* despite positive initial reviews of its fresh new sound. Buckingham was replaced by not one but two guitarists, Billy Burnette and Rick Vito, who had stood in for him on the *Tango in the Night* tour and other Fleetwood Mac initiatives. Nicks collaborated with Vito on the blues-rock songs "Love Is Dangerous" and "The Second Time," the second and final tracks on *Behind the Mask.* Mike Campbell collaborated with her on "Freedom." "Affairs of the Heart" is entirely her own creation; the lyrics quote canto 27 of Alfred Lord Tennyson's 1849 poem "In Memoriam A.H.H." (aka "The Way of the Soul") in a country-rock context. This quatrain is the basis of the song's chorus:

I hold it true, whate'er befall;
I feel it, when I sorrow most;
'Tis better to have loved and lost
Than never to have loved at all.

Nicks inserts the line "Ah but it's better not to lose" in response to Tennyson's lament for his beloved, the poet Arthur Henry Hallam, who died of a stroke at age twenty-two. It's a bookend to her setting of Edgar Allan Poe's "Annabel Lee," a poem (also from 1849) that brings death to a bride. Poe wrote about doomed love elsewhere; this text relates to the loss of his own wife from tuberculosis. The narrator's love for the maiden he encounters in a fairy-tale seaside kingdom makes the angels jealous. She dies, and he lies down beside her corpse in her sepulcher. Nicks wrote "Annabel Lee" in her senior year of high school, after reading the poem for Mr. Clements's English class.[35] She played it for her mother on guitar. The song floated around as a demo intended for *Trouble in Shangri-La* but was not recorded and released until 2011 on *In Your Dreams,* an album Nicks cocreated with Dave Stewart. Like "Affairs of the Heart," Nicks held "Annabel Lee" close for decades, recording it once she had exorcised the demons of the past, the bad loves, the toxic habits. "Garbo" is another example, though its subject is exploitation. Buckingham lurks, but less frighteningly. To reference a gothic Romantic novel from the same time as the Tennyson and Poe poems—Emily Brontë's *Wuthering Heights*—she was done playing Catherine to Heathcliff.

Nicks's mother, Barbara, had undergone major heart surgery in the summer of 1989, so Nicks decamped to the desert to be with family, recording the vocals for *Behind the Mask* in Phoenix.[36] Producer Greg Ladanyi flew down to assist and recorded a stripped-down, more spacious album than *Tango in the Night*—no eclecticism, no decadence (compared to Buckingham's projects), but flat sales. The band cranked itself into motion with the two hotshot guitarists and toured extensively following the April 9, 1990, release. The magic, however, belonged to the past, with Mick Fleetwood devoting himself less to music than to his memoirs. He dumped a tell-all autobiography (the first of two) on the band in the middle of the tour. It didn't, in fact, tell all, and Nicks reacted with indifference to his prattle about their romance long past. The band once again fell apart after the tour, each core member angry at the others for reasons nobody could remember. Nicks forgot the hotels, the cities, and what happened afterward—her recording an album that Rob Sheffield, who almost never has a bad word to say about her music, called a "tranquilized dud." Few heard it. For Sheffield, *Street Angel* was the nadir: "The benzos had taken over."[37]

Benzodiazepines had taken over her life, true, less so her art. After receiving treatment at Betty Ford for cocaine addiction back in 1986, Nicks had also decided to quit drinking. She reached out to a West Hollywood psychiatrist (fortunately for him, she has not publicly revealed his name) who prescribed clonazepam, which sank her into depression. Rather than have her taper off the anticonvulsant, he upped her dose, which increased her listlessness and caused weight gain. The malpractice lasted eight years, through several albums, the period of her mother's heart surgery, and no end of performances. According to Nicks, "I started to notice that I was shaking all the time [a common side effect of large doses of the drug], and I'm noticing that everybody else is noticing it too. And then I'm starting to think, do I have some kind of neurological disease and I'm dying?" She lived in a blank state and might have remained there were it not for her mother raising the alarm, and for Glen Parrish, who had been her live-in personal assistant during the worst period of her cocaine addiction (1980 to 1986) and who was later a member of her management team. He offered to take her huge daily dose of clonazepam—just once—to gauge the effects. Thirty minutes later he was numb and dizzy, unable to drive. Nicks called her psychiatrist, who upbraided her for sharing her meds. "The first words out of his mouth were, 'Are you trying to kill him?' And the next words out of my mouth were, 'Are you trying to kill me?'" In 1993, she checked into the chemical dependency unit at Daniel Freeman Marina Hospital in Marina Del Rey for treatment. "I molted," she said of the sudden withdrawal from clonazepam. "My hair turned gray. My skin started to completely peel off. I was in terrible pain."[38] The small nonprofit hospital is no longer in operation. A Catholic health provider touted for its combined physiological, spiritual, and psychological approaches to addiction, it treated high-profile patients as well as individuals placed there by the legal system. Nicks would have stayed for a month, the maximum permitted, and would have submitted, as required, to acupuncture treatments for help at this, her absolute lowest point.[39]

Street Angel dates from before and after this terrible time and involved more than one producer. Glyn Johns initiated the project in 1992, and Thom Panunzio completed it. The album began with a month and a half of prep work at home in Los Angeles. Nicks collaborated with guitarist Andy Fairweather Low, of Eric Clapton fame, and guitarist Bernie Leadon, an original member of the Eagles. The initial thought was to make an album with a strong acoustic feel (Leadon played several string instruments and was steeped in traditional country music and bluegrass), recorded in a positive atmosphere with incense and candles.[40] There would be a focus on social issues. Nicks didn't want to be a rigid "taskmaster," she said about the recording of the demos.[41] The music came out no happier than *The Other Side of the Mirror,* but the approach to making the record was, at least at first, positive. "I'm real excited about what's to come because I'm so not excited about what just went by," she told Mary Turner.[42]

Johns was hired for his discography, not his manners. Irritable, snippy, generally rude, he treated Nicks like other artists he thought distracted or unproductive: by policing her art, to the point of barring her from the studio. He had brought immense success to the Eagles, Rolling Stones, Led Zeppelin, and Clapton (whom he called "lazy") so, like a true authoritarian, was not to be questioned.[43] When he was, he packed up and left, paycheck in hand, name scrubbed from the liner notes. "I definitely knew what it was to come up against a really strong-willed Englishman," Nicks said of their failed collaboration. "I knew that it would not be easy. But I never dreamed that I would lose."[44] The bottom line felt the loss more than her dignity. She accepted the risk of dooming the album and her initial good feeling about it.

Glyn's memoir, *Sound Man,* doesn't mention *Street Angel.* Before Panunzio got involved in the record, he handed off some of his duties to his twenty-three-year-old son, Ethan, an aspiring producer who played percussion on *Street Angel* and presented two songs to Nicks that ended up in the land of bonus tracks. "I was called in initially because I had written a couple of songs they wanted to record," Ethan confirmed:

> I went out to LA to help with those. They didn't make the final cut. I remember a few fun days of pre-production at Stevie's house with Mike Campbell, we all got on well, and I ended up playing on about half the record. Meeting and playing with Benmont Tench was very special. Ben and I went on to become good friends. I was surprised on listening to the record how much I played on it. I wasn't there for more than a couple of weeks.

Ethan later returned to Los Angeles with his own band for a show at the Troubadour. "Stevie came down to that show and threw us a great after-show party at her house," he recalled.[45]

His father used Ocean Way Studios in Hollywood to produce the album. "Glyn was one of our best clients," the owner, Allen Sides, explains, "and was definitely working on Stevie's album at Ocean Way. Rob Cavallo was producing a Lindsey Buckingham solo album that had gone on forever in another one of our rooms around the same time, and I remember seeing them together during that time."[46] In fact, Buckingham's album, *Under the Skin,* took him almost a decade to realize. Nicks, in contrast, felt that time was running out on her. And it did. At the end of 1993, after her discharge from the hospital, she heard an album that wasn't her own and distanced herself from it. *Street Angel* was released on June 7, 1994.

It's true that Nicks, Panunzio, and Waddy Wachtel tried to repair the record during her convalescence. The music required animating and enriching; tracks were reordered and, in some instances, replaced. In music as in real estate, however, renovating can be more costly than new construction. The case of "Unconditional Love" is instructive. Eight takes float around online, differing from one another in affect and tempo and arrangement. Johns conceived it as a syrupy ballad, then worked it into a well-ventilated country acoustic. Nicks opted for the ballad and its ethereal potential. The guitar part was enriched, the drums supplemented, and the backup singers assigned a catchy refrain à la the Ronettes. Nicks struggled through the takes; it is painful to hear the frailness of her voice after years spent trying to bolster her technique. The song never quite gelled. No single take is superior to the others. What Nicks was searching for she never found.

Campbell and Wachtel saved the day on the do-over of the first track, "Blue Denim." The synths are gone, with Benmont Tench back on Hammond organ. It's a down-to-earth rocker that appears to reference Buckingham. Nicks's brother contributes harmonica to the second track, "Greta," which had come out of the *Rock a Little* sessions. It derives from "Garbo" but arguably also bears the imprint of "Betty Davis Eyes" as recorded by Kim Carnes. Nicks gathered other songs from years long past, too few for a chronicle about youth, but poignant nonetheless. "Rose Garden" is from her high school days—the guitar timbre and the opening chords, G, Cadd9, and D, are exactly those of Green Day's much later song "Time of Your Life"—and "Destiny" dates from her decision to leave college in 1973 for music. "Unconditional Love" is recovered material from *Wild Heart*. "Jane" was drafted in Dallas in 1991 and dedicated to primatologist Jane Goodall, a friend of a friend, an "angel" who found herself "up against the wall."

Rummaging through her cassettes hadn't always turned up hidden treasures, in Glyn Johns's opinion, so he suggested a pair of covers: Bob Dylan's 1966 "Just Like a Woman" and a 1988 Trevor Horn and Betsy Cook song called "Docklands." Tom Petty knew Dylan, as did Johns, and Nicks worked the connection to convince Dylan to play guitar and harmonica on "Just Like" 2.0 (the backup singers replaced the harmonica in the final mix). Dylan liked her cover, he told her, even though Nicks's mimicking of his vocal mannerisms suggests a parody. The controversial trailing line of the chorus, "she breaks just like a little girl," is preserved. Its meaning is endlessly mooted by Dylan fans. The consensus is that he's upset about being dumped by a grown woman (Joan Baez?) who has acted like a child or made him feel like one. Dylan's defenders claim it's not sexist; because it is, Nicks breaks it just like a little girl. She deadpans her disaffection to the accompaniment of a muffled snare drum, pushed too far forward in the mix. (I'm reminded of the empowered coarseness of Diamanda Galás singing "Do You Take This Man?" over a walking bass line supplied by Led Zeppelin's John Paul Jones.)

"Docklands" is sung with matter-of-fact detachedness until Nicks and her backup singers sing "hold on," at which point the song almost grinds to a halt. The lyrics describe the dispossessed of southeast London and have a connection to the lyrics of the title track, "Street Angel," sung by Nicks and David Crosby, with whom Johns had been working on the album *Thousand Roads,* a lost-sounding flop. Their voices blend all the more effectively for being so held in. She had sung with men in the past on big hits, and that must have been the thinking here—a hetero musical-bonding experience—but the result has a disturbing double-edged ambiguity: the song is lonelier by virtue of being a duet. It's about homeless kids, giving up and not caring, and also an addict's nihilism. The spur for its creation was typically ad hoc. Nicks had to relocate to the Peninsula Hotel in Los Angeles because her house had been inundated with bees. "We had to go," she said, "'cause the bees were so intense that they had to be moved, not killed, but moved."[47] In her hotel suite she watched a couple of movies about homelessness on television, which inspired a song about a wastrel who is given the chance to escape the streets through romance but can't leave.

The LinnDrum pattern is akin to Phil Collins's "In the Air Tonight," though without that song's explosive release. Toward the end Nicks references Charles Dickens, who protested the plight of street angels in his fiction. It's a lateral move, a detour from the song's autobiographical content. The scariest and most fatigued line, "I fell down the stairs a broken rag doll," is enacted throughout *Street Angel,* the bereft, besieged artist's most disconnected, disarticulated album. Her handlers willed it into existence because their livelihoods depended on hers. She willed herself to resist the producer, surrendering the project when she could do no more.

Her angels looked after her in the studio and on the budget-conscious road tour. She traveled with friends. Her longtime familiar Sara Recor (aka Sara Fleetwood) sang backup, together with Sharon Celani and Lori Perry Nicks. They were a fetchingly peppy presence on the tour, which lasted from July 14 to September 18, 1994, highlighted by an appearance on *The Tonight Show with Jay Leno* and a performance at Compton Terrace in Phoenix, Jess Nicks's venue. The reviews are mixed, and partially a Rorschach test of the reviewers' attitudes toward female artists. "The public's desire to have Nicks conform to the gender trends that flourished in the 80s and 90s was unappeased with the 1994 release of

Street Angel," a brief study of her career concluded. "Audiences were bored with Stevie's subtle power demonstrated through songs like 'Rhiannon' and 'Dreams'; they didn't want to look for hidden strength; they wanted overt brashness and a masculine driving energy."[48] Gary Graff, however, loved it: "If that's the case [he mentions her oft-stated plan to work into her eighth decade], *Street Angel* is the beginning of the rest of Nicks' career. And it does sound like a new beginning. Straightforward and rocking—with songs about Greta Garbo, Jane Goodall and a guest appearance by Bob Dylan on Nicks' remake of his 'Just Like a Woman'— it's reminiscent of her first solo album, 1981's *Bella Donna*. And it's hard not to hear the spirit of liberation in the 11 songs on *Street Angel*."[49] The music writer for the *Hartford Courant* called it a "hip return"; the *New Jersey Record* praised her for trashing the "cheesy synthesizers"; and the *Pittsburgh Post-Gazette* celebrated her "smoky-bar-at-3-in-the-morning voice. It proves itself again a formidable weapon, glorious in its inability to hit all of the notes, and captivating in the feeling it conveys."[50] Nicks summarized her experience in five words: "It's not my favorite record."[51] Stephen Davis took this line and excessively elaborated it: "She said she wanted to go back to the hospital because she hated her new record so much. She said it was the saddest, lowest-energy music she'd ever made."[52] Sad music, of course, can also be great music.

Street Angel was the last album Nicks recorded on Modern Records. The label folded five years after its release, in 1999. Her next album belonged to the Reprise label, distributed in the United States by Warner. The time in between was largely her own; she looked after herself, dieting and exercising and maintaining a strict vocal calisthenics routine and spending time with friends and family amid occasional creative projects and performances, including, but hardly limited to, the indispensable *Enchanted* compilation; an appearance at Woodstock on August 14, 1998 (flying over the crowd in a helicopter thrilled her); several Stevie Nicks & Friends benefit concerts for the Arizona Heart Institute; and a greatest hits collection released in Europe, *The Divine Stevie Nicks* (2001). She inspired younger balladeers and rockers, including Tori Amos and Courtney Love, and the gothic fashions and gewgaws—"black gossamer and velvet, gargantuan boots and glittering beads"—of Isaac Mizrahi and Anna Sui.[53]

TWISTER

Her health restored, Nicks could do things for the sheer fun of it, like writing movie music. She wrote the song "Twisted" for the 1996 summer blockbuster *Twister,* accepting the commission after her friend and former assistant Rebecca Alvarez reviewed the script and said she liked it. Both predicted the movie would break box-office records. In the liner notes for *Enchanted,* Nicks let her fans know that the demo was recorded on "March 10, 1996, on a 4-track Tascam by my [new] assistant extraordinaire, Karen Johnston." She adds some domestic detail: "I was living in a beach house overlooking Sunset Boulevard and the Pacific Coast Highway, and beyond that, always . . . the ocean."[54]

Mark Mancina's background scoring for *Twister* mixes Aaron Copland–esque "wide open spaces" motifs with generic action-adventure ostinato patterns.[55] Nicks's song began as a demo recorded with a beatbox and a mandolin overdub, then she picked up the phone and called Buckingham. Perhaps he wanted to have some fun too. He transformed the song into a forceful, closing-credits duet, adding some words of his own. Mick Fleetwood agreed to drum, also for fun, bringing three-fifths of Fleetwood Mac together for the one-off. The song as conceived— before Buckingham's transposition—is playfully macabre, populated by demons within and without, "crazy men, crazy women" needing love. The mandolin "fills the air with colors." It wraps around the voice, the timbre sparklingly bright. There is no A to B to C in the sung line; the lyrics are incantational, moving through a chain of inference from obsession to possession. Nicks references the film, but only generally: "You live for the danger . . . you play with God." "You" would be the male hero, a Midwestern storm chaser, but the voice is his wife's—a university professor and serious scientist, played by Helen Hunt. The cat-5 funnel clouds dramatize the forces that pull them together and fling them apart.

The finest moment in the demo is the musical close-up, when the dynamic level on the voice is punched up. The drum machine maintains its clip as Nicks sings about "chasing down the demons." The song might be an exorcism; it might also be an embrace, since tornadoes involve centrifugal force, sucking things into a vortex (but still casting things out far and wide). The demons belong to the twisting Nether, which Nicks mimes with circular phrases.

She kept the song in mind for her most recent solo album, *24 Karat Gold,* noting that "when songs go into movies you might as well dump them out the window as you're driving by because they never get heard." She, Buckingham, and Fleetwood collaborated friction free, and Fleetwood subsequently, for the twentieth anniversary of *Rumours,* engineered another Fleetwood Mac get-together. The band recorded a live show for MTV in Burbank and then embarked on a twenty-six-city tour called (like the Burbank recording) The Dance. Davis claims that Nicks was "over the moon with relief about the reunion, since it meant putting her next solo album on hold. It meant she didn't have to come up with lots of new songs right away. It meant she could enfold herself in the first-class luxuries of a big Mac tour without having to make any decisions or take on the daunting responsibilities of a band leader."[56] There is no basis for this claim. It seems entirely made up.

TROUBLE IN SHANGRI-LA

Fleetwood Mac had long been less important—creatively speaking—to Nicks than Petty's band, the Heartbreakers. Producers came and went, so Nicks assumed certain production duties for herself, renting different studios and recording in grabbed moments between tours or individual shows. Coming up with "lots of new songs right away" was not an issue. She had one short-lived bout of writer's block—a matter of weeks, not months. Petty shook it out of her over dinner in Phoenix: "What the hell's the matter with you?" he chided her. "You can be miserable or you can just get over it."[57] Then he grinned his impish grin, told her that she sounded great, and reminded her of her superior songwriting skills.

She brought those skills to her sixth studio album, *Trouble in Shangri-La*. It came together casually, with the participation of old and new friends, between 1995 and 2001. Writer's block aside, she felt no need to rush with it until her management team started getting antsy. Just six weeks after its long-awaited release, it reached gold, signaling both her return to top form and the successful reboot of her career for the new century. Nicks initially wanted to call the album *Trouble in Paradise*, in reference to her family's suburban Phoenix neighborhood, Paradise Valley, and to a 1932 film called *Trouble in Paradise* (about thieves in disguise, grand hotels, and a purse made of diamonds, with a disapproving communist making a single hilarious appearance), but Randy Newman had already given his 1983 album that name. Nicks replaced "Paradise" with "Shangri-La," referencing the 1933 James Hilton novel *Lost Horizon*. Shangri-La is the fictional name of a spiritual enclave in a locale east of the Himalayas, where residents live cloistered, peaceful, and impossibly long lives. Nicks claimed the album has a theme—fame isn't all it's made out to be, so "be careful what you wish for"—but, besides the title track, few songs make this point.[58]

John Shanks produced most of the album, but seven others, including Nicks herself, worked on it before he was hired. Rick Nowels helped, as did Sheryl Crow, who had met Nicks in 1996 at the Grammy Awards. She fell into Nicks's orbit two years later in Hawaii. Crow wrote one of the songs on *Trouble,* "It's Only Love," and contributed to others. Nicks enlisted her as producer in chief, until Crow, saddled with other obligations, had to leave the project. She suggested Natalie Maines, lead singer of the Chicks (formerly the Dixie Chicks), as her replacement. Nicks heard Maines and thought, "She and I have very similar country voices, and I could definitely sing with her."[59]

"Too Far from Texas," the song on *Trouble in Shangri-La* that Nicks and Maines recorded together, imagines that "love could fly over the ocean" to chase a man jetting to London while the protagonist pines for him in Houston. Maines's duet with Nicks is simple, heartfelt, and tuneful. As a country song, "Too Far from Texas" would pair well with the Chicks' "You Were Mine," the number-one hit written by Martie Maguire and Emily Robison, the sisters who compose two-thirds of the Chicks. Although Crow's bass playing is often singled out, the truly country twangling guitar work (along with the soulful Hammond organ) stamps the song more forcefully. Maines's voice is subordinate to Nicks's but sharpens the edge of the timbre to give the lyrics more bite; her higher pitch also elevates the song—literally and affectively. The structure, with an emotional payoff at the end plus a quick close, also echoes the Chicks' quick endings in songs like "Wide Open Spaces." Maines would later cover "Landslide" (mixed by Crow) on the Chicks' *Home* (2002), marking a move away from the pop-country blend that first made the group so successful to an acoustic, bluegrass idiom that more perfectly suits Maines's high, lonesome sound. "She's very supportive of other females in the industry," Maines said of Nicks. "I think lots of women are competitive and she really wants you to succeed."[60]

"Bombay Sapphires" is driven by a guitar part that derives from a 1993 song by Sting, "Shape of My Heart." The reference is explicit on the demo but concealed on the produced track. R&B singer Macy Gray takes the upper part, but Nicks had in mind Sting, informing *Q* magazine that "the only reason Macy is on the record is because we're managed by the same people. Originally I wanted Sting to sing that little high part on Bombay Sapphire[s], but I chickened out on calling him and I asked Macy to do it."[61] Gray does not have extraordinary range but sings with an eclectic gamut of affects, from a childlike whisper to exhausted discontent. She was near her peak in 2001, and management must have been thinking about market appeal when recommending her to Nicks. "Bombay Sapphires" came together in three takes: the first too

R&B, in Nicks's opinion, the second too "dirge-like," and the Gold-ilocks third "its funky little reggae self."[62] Gin (nicknamed "the mother's ruin") is not the subject, though Nicks knew that Bombay Sapphire afi-cionados would make the connection. Using the plural in the title avoided copyright infringement. She conceived the song in Maui, and the lyrics reference the reset she experienced in that aqua-blue environment after The Dance tour. It's a chill riposte to the scandalous fecundity of the Fleetwood Mac enterprise—bright and beautiful, with no hint of shadow.

Also involved was Sarah McLachlan, who had moved from the alter-native singer-songwriter scene to the musical mainstream. She bristled at the sexism in the business, especially the resistance to programming and scheduling more than one female artist at a time. In response she curated a festival in the late nineties called Lilith Fair, referring to the divine entity of kabbalistic mysticism. It was a multistage traveling production like Lollapalooza but "women-centric" (as opposed to "women-exclusive," excluding men from the bands).[63] There was a predictable backlash from the male rock establishment and Christian right-wing media before and after Lilith Fair's three-year run. And *Trouble in Shangri-La* was subject to misogynist attack for its "Lilith Fairian posse of special guests," which merely proved both the importance of the festival and the significance of Nicks adopting a "protective attitude" toward Crow and other young women artists.[64] "It had taken a long time for [Nicks's] own status to be restored," popular music expert Lucy O'Brien writes, and she helped pre-vent her protégées from losing theirs.[65]

The Nicks-McLachlan collaboration wasn't planned, yet it became the heart of the album. McLachlan's producer, Pierre Marchand, whom Nicks enlisted for the song "Love Is," was delayed crossing the border into the United States from Canada. Unable to record with Nicks in Los Angeles, he suggested she travel to Vancouver, and there introduced her to McLachlan. He knew that she admired McLachlan's 1994 song "Possession," which has an unpleasant backstory. The lyrics were inspired by poems sent to McLachlan from an obsessed fan, and her harrowing experiences with him. Upon the song's release, the stalker sued her for stealing his words (she didn't), then committed suicide before the case went to trial. The song is eerie, unearthly, and strangely soothing, with a presence and ambiance that fans have associated with the popular nineties witchcraft films *The Craft* and *Practical Magic*. McLachlan and Nicks seem attuned to the distinctly feminine energy of that era. Crow's duet with Nicks, "If You Ever Did Believe," landed on the *Practical Magic* soundtrack.

McLachlan sings backing vocals and plays piano on "Love Is," which Marchand made wondrous. Breathing sounds, staccato "oohs" at the third and fifth above the bass line, and a polished interwoven harmonic texture embrace Nicks's ennui-laden recitation of the words:

So she stood there in the hallway frozen
In the dark
And her heart broke down
She cried
She fell to the floor

One tear
Slid across her lips
To the corner of her mouth
Love is
And dropped to the floor

"Planets of the Universe" dates back to *Rumours* and the breakup with Buckingham. Lyrics about planets moving out of sight of one another, blocking one another's light, seem sadly romantic. Tracing the song from demo to record reveals subtleties beyond the biographical. The piano-vocal demo from the Sausalito recording sessions for *Rumours* moves through three parts; melodic ideas form circles in waltz meter. The rotating planets are "not astounded by the sun and moon." In the second verse, his "rule" ends, yet she responds to his command. The next part is more recitational, and the three arpeggiated harmonies in the accompaniment are reversed with the words "you will remember." The concluding section is akin to an arioso, between singing and reciting. The piano postlude elaborates the three-chord pattern, lending nobility, seriousness, and even dignity to the whole. The song would be bleak without the closing, which pulls down the curtain on a relationship by moving down from C major to A minor and shifting the pitches of each scale down the octave. At the end of the demo she says, "I forgot how to go back into it [to repeat the opening lines]. Did you get that? It wasn't wonderful or anything but . . . at least it has the . . . I just wanted him [the producer] to get the, you know, the B thing."[66]

Another take excludes piano. Buckingham accompanies her on guitar, while Fleetwood fusses with brushes on the snare, trying to displace the triple meter. The bass enters, and vibes provide the twinkling "sound" of stars. It's a little more forceful than the first demo. The version she recorded for *Trouble* is set in a clearer verse-verse-chorus structure. New words enrich the metaphoric content: days disappear into an ocean without shores; there are burning skies, a closed door, and nothing left to discover. Fleetwood Mac diehards tut-tut the remix because it settles into a formula, losing the dreaminess of the original. But that first version is about renouncing dreaminess to look at the movement of the planets with indifference; it's astronomy, not astrology, observation rather than divination. Music as a medium perfectly captures the mechanics of movement, because pitches—with their overtones and undertones—are both an infinite series and a steady state. The song as remade for *Trouble* feels translucent despite the almost-speech, the strumming, and the secure bass line. Computer-based sequences are added, and the sound becomes at once soulful and starlit.

"Candlebright" (aka "Nomad") dates back to the coffee-plant tapes Nicks did with Buckingham circa 1970. It was considered for Fleetwood Mac's "white album," then replaced by "Rhiannon." Peter Stroud (a Crow and McLachlan regular) starts things off on mandolin, and the song soon becomes entangled in a thicket of effects. Real or synthesized strings plus two distinct drum loops are heard simultaneously at the richest, brightest moments. Nicks whispers about shedding a friend while the backup singers contradict her with "still I love you."

Nicks retrieved "Sorcerer," another song from the first years of her career, for a scaled-back duet with Crow. She loves to perform it live, and it seems specially calibrated for large halls with impressive light shows. The chorus is the hook, defined by a rhetorical question, "Sorcerer: Who is the master?" The lyrics allude to showbiz and the Los Angeles she and Buckingham descended into back in the day, long before their music was heard at the beach and in the office, before rock—their rock—became classic. The song includes fairy-tale references to star streams and snow dreams and has a peculiar middle stanza with scrambled grammar:

And who found lady from the mountains
All around black ink darkness
And who found lady from the mountains
Lady from the mountains

The folklore of California miners allegorizes Mountain Annie and female spirits that live underground.[67] Perhaps Nicks has this subject in mind. Or perhaps she is reaching once more back to her childhood, to grandma Alice's stories and the bluesy, folksy, soulful magic of songs sung in small southern towns in vintage America.

Nicks and Crow jointly toured the record in the summer of 2001, until severe bronchitis forced Nicks to cancel four dates and postpone

six others. Reviews were respectful, even from curmudgeons like Mark
Guarino at the *Chicago Daily Herald*. He liked the music and admired
Nicks putting it all out there emotionally. His problem was the fans,
and maybe his own biases; he could not countenance the "goddess wor-
ship from [Nicks's] faithful, spotted in more black lace dresses than the
serving wenches at King Richard's Faire."[68] Had witches rather than
wenches been in the audience, his codpiece might have been cursed and
his tickets to Iron Maiden or other cock-rock costume shows beloved
by boys sent up in smoke.

SAY YOU WILL

Fleetwood Mac sold records and tickets reliably until the Napster era,
when royalties disappeared and concerts lost some of their sparkle: boot-
legs of performances, demos, outtakes, and remixes cannot replace the
aura of a live show, yet they allow listeners to imagine something close—
with better intonation. The trips down seventies lane and antiques road
shows generated income and reminded devotees of their salad days.
Arkansas governor Bill Clinton's unauthorized use of "Don't Stop" as
rally music for his 1992 presidential bid led to a pretend-furious phone
call between Fleetwood Mac's lawyer, Mickey Shapiro, and Clinton's
campaign manager and the promise that "if he wins the presidency, Stevie gets to play at the inauguration."[69] He did; she did.

   The Dance (the live album recorded in Burbank that preceded the
tour) cast the old spells and, with promising results, some new ones:
Nicks sings about a "Sweet Girl"; Christine McVie suggests she's a
"Temporary One." McVie's commitment to Fleetwood Mac wavered,
however. She said no to touring, only changing her mind in 2014.

   McVie's contributions to the Fleetwood Mac record *Say You Will*
(2003) are slight: Hammond organ on one track, vocals on another. The
album's artwork was fittingly inspired by Masahiro Shinoda's film *Double Suicide* (1969), a highly stylized tragic romance. Nicks and Buckingham lie "dead" beside each other on the front cover, their bodies almost
interlocking. John McVie and Fleetwood imitate the same pose on the
back cover. Christine is gone. Fleetwood Mac had become a quartet as
well as its own tribute band. *Say You Will* adhered to what *Rolling
Stone* called "Fleetwood Mac's best instincts: Buckingham's bittersweet
tunes about playing for keeps; Nicks's tough, swirly songs about fragile
and wicked women; and the experiments the group can't stop indulging
in"—including hocket, falsetto, snippets from radio and television,

touch-activated modulations, and a morphing of Nicks's voice into a children's sing-along at the end of the title track.[70] She contributed nine songs, six entirely her own. In a 2013 documentary, she recalled a squabble with Buckingham over the lyrics to "Thrown Down":

> *Nicks:* There is a way to work with people where you suggest, and there's a way to tell people what to do that doesn't work. I laughingly always say, and I say it with great love that, you know, there was a point when we were doing "Say You Will," and there was a song called "Thrown Down." Sometimes I write and I'm in first person, and then, all of a sudden, I'm in second person, you know? And I don't care, because I have no rules. And he's going, "You know, well, you need to change the person of that. So you need to change that line."
>
> *Buckingham [flashback]:* But I'm saying if you put that in the third person and in the past tense, it hangs with the first verse more.
>
> *Nicks:* And I just snapped up and said, "Would you say that to Bob Dylan?"
>
> *Buckingham [flashback]:* I'm just saying that, you know, it's sort of a . . . a rule of thumb in writing that you don't shift your tense and . . . and your person.
>
> *Nicks [flashback]:* Well, I don't think you could say that to Bob Dylan [silence]. 'Cause he would say to you, "I write what I want to."
>
> *Buckingham [flashback]:* Ok![71]

A woman who doesn't play by the rules is by definition unruly, or so Buckingham implies in a conversation with the rule-breaking woman he'd known from adolescence. The arc of the set-to suggests old grievances, with Dylan just the flash point. As to Nicks's lyrics versus Dylan's, Stephen Holden's remarks recall, wittingly or not, the kind of bias that celebrates male lyricists as poets whose insights penetrate the soul while dismissing women as girls writing in their journals. Reviewing the *Wild Heart* album in the *New York Times,* Holden asserted that

> the quality of Miss Nicks's symbolist, free-associative lyrics remains uneven. At their most self-indulgent, Miss Nicks's reflections suggest the diaristic jottings of a high school girl with literary pretensions. But in her more disciplined verses, she manipulates striking, archetypal imagery into a half-comprehensible personal mythology. Miss Nicks's "poetry" is ultimately a very feminine extension of the stream-of-consciousness symbolism that Bob Dylan legitimized as a pop lyric style and that Joni Mitchell refined into a journalistically precise pop poetry. Miss Nicks, though not as powerful as Dylan or as precise as Mitchell, at least has the courage of her esthetic convictions. She weaves frank evocations of erotic turmoil with occult speculations into a pop vocabulary that is all her own.[72]

The repeated invocation of "Miss" aside (neither Dylan nor Mitchell is defined by honorifics tied to gender or marital status), this is still quite a statement. Nicks's "poetry" only becomes poetry without the scare quotes when legitimized by the genius Dylan, yet even then it remains "pop"—likewise Joni Mitchell's "pop poetry." Symbolism and free association are impugned, and high school girls as so often a point of invidious, dismissive comparison. True, Nicks shuns cause-and-effect storytelling, finding, like poets do, greater lyrical and musical power in the amorphous mutations of states of being. Dylan received the Nobel Prize in Literature in 2016 "for having created new poetic expressions within the great American song tradition."[73] Mightn't Mitchell or Nicks be valued for comparable achievements?

The song Nicks and Buckingham had the argument about, the fourth track on *Say You Will,* had a second life as the theme for a 2003 episode of *Friends* titled "The One with the Soap Opera Party." The title perfectly suits the context of the song's making but doesn't excuse Buckingham's condescending unwillingness to recognize a change of tense as perfectly suitable for internal dialogue. The tenth track, "Smile at You," originated from the *Tusk* sessions. According to Ken Caillat, Nicks first recorded it with friends Annie McLoone and Tom Moncrieff.[74] She "couldn't get [the song] past Lindsey," Caillat writes, because of Moncrieff's "smoking guitar solo." Caillat, to his credit, considered it a "potential classic," in which Nicks's smoldering resentment explodes into rage as a "vicious answer song to Lindsey."[75] He didn't get to work on it, however, neither for *Tusk* nor, as was briefly contemplated, for *Mirage.* The song mellowed over time, tracking the course of the Nicks-Buckingham creative dialogue. By the time Fleetwood Mac recorded *Say You Will,* Buckingham had no role in Nicks's life. The five leaked takes of "Smile" from *Tusk,* two from *Mirage,* and the final version from *Say You Will* range in affect from hostile to defiant to circumspect. Some of the demos suggest "Sisters of the Moon"; the last take is overdubbed with prickly acoustic guitar and shamanistic percussion. John McVie revisits "The Chain" in the throbbing bass line. Unresolved feelings are preferable to resolved feelings in the Fleetwood Mac cosmos, and when Nicks sings "I shouldn't be here," it's hard not to believe that she's done with lack of closure.

"Illume" concerns the September 11, 2001, terrorist attacks on the World Trade Center and the Pentagon. On that day Nicks had performed in Toronto on the *Shangri-La* tour. The air traffic shutdown and blackout that followed the destruction of the Twin Towers forced her to cancel her shows in Rochester (scheduled for September 12) and New York City (September 14). She wanted to cancel all the dates that month and the next. Petty and Henley convinced her that performing would be an act of service for a shaken public. A month later, back in California, she wrote the poem that became the song "Illume."

> It's just about making it, you know. I was sitting there, thinking about those horrible tragedies in October of 2001, and I was sitting there with just me in the room, and the candle was lit. I love candles, you know. And my heart was still so heavy from everything, and I didn't know quite what would happen, and we were all like that, confused.
>
> I didn't set out to write a September 11th song, it just happened. It goes "Illume, says the candle that I burn, a reflection in the window," and that's just about the inspiration for the song. And I tell you, my heart was so very heavy and full at this time, I was so confused. And then there are some other parts. . . .
>
> "And I am alone with my thoughts, And how we could make it—And what we have been through, all of the trauma." I also wrote one called "Get Back on the Plane," and a song called "The Towers Touched the Sky," but it was just too depressing.[76]

"Illume" begins as though completely self-involved. The lyrics of the second verse emphasize the personal and individual, as in "I like," though "like" is later liberated to produce a simile that evokes the Hudson: "like living on a working river." The chorus addresses loss:

I am alone now
With my thoughts
Of how we could make it
Of how we could get out
What we've been through
All of the trauma
The smell of Nag champa
Shadow of a stranger

She leaves the confines of the self, and "I" is changed to "we" and "we could," though the plural pronoun isn't specified. Friends? Neighbors? Everyone in the United States? Perhaps the most important aspect of "Illume" is the expression of heartache, her own as the metonymy of grief, and the message she has about suspending such sorrow. It simply can't be done, certainly not through nationalism, jingoism, or retribution. Her mention of "trauma" puzzles. She passes quickly over the word, exploring instead the collective condition, the need to cope. Incense (Nag champa) burns; self and other, individual and collective, coexist dreamily. We are alone yet bonded by grief. The percussion also fuses opposites: a standard drum kit and bongo line adding rhythmic freedom, sometimes falling on the second sixteenth of a four-note subdivision. It seems ornamental in the quick fills, comparable in timbre to raga tabla. So too the simulacrum of competing first-responder announcements: Nicks supplies all the voices, and these are mixed to sound like telephone messages or radio broadcasts while also expressing her own cognitive dissonance.

The lyrics are a mixture, and the tune fragmented, composed of short phrases and small pieces. The grittiness of the singing stands out, with the self-contained tracing of the path from D to G and down to E. The pitch B alternates with A. The persistence of descending figures gives it an incantational aspect. It's a modest, humble, spare chant, the utterances bending forward, or trying to. It becomes unified in its own way and rewards the ear for holding on to it. There is something alluring and assuring about a songwriter trying to process what, for a long time, could not be processed. The tune, such as it is, goes down, descends, falls, and flickers between adjacent pitches, as did buildings and candles. The word "alone" and the condition of loneliness are crucial, not only in the context of 9/11 but also in relation to the COVID-19 pandemic, which Nicks has spoken publicly about. In "Illume," and in the politics of the present, alienation is allegorized in the divide between the coasts and the interior.

It's an unnerving song, with brittle vocals and jangling guitar tracks. Buckingham's first guitar track is panned hard right, and then, just before the chorus, that part is doubled or maybe tripled, adding to its impact. The minor key and the strumming, fluttering effects enhance the sense of anxiousness. Fleetwood's drumming is both meditative and urgent, mixed closer to the foreground of the song than is typical. The hi-hat skims along the top of the register. The distances between the instruments collapse as Nicks sings about the presence of the stranger, and the river flows, connecting different places.

SOMEONE SHE USED TO KNOW

The *Say You Will* tour was fractious, and Nicks soon left it behind in favor of a benign concert series with Henley, the successful Gold Dust solo tour, and another tour honoring the release of the management-driven compilation album *Crystal Visions*. Nicks increased her involvement in philanthropic causes. Her father died. She still, for a few more years, had her mother. In 2006 she attended the fortieth reunion of

Arcadia High School's class of 1966, at the Westin Pasadena. Despite spending her final year of high school at Menlo-Atherton, she accepted the invitation to reminisce. She had met Robin Snyder at Arcadia and sang in Changing Times there. Someone she used to know told her, "You know what? You haven't changed a bit. You are still our little Stevie girl." Tears welled up "because it was the nicest thing anybody had said to me, that I'm still the same. Because I've always tried very hard to stay who I was before I joined Fleetwood Mac and not become a very arrogant and obnoxious, conceited, bitchy chick, which many do, and I think I've been really successful."[77] She read each of the *Twilight* novels when they were published. Romantic tales of star-crossed lovers, vampires, everlasting life, impossible love, and the delight and danger of corrupted innocence. Much of course had changed, but her fascination with teenagers getting into trouble thanks to their "desire, will, and imagination" remained.[78]

IN YOUR DREAMS

In 2011 Nicks released her seventh album and first in a decade, *In Your Dreams,* surrendering about half of the song-writing duties to Dave Stewart. He coproduced it with Glen Ballard, whose career has spanned rock, pop, movies (*Batman, The Polar Express*), and musicals (*Ghost, Back to the Future*). Both Stewart and Ballard enlisted a large number of session musicians to replace the programmed loop parts on the demos. Simon Smith was part of this collective. He provided bass on "Everybody Loves You" in a two-hour session at Ballard's studio and remembers the lyrics changing between the demo and final version. He didn't meet Nicks.[79]

On the cover of *In Your Dreams,* Nicks stands behind a translucent orb, beside a white horse in a glade somewhere—an unapologetically innocent romantic imagining. Less innocent is the song inspired by her summer reading: "Moonlight (a Vampire's Dream)." Jonathan Keafe scorned it: "Inspired by her viewing [*sic*] of *The Twilight Saga: New Moon* while on tour[,] it boasts exactly the same degree of depth as Stephenie Meyer's vapid, wooden prose." He's less charitable describing the fifth track: "Even worse is 'New Orleans,' with a howlingly bad chorus that finds Nicks singing, 'I want to dress up/I want to wear beads/I want to wear feathers and lace/I want to brush by Anne Rice,' with an inexplicable reverence. That the melody lifts at the end of each line overemphasizes the final word of those lines, giving the song an obnoxious, stilted cadence. It's perhaps the worst song in Nicks's entire catalogue, reducing the culture of New Orleans to Bourbon Street and vampire lore."[80]

"New Orleans" is not supposed to be serious, and "Moonlight" shouldn't be dismissed so casually—especially given its ties to the four *Twilight* novels and movies. The hero, Bella, is a seventeen-year-old from Arizona, and in *New Moon*, the second book in the tetralogy, she meets her grandmother, or thinks she does, unless she is seeing herself at her grandmother's age. Nicks begins her song with the line "some call her strange lady from the mountains." She's referring to her own relative, the Alice of "Alice." Jenny Turner, an expert on Meyer's novels, highlights the obvious connection to Dorian Gray.[81] And then there is the central conundrum of Bella's romance with Edward. He keeps her at a distance and encourages her to keep her clothes on, because both of them won't be as cute on the other side. The upshot: he's a beautiful monster until they have sex, then he's something else. Nicks doesn't tarry with this particular negative. Her song is shiny bright, and the video, a modestly made party for her guild of backup singers, plus slender man Waddy Wachtel, Stewart in magician's guise, an owl, and select session players— an innocent thing.

The electronic distortion could, I suppose, represent dysrhythmia, but if "Moonlight" is vampiric, then so is the entire popular-music industry. Everything is in its right place in the carefully produced song. It's the perfection Bella sees in Edward, the undead orphan with flawless skin. He's a studio technician who's stayed out of the light. Meyer makes him at once artificial and ideal, thus attractive to the girl who hates fake people and fake things. There's no escaping Edward, just as there's no escaping fashion magazines. Fake things are ideal images are dead things, which means, as Turner writes, our world, just like Meyer's world, is full of vampires:

> In the old days, the Gothic was said to focus readers' deepest fears about their future: blood-sucking aristos; mills, engines, new technology, with its way of shifting boundaries between the human and the not-human; infant mortality, post-mortem flatus, doubts about the afterlife and, of course and always and mainly, the problem of death. In our day we don't have to visit a cinema to hallucinate life into images of immortal perfection; they flicker everywhere around us, emptied of the animal and plumped up instead with plastics. And so, the question is not so much about entering the "labyrinthine realm of undeath" as whether anyone can ever really be said to leave it.[82]

Welcome to the Hotel California. You think you've handed in the keys and are ready to leave, as does Bella, but you're still one of the guests.

Does Nicks, as image-conscious as she is self-aware, even want to go? She sings as though no time has passed in her career and expresses no embarrassment about her enduring affection for things others dismiss as adolescent. To be ashamed of girlish things is often imagined to define womanhood, yet might maturity also honor the younger self's feelings and loves? The girl doesn't have to die so the woman might live.

Nicks had reconnected with Stewart five years before the release of *In Your Dreams,* when, on Iovine's recommendation, he had asked her for an interview to be broadcast as the pilot episode of the HBO series *Off the Record,* which he hosted. Nicks sang an "epic," fifteen-minute-long version of "Rhiannon" for the broadcast. Afterward, Stewart drafted a song for her: "Everyone loves you, but you're alone," the hook begins.[83] She took to it, added the missing verse material, and invited him over to record it in her private studio, taking advantage of the acoustics in the rotunda and winding staircase of her Pacific Palisades residence.[84] Stewart rummaged through a book of poems, forty in all, that she'd assembled over the years, for additional songs. "I don't know a thousand chords, and Dave doesn't have a book of forty poems," she said of the long, thirteen-track album they made intermittently between February and December 2010. "When you put those two things together, you have this amazing amount of wisdom and knowledge."[85] Stewart had long had an interest in film—as a child he traded a gold bracelet he found on the street for an eight-millimeter camera—and proposed monetizing their collaboration by making a movie of it.[86] Footage from the HBO episode and old photographs (those of the tavern her father operated and grandfather frequented in Pasadena) enhanced the chronicle of the making of each song.

It was a pleasant months-long reunion involving dress-up parties, masquerade masks, running children, barking Yorkies, and Reese Witherspoon, cocktail in hand. (Witherspoon's casual invitation to Stewart to crash at her place in Nashville provided the title of "Cheaper Than Free.") "Suddenly everybody started turning into characters," Stewart wrote in his biography, "influenced, no doubt, by the house and by Stevie's obsession with Edgar Allan Poe [the song "Annabel Lee" is on *In Your Dreams*]. People dressed in Edwardian costumes started turning up. Even my daughters, Kaya and Indya, were involved, dressed as spooky little characters, holding owls and walking through halls."[87]

The headdresses, boas, and flowing trains were put away when it came time to work. Nicks has an extraordinary ear, the documentary affirms, and terrible eyesight: the film shows her going through numerous pairs of glasses and using a magnifier to read lyrics. Her assistant

Karen Johnston kept the grand pianos tuned and helped outfit the studio for the increasingly robust roster of guest musicians. Nicks called up Buckingham for help with one of the tracks, then had a row with him for challenging her musicianship. Fleetwood turned up as well, as did Mike Campbell, Waddy Wachtel, and Neale Heywood. Nicks's devoted backup singers perform, as do two violinists, four Hammond organists, several bassists and percussionists, and a single mandolinist.

The single "Secret Love" is a *Rumours* discard, a demo that didn't make the initial cut. The protagonist takes comfort in a former lover who's mistaken in thinking there's a chance of reconciliation. The tightly focused, jangling accompaniment contrasts with Nicks's leisurely, calm-in-the-center-of-the-storm singing. She put more time into "Soldier's Angel." Inspiration came from visiting wounded Iraq War veterans in Washington, DC, in 2005 and reports of a massacre of British soldiers in the same conflict. In the documentary, Nicks rehearses the song on her red satin couch by the fireplace and in the rotunda, a milieu of extreme privilege—the privilege of someone wholly protected from the world's sorrows. Nicks comes close to calling herself out for it. The song's narrator is a soldier's "girl" as well as his "memory," "mother," and "widow." She protests war because the soldier's sacrifice has given her the right to do so. The music is dirge-like, with the falling fifth in the guitar becoming a falling sixth on the way to completing a descending tetrachord—a musical symbol of lament. The bass drum trudges through the verses. The texture brightens in the chorus, which pushes "ghostly shadows . . . back into the light." Buckingham, who helped compose the song, harmonizes with Nicks in thirds in the chorus, recalling the starkest passages of their 1973 debut album.

"Soldier's Angel" was recommended, enthusiastically, by Rob Sheffield in *Rolling Stone*: "Nicks finds storytelling inspiration everywhere, from the *Twilight* series ('Moonlight [A Vampire's Dream]') to Jean Rhys ('Wide Sargasso Sea')," he added.[88] Superfan John Seger also singled out the storytelling for praise but couldn't muster much detail about the structure of the music, excluding a generic comment about "Wide Sargasso Sea": he notes the song's slow buildup of intensity and Nicks's "trademark wailing" at the end.[89] In an interview with Marjorie Hernandez of the *Ventura County Star*, Nicks offered only that "there is a song about a novel called *Wide Sargasso Sea,* the precursor to *Jane Eyre.* It was a crazy movie in the '80s [sic] that I loved."[90] In an interview with Lynne Margolis, Nicks noted the diverse nature of *In Your Dreams,* saying, "I think of these songs and they're all so different, and that's what I love."[91]

Published in 1966, *Wide Sargasso Sea* narrates abject suffering within a dreamscape of stifling heat. The hero, Antoinette Conway, is the Creole child of the owner of a former sugar plantation in Coulibri, Jamaica. Since the abolition of slavery, her childhood home has fallen into disrepair. Abuse disintegrates her sense of self. "I knew the time of day when though it is hot and blue and there are no clouds, the sky can have a very black look," Antoinette says in one of the novel's famous lines.[92] (Consider, in contrast, Nicks's comment about her view of the ocean: "so heavy and so big and so massive and so dangerous. It just makes me feel better. It's way better than Prozac.")[93] Antoinette enters into an arranged marriage with an Englishman who flaunts his unfaithfulness, changes her name, and confines her to an attic in his remote English mansion, Thornton Hall. Antoinette falls under the malevolent guard of Grace Poole, a character in Charlotte Brontë's 1847 novel *Jane Eyre*. *Wide Sargasso Sea* is its feminist, anticolonialist prequel, the conjunction of two transatlantic tales.

Nicks's lyrics touch on the mistrust between Antoinette and her husband and evoke the novel's final chapter, in which Antoinette escapes her room by burning down the house of her captor—just as her childhood home had been incinerated by emancipated slaves. Nicks, not Antoinette, dies in the fire, and Stewart is responsible—for the superslick production that negates affect, emotion, and sentiment; for slapping one screeching guitar solo on top of another; for the synthesizer interjections and abrupt shift from hushed romantic ballad to din-filled blues rock; for the heartbeat rhythm of the coda; for encouraging Nicks to sing with a Nashville twang; and for evincing that he had absolutely no idea what to do with the text. Sheen probably suited the song about Stephenie Meyer. It doesn't suit this one.

Nicks fixated on the voodoo scenes in the novel and movie, along with the supposed drumming of cannibals. "When those drums stop," she says, "you'd better start running."[94] It's a curious comment to make about such a mild track. The artist of gothic legend looms a little less large on the album, excluding the track she rescued from her youth, "Annabel Lee." Rhys's melancholic streak—the feeling that she was living in a dream, "the sense of loss, and a consequent sense of being at a loss"—didn't filter down to Nicks, even though Robin had left her life and by 2012 both of her parents were gone.[95] Tom Petty would leave too, which told her that the whole rock-star thing was indeed over, except for the part about living in the moment, permanently.

FRED AND GINGER

On July 21, 2017, Lana Del Rey released a gorgeous duet with Nicks called "Beautiful People Beautiful Problems." Ten weeks later, on October 2, 2017, Petty died at sixty-six of an accidental overdose of pain medications for a bone fracture. He had slipped and cracked his hip during a tour rehearsal with the Heartbreakers, after earlier electing to postpone hip-replacement surgery. "My audience is what's made me survive, honestly," he fatefully declared. Standing onstage night after night with a guitar slung over his right shoulder increased the pain; eventually the fracture turned into a break. The *Los Angeles Times* added details of his mental health to the report of his death: "Petty struggled with depression, anxiety and insomnia as well as pain from the hip fracture, as evidenced by substances the coroner found in his system when he died: fentanyl and oxycodone (painkillers); alprazolam (Xanax) and temazepam (to treat anxiety and insomnia); and citalopram, an antidepressant."[96] The litany suggests a tortured male genius, mythologizing Petty.

As ever, fans and family members were left wondering what could have been done differently. His second wife, now widow, Dana York said that "he was very stubborn" and "would still be with us" if he had received hip surgery instead of hitting the road.[97] Nicks filmed a solo show with him, released after his passing, and remarked that

> even when I talk about him now onstage, I talk about him like he is not dead—because I don't want him to be dead. So I talk to him like he's still down the street [she once lived near him in Encino] and I can, like, pick up the phone and call him. I'm really glad that this show was recorded before he died, because I think if he had already died, it would've definitely changed the way I spoke about everything. There would've been more of a sad pang to it. And as it was, it was all joyful.[98]

She liked his company and his music, which communicated directly and pleasurably. "It's real easy for Tom and I to be theatrical on stage," she once told MTV, like "Fred Astaire and Ginger Rogers."[99]

Maybe she had in mind "Let's Face the Music and Dance," the fabulous pose Fred and Ginger strike when she arches back, or Ginger's fabulous feathered dress, or the paradoxical authenticity of her and Fred's duets, the genuine moments amid the scripted ones. Or perhaps she was thinking of the line Texas state treasurer (and later governor) Ann Richards made famous in her keynote speech at the 1988 Democratic

National Convention. Advocating for women to have a place in politics, she asserted, "If you give us a chance, we can perform. After all, Ginger Rogers did everything that Fred Astaire did. She just did it backwards and in high heels."[100]

Nicks still senses Petty's presence in her life, and she recently told Tavi Gevinson in a *New Yorker* interview about their connection even on the night he died:

> I feel Tom. I was up watching TV in my apartment that has this view all the way to the pier, and then all the way back to Point Dume. And, all of a sudden, I just looked over to the right and I saw this little red dot way far away down toward Malibu, and I went over to the window and I just stood there and I watched it come all the way up and kind of slow down, when it stopped at the street before me. And I realized, after Tom died, that that was Tom in that ambulance.[101]

MUSICARES

Nicks joined the Fleetwood Mac reunions while pursuing her solo career through the first month of 2018, when the band performed at the MusiCares Person of the Year celebration at Radio City Music Hall. For the audience it was an evening of positivity, with Lorde, Haim, Harry Styles, Alison Krauss, OneRepublic, and other artists paying tribute to Fleetwood Mac. The band filed on stage, Fleetwood leading the way; Nicks entered last, after Buckingham, as usual. Excluding the reticent John McVie, each of them spoke, acknowledging the good work of MusiCares, which raised $7 million that night to assist struggling musicians. Buckingham, the Prospero of the Fleetwood Mac tempest, noted the band's complex history and the love underpinning it all. Fleetwood and Christine McVie feigned a waltz during Nicks's self-effacing turn at the podium, where she talked about talking too much, then acknowledged the loss of the luminaries, Petty chiefly, who had lit her path and kept it shining. The curtain came down in preparation for the band's mini-set, which, Nicks pledged, would tickle everyone's fancy.[102] Backstage, tension spiked. Foul of mood, Buckingham mocked the choice of "Rhiannon" as walk-on music when the curtain went back up. He hated the old stuff, he made clear; he had returned from self-imposed exile with new material that the group did not want to play.[103]

After the show, Nicks's manager Irving Azoff told Buckingham that Nicks would never again appear with him onstage. Nothing was fun anymore; the arguments were ancient and endless and, worst of all, boring. He said, she said; she said, he said: they'd both said a lot. It was over. Yes, Buckingham felt underrecognized. And yes, he had largely ignored *Bella Donna* and Nicks's other solo albums, even those he lent a hand to. He showed little appreciation for her creativity, her voice, and how it resonated with the experiences of people—especially women—who didn't run record labels or decide what would be heard on the airwaves or streamed. Had he given "Joan of Arc" a chance, as an arranger, performer, and producer whose instincts Nicks deeply respected, it might have topped the charts. That did not happen, just as the sequel to *Buckingham Nicks* did not happen, and how great that sequel would have been.

Buckingham had a heart attack in February 2019, as had his brother Greg and father Morris at much earlier ages. Photographer and interior designer Kristen Messner, who married him in 2000, regularly posted updates on his recovery from emergency triple bypass surgery, and Nicks sent Buckingham a note asking him to please take care of himself.[104] His vocal cords were damaged by the ventilator that saved his life, slightly lowering his voice; his straight-up, socket-finger hair went gray. In June 2021, he announced a club tour and released a self-titled album with a conciliatory single, "I Don't Mind." Consolation, however, doesn't sell music quite like dysfunction does, and Buckingham coarsely tried to bait Nicks in the *Los Angeles Times, New York Times,* and *Rolling Stone*— and all of the publications aggregating them—by calling her "lonely" and low energy.[105] The pigtail-pulling hasn't gotten much of a rise out of her.[106] Meantime Messner announced that she had filed for a divorce. That matter, too, has been made to seem acrimonious.[107]

No one contests Buckingham's gifts, and myriad blog postings and YouTube comments insist that had Nicks stayed with him her music would have fared better commercially, never mind her second inauguration into the Rock & Roll Hall of Fame in 2019 and subsequent $100 million sale of the rights to her catalogue, name, and likeness to the publishing and talent management firm Primary Wave.[108] Buckingham has recently sold his catalogue as well—the mega-selling music he wrote for Fleetwood Mac as well as his solo endeavors, which range from delicate acoustic tracks to garage rock, generic pop, and covers of his father's forty-fives. Some of the songs are grievance filled, others coolly indifferent. He expressed his dismay with Mick Fleetwood's tattle-telling memoirs in a 1992 song called "Wrong." It refers to Fleetwood as "Young Mr. Rockcock."

Boys will be boys.

CHAPTER 5

24 Karat Gold

And girls can become divas.

The illustrious women of stage and screen to whom Stevie Nicks has been compared include Judy Garland, Billie Holiday, Dolly Parton, and Barbra Streisand. She personally aligned herself not with these treasured divas but with two others: Greta Garbo and Mabel Normand. The latter is lesser known and, Nicks felt, deserves attention. A stream-of-consciousness song about Normand features on Nicks's eighth and most recent album, the capstone of her resurgence.

Titled 24 Karat Gold and subtitled *Songs from the Vault*, it includes demos and drafts of songs she had all but forgotten until purloined copies began to appear online, some from a suitcase of cassettes that her ex-husband Kim Anderson had sold at a yard sale.[1] Internet averse (she writes with pen and paper and uses her iPhone only as a phone), Nicks learned belatedly that her archive had been looted; bootleggers had assembled their own versions of 24 Karat Gold. Her lawyers decided she needed to reassert her copyright, so the archive became a vault and 24 Karat Gold a gathering of new songs built atop old and old atop new. Dave Stewart and Waddy Wachtel produced the album with her at Blackbird Studios in Nashville, drawing on Sound City, producer Keith Olsen, and the *Buckingham Nicks* electroacoustic sound. It's an album of polished rawness, a bold, rich blend of the pre- and post-coffee-plant tapes that explores how things might have been different. In this sense it's not a reinvention—anathema to the true diva—but a revelation.

The reviews varied but don't matter, since the album was for Nicks's longtime fans.[2] She took to the road in 2016, starting on October 25 at Talking Stick Resort Arena. She confessed to being "a little freaked out [from nerves]—just a little—but I'm in my hometown, Phoenix, where I wrote a lot of my songs." The Pretenders opened for her; she moved through her roles as commercial music's mercurial genetrix—up-market urban siren, down-market desert heart—for listeners aged "15 to 93."[3] Over two nights in Indianapolis and Pittsburgh, Joe Thomas made a concert film, *Stevie Nicks 24 Karat Gold the Concert*. It's almost as preoccupied with Nicks's biographical stories (including generous tributes to Prince and Keith Olsen) as with the music, though Thomas edited out some of her diva-ish "stream of consciousness" longueurs.[4] The film was released on October 21, 2020, in nine hundred theaters worldwide, but the pandemic spoiled the party.[5] It ended up online instead. The *Daily Californian* thought it "wonderful" but too long.[6] *Digital Journal* called it "unforgettable."[7]

EXCEPT FOR MABEL

There are fourteen tracks on *24 Karat Gold,* thirteen of which are do-overs of material written between 1969 and 1995. "Night Gallery," the grim demo from the *Rock a Little* sessions, was excluded; its time has yet to come. The deluxe edition includes two more tracks: "Twisted" and "Watch Chain." The demo of the latter dates back to the seventies, with Nicks doubling herself on vocals to a reggae-inspired guitar lick and laid-back beat. Mick Fleetwood supplied the metaphor. He liked watch chains, even when wearing (as the lyrics note) faded blue jeans. The inspiration for the clumsier alternate title, "Watch Devil," is unclear, though there's no shortage of folklore about clocks and the ringing of the hours as devil's work. It's a seventies song that sounds like a sixties song, with lyrics about old age presented in paradoxical fashion as a remembered now.

"Blue Water" dates from the start of the eighties and *Bella Donna.* Nicks recorded it with the Nashville trio Lady A (formerly Lady Antebellum), with whom she had been trading songs for five years, even performing with them at the Academy of Country Music Awards. Lady A's harmonization considerably brightens the texture, adding Christian "soul" to Nicks's paean to the vibey Hawaiian Pacific. Dave Haywood's guitar curlicues suggest alternate, less austere, melodic possibilities for the accompaniment. Cognoscenti love the intimacy of the piano-vocal version Nicks recorded for a January 2015 cover story in *Rolling Stone,* her first since 1981, but the Lady A transposition pushes past the narcissism of the text (the water gazes back at her while she awaits her gypsy) to enhance the romantic nature imagery. The harmonization imitates the magical opening and closing of a blue water lily.

"Blue Water" describes a situation in flux, perhaps permanently so, and Nicks translates instability into sound. It's a problem for critics like Jim Farber, who considers the looseness of 24 *Karat Gold* somehow a shortcoming: "Unlike her beautifully pruned work with Fleetwood Mac, many songs on her latest solo work fray at the seams, or wander outside the confines of an ideal melody. The album does contain a few must-have highlights, but key parts feature lyrics that wobble awkwardly on their tunes. Yet those very flaws and indulgences wind up casting a clearer light on Nicks' character, and concerns, than ever."[8] Farber doesn't explain what those concerns are, but the tides and whirlpools referenced in "Blue Water" present different perceptions of time. There is the pull into the abyss and a denial of it that suggests Michel de Montaigne's formulation: "Our desires incessantly grow young again; we are always re-beginning to live."[9] Nicks's recent interviews emphasize the "adventure just waiting around the corner" (a phrase Stewart gave her) and the fact that there's never been a clear artistic goal toward which she's been striving.[10] Unsettledness and discursiveness are a bane to music-business execs, but they are the stuff of art. Commercial entertainment in general privileges the fantastical messiness of dreams as long as the mess gets cleaned up before the end. Nicks gave up cleaning a long, long time ago.

Nicks's voice has changed, but that has its advantages for the redo of the 1971 song "Lady." The 2014 version benefits from the richer lower-range timbre of her present-day voice. She has essentially surrendered the mezzo-soprano register of the eighties and seventies, when she could navigate the octave and a half above and the octave below middle C with her trademark fierceness and tenderness intact. The wear and tear of the road and passage of time have gradually compressed her sound.[11] She didn't have years of professional training and so intuited, with her friend Robin Snyder's help, the tricks of the trade: slowing and pausing rhythms; taking the thinnest thread of a phrase and shrouding it in breath; increasing and decreasing pressure on discrete pitches—depending on the points she wanted to make.

In the official video for "Lady," she represents herself not as a different kind of singer but as a performer from another era. She sings without a band in a theater with a royal red curtain, plainly and directly at the mic and in the rhythm of a cradle song, a superstar of the digital age trying to catch a break in an old-time music hall in Nashville. "Lady" is unprepossessing, withdrawn. It's not instantly catchy; it requires a few hearings to appreciate the gradual increase in emotional investment through the first verse and pre-chorus until the soaring breakout moment—"what is to become of me?"—at the heart of the song. Nicks's older self knows the answer to the question posed by her younger self. She pulls back for the second verse, a modified repetition of the first. She pauses, wearied, after singing "knockin' on doors when there's nobody there." Then she gives a final push before the lights go out.

One of the songs is based on music written by Mark Knopfler, the bard of Dire Straits. It comes from a brooding 1984 film, *Cal,* set in Belfast during Northern Ireland's religious war. The plot centers on the doomed, Tristan and Isolde–like romance between the Catholic Cal, an IRA lansquenet, and the widow of a Protestant police officer killed by the IRA, with Cal's participation. Cal tries to hide from those seeking his arrest and from his own conscience. It's impossible, just as it is for the widow, Marcella, to suppress her combined love and hatred of him. Knopfler's Celtic-influenced soundtrack greatly benefits from Liam O'Flynn on uilleann pipes. It's typically beautiful, haunting, and reserved, representing both the setting of the film and the psychologies of the characters. Nicks's setting excludes the pipes in favor of six-string and twelve-string guitars, panned on opposite sides. The final track on *24 Karat Gold,* it seems dedicated to one of the men in her own life but also suits the film, since it relates a love that "no one understands" and references the (Irish) sea. Titled "She Loves Him Still," it's a straightforward ballad with a spoken-word bridge to the final chorus.

There's also a cover of a song by Vanessa Lee Carlton, whose career benefited from Nicks's spiritual and creative mentorship. Carlton rose to fame with the song "A Thousand Miles" in 2002, the one hit on her album *Be Not Nobody.* It has since become her signature. Carlton has continued to perform and to record albums, six in all, and has opened for Nicks, who considers her a friend and a protégée. Nicks's mother, Barbara, liked Carlton's 2011 "Carousel," which inspired Nicks to cover it with Carlton's involvement as singer and instrumentalist. (Nicks's niece, Jessica, also performs on the track.) The original version is the first song on Carlton's *Rabbits on the Run* (2011). It was recorded direct-to-tape in the acoustically sublime "wood room" of Peter Gabriel's Real World Studios near Bath. The video has the feel of a fashion shoot; the rural life never looked so posh. The vamp replicates the spinning of the carousel, plus recalls the chord progression of Cyndi Lauper's more earnest "True Colors." There's also a children's chorus, though Nicks eliminates it.

In Nicks's version, nuance comes from violinist and fiddler Ann Marie Calhoun. She performed on Nicks's *In Your Dreams* in a conventional style. On "Carousel," however, she demonstrates her knowledge of US folk traditions, in indirect homage to Barbara Nicks. (Calhoun's father, a self-described hillbilly and descendant of Pocahontas, played banjo; her sister is an accomplished bluegrass musician, and she herself has performed Appalachian music.)[12] The words use the carousel metaphor for the comings and goings of relationships, the presences and absences. The original has an Edenic Enya-like gloss, but Nicks prefers corn-syrupy sweetness, as does Calhoun, who extracted it from different sources. A native of Gordonsville, Virginia, she once rode the rails with an African American ensemble specializing in Afro-Appalachian music. She has also recorded bluegrass, played on soundtracks about the super-human *(Man of Steel)* and inhuman *(12 Years a Slave),* and collaborated with Damian Marley and Ringo Starr. Like Barbara's daughter—A.J.'s granddaughter—she embodies a cosmopolitan hillbillyness.

The album's title track establishes a hypnotic vamp—a tripping, chick-a-boom pattern in the bass complemented by precise eighth notes in the backbeat. The harmonic progression is close to that of the twenty-four-karat-gold song "Dreams." The guitar playing involves a standard layering of electric and acoustic sounds, with a sparkling conversation between a clean single-coil instrument and an overdriven one in the bridge to the final chorus. The song alternates verse and chorus, but on the 1979 demo (intended for *Bella Donna,* not *Tusk*) the contrast between the two sections breaks down, thanks to a cadential move underneath the trailing lines of the chorus, which question "What kind of freedom? What kind of game?"

The piano and guitar lines arpeggiate a pair of major chords on the demo, and the singing is clipped in a narrow range. The strophe-ending declaration, "You said you might be coming back to town," relies on a single pitch, F, that is excluded from the rest of the tune. The threat or promise of coming back to town (Nicks's delivery combines the sensations of both hope and fear) is typical of country rock and could have been dropped into any number of her songs. There follows a shift from major to minor for "let me be . . . face down" on the ground "in the rain." The bond between melody and accompaniment severs when she repeats the declaration ("set me free") and an F major seventh chord is introduced, the E pointing outside the harmonic confines until the astonishing moment when the song folds back on itself, elaborating, according to the lyrics, a collapse of the world into the wind. When Nicks announces "Here comes the cold chill," the opening vamp returns. Far from familiar pop-music fare, the two major chords of the vamp are brittle and harsh. The snarling bass in the produced version expresses that frostiness, but the line "here comes the cold chill" is no longer sung. It belongs to the demo alone.

Gold is for saving and hoarding, not spending, yet is currency in songs about love. The "golden wings in the sunset" suggest escape through flight but also death, and the protagonist asks to be brought "back" from that horizon, since there was "no one, out there" (a line that is hollowly harmonized, which makes it sound lonelier). The title words "24 karat gold" are punctuated by "chain of chains," unsustainable as a reference to the ever-expanding family called Fleetwood Mac or to Hollywood's dream factory or to a best-selling record—unless all of those references are combined in a golden excess of signification. Chimes and triangle and the reverberating backing singers make the chorus twinkle.

Production is like gold dust, but 24 *Karat Gold* reveals that the most important elements of Nicks's music are the raw ore: fragmented melodies, half-realized ideas, loosely organized declamations, cut-and-paste structures, and playfulness and whimsy (both on the expressive and referential level). Country singer Loretta Lynn makes an appearance, and rocker Janis Joplin too. Whereas Nicks's first two solo albums offered an unnerving emotional intensity at the expense of nuance, the abandoned songs, recovered for 24 *Karat Gold,* reveal her imagination as presented in disconnected poetic images and asynchronous melodic-accompaniment relationships. Her self-awareness, as unregulated in art as in life, is present throughout the album, mostly on the song dedicated to her newly discovered alter ego, a track called a "mess" in Farber's mixed bag of a review.[13]

The implication is that the song, "Mabel Normand," needed an overseeing hand, a more involved producer than either Stewart or Wachtel. There are shockingly few women producers in the business (just 2.6 percent of the songs topping the Billboard Hot 100 songs list for 2020 featured women at the console), and Nicks has not to date worked with one.[14] Sheryl Crow's involvement on *Trouble in Shangri-La* is a partial exception. But perhaps this song, about the short-lived actor Mabel Normand (1892–1930), is meant to sound as it does. Perhaps Nicks intended it to be a perfect mess.

MABEL

Biographers have represented Normand as just that: both flawless and deeply flawed. Normand played the clown and put on faux aristocratic airs, but she also had an introverted, melancholic side. Though she steeped herself in Henri Bergson, Sigmund Freud, and Oscar Wilde, the "I don't care girl," the actor of "pure emotion," could not professionally escape the company of crass "slapstick guys." She became a star of the silver screen before the introduction of sound—frankly, even before the introduction of scripts. Just as the silent era was ending, she died (of tuberculosis), her reputation mired in intrigue, self-abuse, and gossip and wedded to Gloria Swanson's disturbing representation in the Hollywood horror story *Sunset Boulevard*.

Normand was born before most of the boulevard was built, and came from about as far away from it as possible in America: the north shore of Staten Island. Her father, Claude, played piano and worked as a carpenter at a retired sailors' residence, and her mother, Mille, sang. After boarding school Normand modeled clothing, endorsed cosmetics, and posed for lantern slides before lying about her age to get an acting job with Vitagraph Studios in New York, earning $25 a week (about $680 in today's currency). "A frisky colt that knew no bridle," she moved to the West Coast and Keystone Studios in Echo Park, Los Angeles.[15]

Normand made dozens of eight- and fifteen-minute-long slapstick comedies, diving off cliffs and getting tied to the railroad tracks. Her on-screen partners included Charlie Chaplin—whose early career she advanced but who vastly out-earned her and eclipsed her as a star—and Roscoe "Fatty" Arbuckle, with whom she appeared in a string of low-key romantic comedies such as *Mabel and Fatty's Wash Day* (1915). Normand showed greater emotional and psychological breadth in the feature films of later years but was never taken as seriously as she deserved. Pulling pranks was her métier. *Mickey* (1918) cast her as a pulchritudinous tomboy pluckily overcoming the odds, and it is the one film released by the company that briefly bore her name. Like Mary Pickford, Normand demonstrated an ambitiousness almost unheard of for women at the time, but she was harassed on the climb to the top. Producer, director, and studio head Mack Sennett proposed to her while cheating on her, and she almost died when her romantic rival bashed her on the head with a vase.[16] Slapstick can be lethal in real life.

Her later years in Los Angeles exposed the dark side of the twenties movie world. Arbuckle was arrested in connection with the assault and death of twenty-six-year-old actor Virginia Rappe in a San Francisco hotel on September 5, 1921. Despite his eventual acquittal—there was no assault; Rappe died from alcohol poisoning—the trial ruined Arbuckle's career and tarnished Normand by association. The press sensationalized the case, as it did the still-unexplained murder of film director William Desmond Taylor on February 2, 1922. (The case inspired an entire forensic subfield: Taylorology.) Taylor loved her like the other men did, but more chivalrously, even keeping a picture of the two of them in a locket. Normand was the last person to see him alive, having purportedly sought his help overcoming her cocaine habit, but the degree of the addiction, if she was in fact addicted, is disputed by her great-nephew, who says that her biographers erred in believing what the tabloids dished about her in the Roaring Twenties. Gin was more her special helper than cocaine, he suggests, failing to mention that both were prohibited during that decade.[17] The Harrison Act of 1914 had severely limited the distribution of the drug, but doctors could still prescribe it. The Miller Act of 1922 targeted importers and the Andean cocaine trade, as journalists warned of the horrors of addiction: "Self-respect and hope are dead, and a cruel and dominant selfishness has taken their place. He must have the drug or he suffers tortures beyond description. Life means the drug."[18] Legend has Taylor pledging to go after Normand's suppliers, and it is thought, though disputed, that the suppliers took out a contract on his life. Normand was gutted by his death.

Two years later another horror occurred. On New Year's Day 1924, Normand was invited for drinks at the apartment of Courtland Dines, a hotheaded, loudmouthed Denver oil tycoon "playing the field in Hollywood." Despite being betrothed to another actor, Edna Purviance, he had set his eye on Normand, even taking her out a few times behind his betrothed's back. The evening went to hell, and Normand called her chauffeur, Horace Green, for a rescue. The chauffeur arrived; Dines refused to let him in, and an argument developed, with Dines moving to "brain" the chauffeur with a whiskey bottle. The chauffeur had brought along Normand's Colt pistol for safety and fired it three times, hitting Dines in the ear and lung. During the trial it was revealed that he was an escapee from a chain gang and living under a false name, Joe Kelly. Normand declined to defend him: "Shush, the poor boob was nuts," she commented in her highly affected, dryly sarcastic style. "He was only one of the servants, and he was treated like one. Why, I didn't even treat him like—well I've had a lot of good chauffeurs. And good gawd, I didn't even hire this egg. My secretary did that." The chauffeur impugned Normand in turn, drawing attention to her excessive alcohol intake. Dines didn't testify, which resulted in the chauffeur's acquittal.[19]

Normand died long before Nicks was born, but there are haunting resemblances in some photographs. The titles of some of Normand's films could even serve as chapter titles in a book such as this one: *[Stevie's] Dramatic Career, Awful Mistakes, Stormy Love Affair, Strange Predicament,* and *Punctured Romance.* Life and art twirl around each other in Tinseltown as in Village Studios. Normand played the role of the "pride of Yokeltown and apple of her mother's eye."[20] So did Nicks.

Nicks "felt the union" with Normand after watching something about her on television in 1985, a low point in her own life. Each song on *24 Karat Gold,* Nicks commented at the time of the album's release, "is a lifetime. Each . . . has a soul . . . a purpose . . . a love story. They represent my life behind the scenes, the secrets, the broken hearts, the broken hearted and the survivors."[21] The album is a woolgathering—containing fuzzy recollections of "walking on the edge" and a "dangerous year in my life," "what drugs can do to you."[22] Nicks filled in the details about "Mabel Normand" in an interview with *Billboard,* believing, or wanting to believe, the tales of the actor's lethal habits, even though it was tuberculosis that did her in:

> *When you went back to listen to songs you'd written years ago, did they each remind you of a specific period of your life?*
> Yes. Give "Mabel Normand" a special listen. Mabel was an amazing actress and comedian from the '20s, and she was a terrible cocaine addict. She eventually died of tuberculosis, but it was really her drug addiction that killed her. She was in love with a famous director, who tried to get her off coke, and he was murdered. Rumor has it, drug dealers killed him. I saw a documentary of her in 1985, when I was at my lowest point with the blow. I was watching TV one night, the movie came on, and I really felt a connection with her. That's when I wrote the song. Less than a year later, I went to rehab at Betty Ford.
>
> *Didn't a doctor warn you in the '80s that if you did one more line of coke, you might have a heart attack?*
> He said I'd have a brain hemorrhage, actually. The documentary really scared me, because I saw this beautiful girl go downhill so fast. Sometimes you can't see it in yourself, but you sure as heck can see it in someone else. And suicide was never my MO. I'm basically a happy person. I was a happy person back then. I just got addicted to coke, and that was a very bad drug for me. It was obviously a very bad drug for Mabel too. She had a gang of rich kids, like Lindsay Lohan today. That same bunch of girls comes around every 15 years.[23]

For *Out* magazine Nicks expanded on her thoughts, expressing surprise that stars living in the twenties waged war on themselves just as she had. She also described taking stark, unsmiling, intentionally unmediated and unfeminine photos of herself on a Polaroid camera every night and looking in fright at addiction's ravages. (The standard edition of 24 *Karat Gold* includes some of the images.) Nicks wrote "Mabel Normand" as a kind of "just say no" warning. "I wanted it to be something that somebody having a problem with drugs can sit down and listen to 5,000 times," she told Michael Martin. "Try to let it be an epiphany for you, 18-year-old person doing a lot of coke and smoking heroin and taking ecstasy on a dead-end road to hell. I want anybody who hears a doctor say, 'Would you like me to write you a prescription of Klonopin?' to get up and run out of the room screaming and take the air out of that doctor's tires. I want them to hear the word 'cocaine' and think *'brain hemorrhage, beauty gone, lines, aging, fat.'*"[24]

The lyrics of "Mabel Normand" (the longest track on the album) mix references to Normand and Taylor's romance with Taylor speaking with Nicks about addiction. It's a bitter, hard-edged, and aimless composition, similar in its acerbic spirit to an article by Jon Boorstin about the actor's almost-greatness. Normand died too soon to make the glorious black-and-white sound picture she could have made, he believes. Her death ended the silent era; she did screen tests for sound films, but nothing more. Comedy was her tragedy. She is the movie business, Boorstin appends.[25] Nicks is Normand's simulacrum in some of the photographs, just one inch taller. She is the music business.

The song tells more than one tale and ends on a note of heavy regret:

She fought a losing battle
She might even make it through tomorrow
So beautiful, so beautiful
Sad we won't know her[26]

There are references elsewhere in the lyrics to the 1973 *Buckingham Nicks* song "Races Are Run," and "Long Distance Winner" is reflected in the phrases, distributed throughout, about winning and losing. Nicks recites the long verses over a crude synthesized pulse and three chords (A minor and F and G major, repeated agitatedly over and over again) in the demo. The redone version is pushed a half-step higher.

The song goes hazily nowhere, but Wachtel fills that nowhere with overdriven solo fills and, as on "24 Karat Gold," layers acoustic and electric guitars in a manner comparable to Jess Lynne's productions with Tom Petty and the Traveling Wilburys. The guitar playing is typical of a general move on the part of "legacy" artists toward more natural and classic guitar and bass playing. Gone are the modulations, reverbs, and delays of the eighties.

The first and last verses describe "Sad Mabel Normand"; those in the middle refer to "you and your friend" and a "Beloved Exile." The point of departure here seems to be a 1984 novel of Arthuriana by the popular fantasy writer Parke Godwin. Titled *Beloved Exile*, it tells the tale of Queen Guinevere following the death of King Arthur. She appears at his funeral under a "sodden blanket of weariness," "naked to the moment," in Godwin's colorful prose.[27] Numerous adaptations of the original Arthurian legend have Guinevere falling in love with Arthur's leading knight, Lancelot, then, following the king's death in the Battle of Camlann, exiling herself to a convent to repent. Godwin picks up where the legend leaves off and represents Guinevere altogether positively. The Celtic Briton queen is captured by Saxons and made a slave but brought around to the side of the "invaders" after learning of the violence inflicted against them by Arthur.[28] She is good-hearted, forgiving, and altruistic in Godwin's account, as opposed to scheming, treacherous, and loose in mores.

The roles of Lancelot and Arthur are up for grabs: there are several contenders, both in Nicks's life and Normand's. What might the song tell us about each of them? Don't look for a simple explanation, because people's lives don't provide them. The singing has attack, conviction, and focus. It critiques; it denounces; it remonstrates with itself; it's adventitious; it has the tired-of-the-sheer-waste-of-it-all edginess of multiple takes that could have been just one; it's free and easy; it's trapped in a three-chord cycle of denial. "Mabel Normand" is also sympathetic and circumspect, like Godwin's reimagined Guinevere. It's a wild ride that doesn't have a tune, going nowhere and everywhere, then just stopping with the delirious, punchy, and ultimately unbearable pair of words "so beautiful."

Conclusion

A Thousand Stevies

Posing and playacting were part of music in the seventies, and at a certain point the "artificial sentiments" and "personal emotion" dissolved into each other, such that Nicks could declare that "everyone can dress up like me, because there's so many different *mes* [Greta, Mabel, the heroes of the Mabinogi]. You can be any me you want."[1] She is addressing participants in the "Night of 1000 Stevies" (NOTS), who have taken up her artistic persona in cosplay fanfests held since 1991.[2] The first occurred in the meatpacking district of New York in a club called Mother, aka Jackie 60, on the passionate initiative of nightclub impresarios Chi Chi Valenti and Johnny Dynell, with input from costume designer Kitty Boots. After that, the annual burlesque expanded from Irving Plaza in New York to the club One Eyed Jacks in New Orleans. May 4, 2019, was the twenty-ninth NOTS event. The 2020 event was canceled because of the COVID pandemic, but the official website promised Nicks's fans, her "Enchanted Gypsies," that the "glitter and doves will return!"[3]

Many LGBTQ+ fashionistas adore Nicks, and she adores them too, for their appreciation of a career that seems to embrace camp, as defined by Susan Sontag in her Oscar Wilde–inspired, aphoristically rendered "notes" on the phenomenon. "The hallmark of Camp is the spirit of extravagance," Sontag commented back in 1964. "Camp is a woman walking around in a dress made of three million feathers."[4] The sentence is as excessive as the thing it describes: three million feathers are just too many, but Nicks did wear a lot of fringe. In the camp world, immense, supremely over-the-top extravagance cloaks impoverishment. Consider camp's aristocratic progenitor: Marie Antoinette, the last French queen before the 1792 fall of the monarchy. Her life was defined by "codes of etiquette," and she maintained aristocrat decorum right up to the end (she apologized for stepping on her executioner's shoe). She was born to her role; martyrdom was imposed on her, and, when she obeyed the "dictates of the heart," she suffered for it.[5]

Nicks loves the "1000 Stevies" events and has promised, or "threatened," an incognito appearance. "I'll be in such fantastic makeup that I'll be able to float around," Nicks said. "Nobody will know it's me, until I walk on stage and start singing 'Edge of 17.' Everybody will faint and they'll have to call ambulances."[6] Performer and diehard Nicks fan Heather Litteer told *Rolling Stone* in 2015 that "Stevie's one of the top rock idols for any woman." She expresses nostalgia not for Nicks in her heyday but for the heyday of the fan events. "Everybody dressed like Stevie. Everybody had blond wigs, tambourines, boas, feathers everywhere. . . . It's like a sea. It's like the ocean of Stevies." A video of Litteer concludes with her rendition of a Nicks rarity, the 1969 brothel ode "Cathouse Blues," with Dixieland-band accompaniment. The evenings have become too overwhelmingly big for Litteer: shows now embrace all ages, genders, and sexual orientations. "I don't think we were really aware of how big her fan base is and how many people—and different types of people—like Stevie," coproducer Dynell noted. "It's a Noah's Ark of Stevie love," Valenti added.[7]

What makes Nicks a diva in this milieu? She refused ordinariness, and ordinariness refused her, ensuring a long reign at or near the top of the music business, through its pre-disco boom and post-disco bust. The singer had been put through (and put herself through) a brutal gauntlet and was hazed in the press as what Lucy O'Brien calls a "parody of her former self, the archetypal blonde-locked spacey Rock Chick in flowing dresses."[8] Yet the parody is broadly associated with fabulousness: Nicks is a "beautiful eccentric," to quote the title of Madison Moore's book on the transformation of struggle into opulence.[9]

In an article wittily titled "Queering the Witch" (in the collection *Queering the Popular Pitch*), Jason Lee Oakes affirms that Nicks "serves as a model of female—and, more specifically, feminine— empowerment." His evidence is, unsurprisingly, "Rhiannon," which he gives a "queer hearing." The song's harmonic, melodic, and rhythmic misalignments, he writes, indicate her (or her persona's) "unwillingness to be pinned down." Nicks and her "feminine-associated tambourine" twirl "in perpetual motion around a seemingly fixed point of arrival that is never reached."[10]

That reading can be compared with Michael Montlack's remarks about Nicks and NOTS. He appreciates her duality: the tear-streaked, furrowed-brow obviousness of the emotions she expresses alongside the ambivalence of their meanings. Trafficking in stereotypes, he explores her performances as representing "the troubled, drug-addicted rock star versus the humble singer-songwriter introduced on stage by her proud 'Daddy'" and "the spinning, black-caped vamp accused of witchcraft versus the doe-eyed angel about to take flight in those layers of white gauze and lace." Ultimately, he concludes (rightly if a little banally) that "fans were left to decipher or just guess what her real story was."[11] Nicks engages directly with those fans on social media, answering benign questions one-on-one while keeping them guessing about the deeper details. Everyone—famous, invisible, and flamboyant alike—deserves the refuge of their privacy.

Nicks's campiest declaration concerns her mountains of fabrics: "I have my shawl vault. They're all in temperature-controlled storage. I have these huge red cases Fleetwood Mac bought, all the way back in 1975—my clothes are saved in these cases. All my vintage stuff is protected for all my little goddaughters and nieces. I'm trying to give my shawls away—but there's thousands of them. If I ever write my life story, maybe that should be the name of my book: *There's Enough Shawls to Go Around*."[12] Hers is the busy life of a dreamer, not that of a bored desirer.[13]

"A long time ago I decided I was going to have a kind of mystical presence," Nicks informed *Interview* in 1998, "so I made my clothes, my boots, my hair, and my whole being go with that. But it wasn't something I just made up at that point. It's the way I've always been. I've always believed in good witches—not bad witches—and fairies and angels."[14] Contemporary feminists reject the bad-good distinction imposed on women by men and so can celebrate all sides of Nicks. The sex-positive online collective *Slutist* describes her as a "leather- and lace-clad celebration of the witch-slut-feminist trifecta."[15] The mystical presence comes from the books she reads and movies she watches, from A.J. and Alice and the real and imagined Saras, from a late-sixties moment in music and its seventies commodification on the Southwest's airwaves, from the fantasies of girls that shape popular culture. Her highs were the music industry's highs, her lows likewise, and when she reached the place in between, the industry was no longer the same. Now everything she says about the past comments mostly on her present.

Nicks declines to be nostalgic. Indeed, her most nostalgic songs rank among her earliest. The text of "Cathouse Blues" dates from 1969 and imagines senses dulling in old age and "I" and "you" pronouns getting confused: "I guess you don't remember/I guess that I was younger."[16] The prematurely jaded ingenue mocks the rumpled seediness of the men in the music business—the six-car flunkies, or the power junkies, as the Eagles put it in "King of Hollywood." She was not seventeen in 1981, but "Edge [Age] of Seventeen" has that age's fierceness. "Her usual pressed-posy lyrics," Greil Marcus commented about a live take, "but rendered with such force and passion that whatever metaphors our lady of the veils might be offering are dissolved in a performance of the purest lust."[17] This song, the most successful of her solo career and, thanks to Wachtel's grinding, the most sex positive, concludes the NOTS events, with a prize going to the best Rhiannon impression. Yet Nicks's achievement, her coven knows, is predicated on more than just scarves and lipstick, leather and high heels—more than appearance alone. Her opulence is her poetry's opulence, and her music's opulence too. Her art is a complicated interaction between free-floating poetic symbols and strict, too-strict forms. When she sings "Set me free, set me free/Is this what you wanted, to happen to me?" she might, yes, be referring to lovers, or to producers, managers, and the arbiters of commercial entertainment.

Stevie Nicks believes she has lived previous lives, and surely every artist of any repute travels a considerable distance. In Nicks's case, she knows the Arizona desert of her kinfolk and aligns herself with medieval lore and revolutionary femmes fatales. Perhaps she lost her head like Marie Antoinette, as her ballet coach teased back in 1982.[18] Her own experiences had distant antecedents: the ancient treatise *Malleus Maleficarum* defines women who live alone, experience illness, or "Sway the Minds of Men to Love and Hatred" as potential sorceresses.[19]

She became a superstar in the year of *Star Wars,* the Concorde, Elvis's death, New York's blackout, Jimmy Carter's inauguration, and FM music that imagined utopia in the midst of stagflation. *Rumours* still sells because people are still trying to imagine 1977 as it never was. Nicks scratched its depth—through the grain of her voice—into a gleaming surface. Her sharp edge is part of her enduring appeal. Her continued presence in the lives of younger enchanters is also testament to the power of music fashioned on a loom—cut fine, then textured and softly woven, like Taylor Swift's "Cardigan." Nicks became who she became by, she says, not being "interested in existing on that critical level most people live on."[20] Her music comes from a place that is much bigger on the inside than the outside, where feelings are more significant than thoughts or actions. She loves what needs loving and embraces "anything that is wonderful," including "some sadness. I don't mind that, but evil, bad things, I don't like them in my life."[21] Audiences at the "Night of 1000 Stevies" choose beauty, as do the fans and superfans who grew up with her—likewise those who have come to know her music via the chill "Dreams" memes of 2020, a year full of evil, its bad things made just a bit better by her crystal visions.

Acknowledgments

This book arose about six years ago in conversation with people who love Stevie Nicks's song "Dreams" just because they do, without needing or wanting to explain the love. I am one of those people, though writing about "Dreams" and other songs meant thinking about that love as opposed to leaving it be.

I owe special thanks to my research assistant Violet Prete. I am also grateful to Samantha Grayson, who gathered material on "Rhiannon" and *Rumours*, and to Nate Radley, guitarist extraordinaire, who guided me through the electric and acoustic playing on the available Fritz recordings and the *Buckingham Nicks* album.

My thanks as well to the illustrious musicians and producers who, as the notes show, indulged my questions about Fleetwood Mac and Nicks's solo career; to the librarians and archivists who helped retrace her upbringing; to Helen Fulton for educating me in Welsh legend; to Liza DiSavino for information about the music of Appalachia; to Kristen Sollée for her insights on witchcraft; and to John Pendergast for his analysis of "Joan of Arc." I am grateful as well to Megan Pugh for developmental work on the book; Susan Silver and Jan Spauschus for their twenty-four-karat-gold copy editing, fact-checking, and help tracking down references; Raina Polivka and Kim Robinson for believing in the project and guiding it from proposal to publication; my friends at the University of Southern California, especially Tom Seifrid, for encouragement; Roland Hui for generously sharing clippings, images, and fanfic about Fleetwood Mac and Stevie Nicks; Katie Adams for advice on the introduction; Elizabeth Rouget for proofreading; and the anonymous reviewers of the book's draft. Last and most important, I am indebted to Elizabeth Bergman for reading and improving each page of the text and, as ever, for her presence.

Demos

24 KARAT GOLD (STANDARD EDITION)
Starshine
Recorded on April 4, 1980, with Tom Petty and the Heartbreakers; intended for *Bella Donna*. Partial audio of the studio session available at Cobius, "Stevie Nicks ~ Starshine Full Session with Tom Petty + The Heartbreakers," YouTube video, 9:30, April 21, 2019, www.youtube.com/watch?v=1KzONQSzNXU. Nicks hears an Otis Redding influence in the music as Petty talks about chord changes, the bridge, and solos. Dave Stewart released an excerpt of the produced song for *24 Karat Gold* on social media on June 2, 2014, as did Nicks on September 15 of that year.

The Dealer
Written in 1979 and recorded in succession for *Tusk, Bella Donna,* and *Rock a Little.* Original version available at Cobius, "Fleetwood Mac/Stevie Nicks ~ The Dealer (Tusk Demo)," YouTube video, 4:55, July 17, 2019, www.youtube .com/watch?v=Q_r8MpKhiFQ. Sharon Celani sings with Nicks on the *Bella Donna* version available at Jeremy Doe, "Stevie Nicks – The Dealer (Drum Machine Demo + 'Haunting' Fleetwood Mac Demo) – Cassette Master," YouTube video, 9:01, March 1, 2011, https://www.youtube.com/watch?v=k__ QI7oluoQ. Released as a single for *24 Karat Gold* on August 5, 2014.

Mabel Normand
Also called "You Change Sides"; written and recorded in 1984 with drum machine and keyboard. Excerpt of the produced song for *24 Karat Gold* released on August 15, 2014.

Blue Water

Written and recorded in Hawaii in March 1978, with Nicks on piano and Celani as second vocalist.

Cathouse Blues

Written in 1969, recorded with Lindsey Buckingham on guitar two years later. Excerpt of the produced song for 24 *Karat Gold* released on September 9, 2014.

24 Karat Gold

Written and recorded in January 1980 with drum machine and piano and improvised lyrics. The version available at Jeremy Doe, "Stevie Nicks – 24 Karat Gold – Vocal Track 23 – Demo (January 1980)," YouTube video, 7:06, October 27, 2014, https://www.youtube.com/watch?v=ykMAiieHFDo, has Nicks reciting "studio on the water, palm trees in Santa Monica, condominiums for $800,000, any one of you could afford it." Intended for *Bella Donna*.

Lady

Also called "Knocking on Doors"; written and recorded with Nicks on piano in 1971, during the Fritz/*Buckingham Nicks* era.

All the Beautiful Worlds

Written and recorded for *The Wild Heart* at Goodnight Audio, Dallas, in 1982 with Lori Perry as second vocalist. Excerpt of the produced song for 24 *Karat Gold* released on August 22, 2014.

Belle Fleur

Written in 1981; first intended for *Bella Donna,* then for *The Wild Heart.* The February 18, 1981, version available at lyannas, "Stevie Nicks – Belle Fleur (Demo)," YouTube video, 4:37, September 22, 2014, www.youtube.com /watch?v=12KyHQfM7Rg, has Nicks asking the keyboardist, "Is that a good tempo, Ben [Benmont Tench]?" Excerpt of the produced song for 24 *Karat Gold* released on August 19, 2014.

If You Were My Love

Recorded with drum machine and electronic keyboard on July 13, 1980, and at a slower tempo with piano on February 20, 1981; intended in succession for *Bella Donna, Mirage,* and *Street Angel.* Excerpt of the produced song for 24 *Karat Gold* released on August 12, 2014.

She Loves Him Still

Written and recorded in 1984 with Mark Knopfler and intended for *Rock a Little*. Three known takes, the last with modified lyrics. Excerpt of the produced song for *24 Karat Gold* released on September 12, 2014.

24 *KARAT GOLD* (DELUXE EDITION BONUS TRACKS)
Twisted

Written and recorded in 1996 for the *Twister* soundtrack; released in 1998 as part of Nicks's retrospective box set *Enchanted*.

Watch Chain

Also called "Watch Devil"; written in 1978 and recorded in 1981 for *Bella Donna*.

Fandom

These are devotee websites. For journalistic opinion, the Rock's Back Pages database, rocksbackpages.com, boasting 235 sources on Nicks and 619 sources on Fleetwood Mac, is recommended.

AMC Stevie Nicks Home Page
  angelfire.com/sc/stevienicks/index.html
  owned by Adam M. Chalmers
  articles, interviews, songs, and quotes

Benzodiazepine Information Coalition
  benzoinfo.com/stevie-nicks
  quotes about Nicks's struggles with Klonopin

Biography
  biography.com/musician/stevie-nicks
  biography from early life to later solo work

Blue White Fire (archived)
  web.archive.org/web/20031118182819/http://www.bluewhitefire.com
  owned by Tiffany Sledzianowsky
  photos, lyrics, downloads, and other links

Buckingham Nicks

buckinghamnicks.net
owned by Nancy Kerns
up-to-date info, news, and sections for each musician with photos and lyrics

Burnish: Ode de Fleetwood Mac (archived)

web.archive.org/web/20001002191131/http://burnish.net
owned by Tracy Garner
archives (interviews, articles), chat room, videos, links, photos, audio files, lyric interpretations, and concert reviews

The Changing Times: Stevie Nicks (active)

stevienicks.bellaillume.com
owned by Sandy Thornton
bio, discography, tour archives, photos, and calendar

Dreams: The Crystal Visions of Stevie Nicks (active)

crystalvisionsdesigns.com/dreams
owned by Claudia Brady-Drake
bio, wallpapers, photos, quotes, and other links

Encyclopedia

encyclopedia.com/people/literature-and-arts/music-popular-and-jazz-biographies/stevie-nicks
biography with sources

Everything That Is Fleetwood Mac (active)

fleetwoodmac.net/fwm
owned by Lisa and Marty Adelson
history, biographies, discographies, news, concerts, and fan chats

The Fleetwood Mac Legacy (archived)

web.archive.org/web/20121226223433/http://www.fmlegacy.com/main.html
owned by Dirk Faes and Jan Freedland
biographies, concerts, interviews, articles, discography, and photos

Fleetwood Mac News

fleetwoodmacnews.com

news, tour dates, recording sessions, discography, tour archives, album reviews, videos, interviews, and links

Fleetwood Mac UK (active)
fleetwoodmac-uk.com
owned by Neil O. Donoghue
articles, shop, concerts, and UK activities

Gold Dust Stevie (active)
goldduststevie.tumblr.com/
Tumblr account

In Her Own Words (inactive)
inherownwords.com
owned by Christine Kilger
quotes from Stevie organized by songs, people, and albums

Inspired Angel
inspiredangel.com
lyrics

Leaping Princess Studios
leapingprincess.tripod.com
owned by Amanda W. Crews
art collection inspired largely by Stevie Nicks and Fleetwood Mac

The Ledge
ledge.fleetwoodmac.net
fan chat boards and FAQs

Madness Fades (archived)
web.archive.org/web/20050207052127/http://www.madnessfades.net/index.htm
owned by Lindsey Buckingham
Buckingham's songs, albums, and experiences

The Morrison Hotel Gallery
morrisonhotelgallery.com
photos of musicians by notable photographers

The Nicks Fix (inactive)

rockalittle.com
owned by John Kinney
tour dates, music, fan chats, archives (articles, interviews, reviews), trivia, photos, lyrics, covers, songbooks, and links

Purple Moon

purplemoon.com/Stevie.html
photos, collectibles, tour diaries, memorabilia, books, and jewelry

The Queen of Rock and Roll (archived)

web.archive.org/web/19990501194506/http://www.queenofrock.com
owned by Brian Humphreys
videos, interviews, articles, photos, links, and audio

Rhinestone Collections

angelfire.com/nf/mjmirabella/index.html
lyrics, poetry, and quotes

Rock on the Net (active)

rockonthenet.com/artists-n/stevienicks_main.htm
biography, timeline, discography, and reviews

Silver Springs

jjshank.tripod.com/stevie_music.html
guitar music (lyrics and chords) from Stevie Nicks's solo career

Stevie Nicks Chain

stevienickschain.com
mailing list and fan club

Stevie Nicks Daily (active)

stevie-nicks.org
daily updates, music, photos, and press

Stevie Nicks FAQ (legacy site)

faqs.org/faqs/music/stevie-nicks
owned by C.L. Moon
FAQs about Stevie Nicks and her music

Stevie Nicks Info (active)

stevienicks.info
news, archives (articles, interviews), FAQs, tours, music, videos, shop, and links

Stevie Nicks: My Fan Site

stevie-nicks.myfansite.nl
photos, articles, news, and lyrics

Stevie Nicks Official Website (active)

stevienicksofficial.com
news, updates, tour dates, music, photos, videos, store, and VIP packages

The Stevie Nicks Underground (archived)

web.archive.org/web/20001018062048/http://www.sararhiannon.com
owned by Sara Maitland
photos, news, discography, audio, store, and links

Stevie Nicks Welsh Witch (Tumblr; inactive)

stevienickswelshwitch.tumblr.com
biographies, discographies, songs, lyrics, and photos

Notes

INTRODUCTION

1. PresenceRO, "Fleetwood Mac: Angel (Live in St Louis, Nov 1979)," YouTube video, 5:02, August 16, 2011, www.youtube.com/watch?v=Pyt250qx9uA. My thanks to New York University dance and theater historian Julie Malnig for her analysis of the dancing (email communication with the author, July 28, 2020).

2. Don Short, "At Last . . . It's a Hit to Be a Mrs.," *Daily Mirror*, November 23, 1968, 9.

3. Meantime, singer-songwriter and guitarist Bob Welch also performed with Fleetwood Mac. His best-known song, "Hypnotized," a swinging shuffle groove in C minor overladen with spoken-word recitation and a soulful chorus, has been likened to a "shamanistic vision" and "spiritual pilgrimage." Camille Paglia, "Too Late for Obama to Turn It Around?," *Salon*, September 9, 2009, www .salon.com/2009/09/09/healthcare_31/.

4. Jessica Hopper, "Fleetwood Mac: Rumours," Pitchfork, February 8, 2013, https://pitchfork.com/reviews/albums/17499-rumours/.

5. Ibid.

6. Arguably the most eclectic book in the Bloomsbury 33 1/3 series about iconic albums is dedicated to it; the first sentence reads, "There's a good chance you won't like this book." Rob Trucks, *Tusk* (New York: Bloomsbury, 2011), 1.

7. Geoffrey Himes, "Can You Make History without Innovating a New Style? A Case for Fleetwood Mac," *Paste*, June 22, 2017, www.pastemagazine .com/articles/2017/06/can-you-make-musical-history-without-inventing-a-n .html?amp.

8. The alternative rock band Camper Van Beethoven released a track-for-track cover of the album in 2003, not because they liked the original, but because they didn't: "I hate 'Tusk,'" Camper's bassist admitted. "It's like the 'Magnificent Ambersons' of rock, a work that's supposed to be good, but is really just a

cocaine-damaged horror of excess." "This Beethoven Is Still a Classic," *Chicago Tribune*, January 17, 2003, www.chicagotribune.com/news/ct-xpm-2003-01-17-0301170222-story.html.

9. Gossip too, some generated by the band members themselves. Christine McVie has been quoted as saying that "Fleetwood Mac rocked" in the "me" decade "thanks to the drugs." Jaymi McCann, "Desert Island Discs: 'Fleetwood Mac Rocked Thanks to the Drugs' Says Christine McVie," *Express*, December 17, 2017, www.express.co.uk/showbiz/tv-radio/893393/Desert-Island-Discs-Fleetwood-Mac-Christine-McVie-drink-drugs.

10. Philip Auslander, *In Concert: Performing Musical Persona* (Ann Arbor: University of Michigan Press, 2021), 28, 114, Kindle.

11. Mary Bartlet Leader, *Triad: A Novel of the Supernatural* (New York: Coward, McCann and Geoghegan, 1973). Nicks has referred to both this novel and the witch as "schizoid." John Grissim, "Look Who's Back: Fleetwood Mac," *Rolling Stone*, April 8, 1976, www.rollingstone.com/music/music-news/look-whos-back-fleetwood-mac-232189/.

12. Kristen Sollée, email communication with the author, August 8, 2020.

13. Amanda Petrusich, "The Resurgent Appeal of Stevie Nicks," *New Yorker*, November 21, 2016, www.newyorker.com/magazine/2016/11/28/the-resurgent-appeal-of-stevie-nicks.

14. See Sara Ahmed, *The Promise of Happiness* (Durham: Duke University Press, 2010), 62–65, who discusses the female imagination contra patriarchal conceptions of happiness. "The figure of the female troublemaker," Ahmed writes, "shares the same horizon with the figure of the feminist killjoy."

15. Amy Kaufman, "The Moonlit Confessions of Stevie Nicks," *Los Angeles Times*, September 30, 2020, www.latimes.com/entertainment-arts/music/story/2020-09-30/stevie-nicks-fleetwood-mac-solo-concert-film.

16. Emily Kirkpatrick, "Stevie Nicks Says She 'Saved' Herself from Cocaine Addiction: 'I Survived Me,'" *Vanity Fair*, August 19, 2021, www.vanityfair.com/style/2021/08/stevie-nicks-cocaine-addiction-recovery-memoir-tim-mcgraw-apple-music-beyond-the-influence-radio.

CHAPTER 1. STEPHANIE

1. Audy toiled in a mine operated by the Phelps Dodge Corporation. Barbara moved with her mother, siblings, and stepfather to Pueblo, Colorado, and Lordsburg, New Mexico. As a child, she was a member of the Masonic Order of the Rainbow for Girls, which practices faith, hope, and charity.

2. Timothy White, "Stevie Nicks: Long-Distance Winner," *Billboard* 110, no. 16 (1988): 3.

3. Brittany Spanos, "Stevie Nicks Asks Spirits for Guidance on Powerful New Song 'Show Them the Way,'" *Rolling Stone*, October 9, 2020, www.rollingstone.com/music/music-news/stevie-nicks-show-them-the-way-dave-grohl-1069754/.

4. "Marriage of Local Couple Revealed Here Yesterday," *Arizona Republic*, November 14, 1947, 27.

5. Sonja Haller, "Scottsdale Store Offers Stevie Nicks' Memorabilia," *Arizona Republic*, July 31, 2010, 16.

6. "Jess Nicks: More Like 'Jess' Lucky—and in Nick of Time," *Salt Lake Tribune,* June 3, 1962, 2C. I am grateful to Paloma Phelps of Archives and Public Records, Arizona State Library, for this reference and for directing me to the Pasadena City Directories for details about Jess Nicks's barkeeping days.

7. Kathy Shayna Shocket, "Parents Are Rocker Stevie Nicks' Biggest Fans," *Arizona Republic,* July 10, 2003, 4.

8. The 1950 Sierra Madre Chamber of Commerce Directory has a listing for J. H. Nicks at 313 Cypress Court.

9. According to area phone books, the Nicks family rented 468 Woodland Drive in Sierra Madre and 214½ North Avenue 66 in Highland Park. Mickie's Tavern had previously been operated by Herman D. Oswald (who named it Ozzie's) and, from 1946, Irish-born Bessie A. Laurence (who renamed it Mickie's Café, after the Irish hypocorism "Mick") at 2427 East Washington Street in Altadena (the address is now part of Pasadena). Nicks sold it in 1955 or 1956 to Louis Feustel, a horse trainer, after which the Nicks family moved to 194 North Holliston in Pasadena. In the sixties, Mickie's was renamed the Old Timer, remembered by locals as a small place with cheap beer, a jukebox and pool table, and three or four tables. It's closed now, used as storage space for the Italian restaurant across the street.

10. "Jess Nicks."

11. Mike Sunnucks, "Evolution Changes Greyhoud *[sic]* from Dial to Viad," *Phoenix Business Journal,* November 2, 2015, www.bizjournals.com/phoenix/news/2015/11/02/evolution-changes-greyhoud-from-dial-to-viad.html.

12. Patty Prado Duke and Ron Ridenhour, "The History of the Phoenix 40: Passing the Torch," *New Times* (Phoenix), April 23, 1975, 3, 17.

13. "Jess Seth Nicks," *Arizona Republic,* August 17, 2005, B8.

14. "Greyhound Forms an Executive Office, Promotes Several Men," *Wall Street Journal,* February 21, 1975, 18.

15. Ed Masley, "Nicks on Phoenix: 'This Actually Is My Home,'" *Arizona Republic,* March 29, 2019, C6.

16. Debbi Radford, "An Evening with Stevie Nicks," Nicks Fix, April 21, 1996, http://stevienicks.net/azreview.htm.

17. Zoë Howe, *Stevie Nicks: Visions, Dreams and Rumours* (London: Omnibus, 2015), 5.

18. Stephen Davis, *Gold Dust Woman: The Biography of Stevie Nicks* (New York: St. Martin's Griffin, 2017), 3. It's impossible to imagine Barbara and Jess allowing their beloved daughter to be exploited in this fashion; Stevie and A.J.'s career as a duo surely began and ended at Mickie's.

19. Rob Sheffield, "Stevie Nicks on Tom Petty, Drag Queens, 'Game of Thrones' and Missing Prince," *Rolling Stone,* February 28, 2019, www.rollingstone.com/music/music-features/stevie-nicks-interview-tom-petty-drag-queens-game-of-thrones-prince-801112/.

20. Aaron Jesse Nicks, registration card, "World War I Selective Service System Draft Registration Cards, 1917–1918," M1509, 572850, Military Records, National Archives, accessed November 8, 2020, www.archives.gov/research/military/wwi/draft-registration?_ga=2.131585743.1116227716.1604942351–1516090316.1604942351#mfilm.

21. "Aaron Jess Nicks Sr. (1892–1974)," WikiTree, accessed December 26, 2020, www.wikitree.com/wiki/Nicks-160; see also James Pylant, "The Family Tree of Stevie Nicks," *Genealogy Magazine,* 2010, www.genealogymagazine.com/stevie-nicks/#easy-footnote-4-7266.

22. "Aaron Nicks," *Arizona Republic,* August 21, 1974, 19.

23. Dave Stewart, dir., *Stevie Nicks: In Your Dreams,* Tubi video, 1:40:46, 2013, https://tubitv.com/movies/501868/stevie-nicks-in-your-dreams, 31:13.

24. Brian Hiatt, "Stevie Nicks: A Rock Goddess Looks Back," *Rolling Stone,* January 29, 2015, www.rollingstone.com/music/music-news/stevie-nicks-a-rock-goddess-looks-back-179984/.

25. "Family," Stevie Nicks: In Her Own Words, accessed December 26, 2020, www.inherownwords.com/family.htm.

26. Ibid.

27. Davis, *Gold Dust Woman,* 8.

28. These details are from Stephanie Vander Wel, "The Singing Voice in Country Music," in *The Oxford Handbook of Country Music,* ed. Travis D. Stimeling (New York: Oxford University Press, 2017), 157–76, esp. 168.

29. Eric Walden, "Stevie Nicks' 'Gothic Trunk of Lost Songs' Filled with Magic Moments," *Salt Lake Tribune,* February 28, 2017, https://archive.sltrib.com/article.php?id=4986620&itype=CMSID. Nicks is mentioned as graduating from Wasatch in "490 Ninth Graders Leave Wasatch Junior," *Neighbor,* May 22, 1963, 6.

30. Lori Buttars, "True 'Rumours,'" *Salt Lake Tribune,* September 12, 1997, E1.

31. Champ Clark, "20 Things You May Not Know about Stevie Nicks," Purple Clover, May 23, 2018, https://purpleclover.littlethings.com/entertainment/8582-stevie-nicks/item/stevie-nicks-top-hat.

32. My thanks to Yvonne Ng, City of Arcadia librarian, for this information. Jess is listed as the homeowner in the city directory, and Stephanie as a "renter," presumably because she occupied a converted maid's quarters in the house.

33. "League Campus Pals to Host Dinner for New Girls at Arcadia High," *Arcadia Tribune,* March 8, 1964, 11.

34. Gary A. Kovacic, ed., *Visions of Arcadia: A Centennial Anthology* (Arcadia: City of Arcadia/Kovacic, 2003).

35. "Robin," Stevie Nicks: In Her Own Words, accessed January 30, 2022, www.inherownwords.com/robin.htm.

36. For more on the male mediation of female-female relationships, see especially Judith Kegan Gardiner's review article "Women's Friendships, Feminist Friendships," *Feminist Studies* 42, no. 2 (2016): 484–501; and Emily Jeremiah, *Willful Girls: Gender and Agency in Contemporary Anglo-American Fiction* (Rochester: Camden House, 2018), 91–115.

37. Nothing is said in the Arcadia High School newspaper, the *Apache Pow Wow,* about the group in 1963–64 or 1965–66.

38. Untitled concert announcement, *Arcadia Tribune,* March 21, 1965, 3. The quotation comes from the 1965 Arcadia High School yearbook, page 92, summarizing the year's events. My thanks to Yvonne Ng for providing a scan.

39. Davis, *Gold Dust Woman,* 14–15.

40. Gareth Grundy, "Stevie Nicks: Soundtrack of My Life," *Guardian,* June 25, 2011, www.theguardian.com/music/2011/jun/26/stevie-nicks-soundtrack-my-life.

41. "Stephanie Nicks," photo, *XV,* 1966, WorthPoint, www.worthpoint.com/worthopedia/fleetwood-mac-stevie-nicks-high-1897179856.

42. Davis, *Gold Dust Woman,* 9, assigns the guitar to her fifteenth birthday and claims the lessons ended when her teacher left for Seville.

43. "Arcadia High School, 1965," Arcadia Apaches, accessed December 26, 2020, www.arcadiaapaches.com/memories/rock_history/stevie_nicks_story2.htm.

44. Fred Schruers, "Fleetwood Mac: Back on the Chain Gang," *Rolling Stone,* October 30, 1997, www.rollingstone.com/music/music-news/fleetwood-mac-back-on-the-chain-gang-243176/.

45. Morris died in 1974, at age fifty-five, and Greg in 1990, at age forty-five.

46. Rhoda Buckingham Montgomery died on December 29, 1971, in Alameda, California. The inheritance was about $75,000 in today's currency.

47. Timothy White, "Lindsey Buckingham Rocks the Cradle," *Billboard,* May 23, 1992, 3.

48. Schruers, "Fleetwood Mac."

49. As Michael Broyles explains in *Mavericks and Other Traditions in American Music* (New Haven: Yale University Press, 2004), "By the 1760s singing schools had become more social than religious. Attended mostly by young people, the singing school met nearly as often in a tavern as in a church. Drinking was common. And particularly if it met in a tavern, the tavern owner or someone else would frequently get out his fiddle and lead in a round of dancing when the singing lessons finished. In a society that provided few opportunities for young people to interact, particularly with members of the opposite sex, the singing school proved immensely attractive" (17).

50. Davis, *Gold Dust Woman,* 14.

51. Stevie Nicks, "The Stevie Nicks Special," broadcast on NBC Radio network's The Source, 1981; quoted in "Lindsey Buckingham," Stevie Nicks: In Her Own Words, accessed December 26, 2020, www.inherownwords.com/lindsey.htm.

52. Kevin Dettmar, "What Bob Dylan Is Doing in 'Murder Most Foul,'" *New Yorker,* March 28, 2020, www.newyorker.com/culture/culture-desk/what-bob-dylan-is-doing-in-murder-most-foul.

53. Nicks might also have taken classes at Cañada College, also part of San Mateo County Community College District. My thanks to Melissa Rohffs, SMCCCD alumni-relations manager, for this detail.

54. Lindsay Zoladz, "Season of the Witch: The Enduring Power of Stevie Nicks," Ringer, November 21, 2017, www.theringer.com/music/2017/11/21/16683772/stevie-nicks-book-career-fleetwood-mac.

55. "Record Total of 1352 Graduate from College of San Mateo," *San Mateo Times,* June 12, 1968, 40. Stephanie L. Nicks is listed under the name of her "hometown": Atherton.

56. My thanks to Darcel Wood of San Jose State University for confirming the enrollment dates.

57. My thanks to San Jose State University archivist Carli Lowe for providing this information.

58. Davis, *Gold Dust Woman,* 17.

59. "Jody Frankfurt," *Los Angeles Daily News,* October 18, 2006, www.legacy.com/obituaries/ladailynews/obituary.aspx?n=jody-frankfurt&pid=196 10734&fhid=10622.

60. Javier Pacheco, "Fritz," *Penguin Biographies,* March 24, 2019, https://web.archive.org/web/20160408222445/http:/www.fleetwoodmac.net/penguin/fritz.htm.

61. "Thanta Flipths over Frithz," *Catamount,* December 8, 1967, 1.

62. "Javier Pacheco (Fritz), July 5–14, 1999," sec. 2, Penguin Q&A Sessions, April 19, 2016, https://web.archive.org/web/20160920053602/http://www.fleetwoodmac.net/penguin/qa/javierpacheco_qa2.htm.

63. Ibid., sec. 4, https://web.archive.org/web/20160920053602/http:/www.fleetwoodmac.net/penguin/qa/javierpacheco_qa4.htm.

64. Bibi Wein, *The Runaway Generation* (New York: David McKay, 1970).

65. "Javier Pacheco," sec. 1, September 20, 2016, https://web.archive.org/web/20160920053602/http:/www.fleetwoodmac.net/penguin/qa/javierpacheco_qa1.htm.

66. Ibid.

67. Nicole Barker, "How the Race Was Won," Buckingham Nicks Info, April 1, 2015, www.buckinghamnicks.info/interview-davidforest. This fan site regularly reposts articles, interviews, and reviews.

68. Richard Burnett, "David Forest, the Starmaker," Xtra, March 24, 2011, www.dailyxtra.com/david-forest-the-starmaker-34187.

69. Jim Keefe, "Fritz Does It Up Right," Buckingham Nicks Info, April 18, 1969, www.buckinghamnicks.info/s/Fritz-Does-It-Up-Right.pdf.

70. "Javier Pacheco," sec. 1.

71. Fritz used the name Action Studios, which Pacheco also refers to as Action Recording and Action Recorders, in 1967 and 1968. It was a makeshift space in San Mateo, not an actual business.

72. Javier Pacheco, "Empty Shell," sung by Lindsey Buckingham, MP3 audio, Buckingham Nicks Net, accessed December 26, 2020, www.buckinghamnicks.net/bn/MP3/emptyshell.mp3.

73. Pachecure, "Lindsey Buckingham: In My World (Javier Pacheco) Fritz Rabyne Memorial Band," YouTube video, 2:47, March 13, 2015, www.youtube.com/watch?v=IA2ozzJbfFo&list=UUNApkEcBUfIvd_138wRiaSQ&index=75.

74. Mary Avila, "Before Fleetwood Mac: Fritz Band Founder Q&A on Stevie Nicks, Lindsey Buckingham," *Santa Monica Mirror,* March 27, 2015, https://smmirror.com/2015/03/before-fleetwood-mac-fritz-band-founder-qa-on-stevie-nicks-lindsey-buckingham/42963/; Davis, *Gold Dust Woman,* 22–23.

75. Ann Powers, "Stevie Nicks: 'When We Walk into the Room, We Have to Float in Like Goddesses,'" NPR, March 17, 2013, www.npr.org/sections/therecord/2013/03/17/174494011/stevie-nicks-when-we-walk-into-the-room-we-have-to-float-in-like-goddessses.

76. John McDermott with Eddie Kramer, *Hendrix: Setting the Record Straight* (New York: Warner Books, 1992), 196. Nicks is referred to as a "pretty

folk singer" who became "red with embarrassment" when Hendrix dedicated the song to her and her "yellow underwear."

77. Martin Kielty, "Stevie Nicks Recalls the Moment Jimi Hendrix Dedicated a Song to Her," UCR, October 19, 2019, https://ultimateclassicrock.com/stevie-nicks-jimi-hendrix-song/.

78. The singer of Count Five, John Byrne, proudly remembers getting bigger applause than Nicks. "I'll never forget [her] coming up to me after we beat her [and Fritz] and saying, 'You're good, but you're not as good as me.'" Paul Kauppila, "The Sound of the Suburbs: A Case Study of Three Garage Bands in San Jose during the 1960s," *Popular Music and Society* 28, no. 3 (2005): 397.

79. Mitch Gallagher, "Studio Legends: Keith Olsen," Premier Guitar, November 5, 2012, www.premierguitar.com/articles/Studio_Legends_Keith_Olsen. Olsen also used the adjective "terrible."

80. Fritz also played in Santa Monica. "Louisa Joy" was recorded overnight on August 12; presumably "In the Dawn" was recorded around the same time. See "History," Buckingham Nicks Info, accessed December 26, 2020, www.buckinghamnicks.info/history.

81. Pacheco addressed the matter in his Q&A session with Fleetwood Mac fans:

The band broke up because Stevie and Lindsey decided they wanted to move to Los Angeles. If you ask the others, they may spread the blame around. They might say I was a tyrant, a rat. Yes, I know I was starting some fights, but I wanted to confront issues in the band while others preferred to just let things ride. We were in Los Angeles when Linds declared that they (he and Stevie) "didn't care anymore" about what happened. Dave Forest might have encouraged that, the bag men in L.A. who were interested only in them may have encouraged that. At any rate, the bottom fell out. Here we were on the verge of a deal with RCA and there was no more enthusiasm anymore. Gee, well if those people pumped up Lindsey and Stevie, I can see why they would feel emboldened to quit this nearly four-year endeavor of ours. The break-up left Brian, Bob and I without the main vocal part of the band. No more weekly rehearsals, no more weekend jobs. Dave Forest didn't come around to console us or offer us any help. The L.A. managers cleaned out our bank account like vultures. I was fortunate in that I knew other musicians and joined a jazz-rock group named Fat Chants. I know the other guys didn't fare as well, in terms of staying active musically right after the split. We acted like it was "everyone for himself," but it was really a split down the middle, encouraged in part by outside forces. We all weathered the storm the best way we could. What hurt was all that material we had rehearsed which fell by the wayside. What hurt was not knowing all the dynamics and foul play that had really been going on around the sidelines (like Bill Graham's interest in the band, which was kept from us), things that we wouldn't find out until years later. And then when you see flakey bands come and go, making it on the strength of some floozy single that you know Fritz could have played circles around . . . well then you realize how strong a band we really were. That's what time does for y'all. ("Javier Pacheco," sec. 1)

82. Alison Martino, "The Tropicana Hotel's Totally Rocking Heyday," *Los Angeles Magazine*, October 12, 2015, www.lamag.com/citythinkblog/the-tropicana-motels-totally-rocking-heyday/.

83. Gallagher, "Studio Legends."

84. Ibid.

85. Jim Harrington, "Lindsey Buckingham, Christine McVie Find Life outside Fleetwood Mac," *East Bay Times,* October 10, 2017, www.eastbaytimes .com/2017/10/10/lindsey-buckingham-christine-mcvie-find-life-outside-fleetwood-mac/.

86. "Timeline," Stevie Nicks: The Wild Heart Press Kit, 1983, www.fleetwood mac-uk.com/articles/presskits/pk_wildheart.html; and partly quoted in Davis, *Gold Dust Woman,* 30.

87. "Keith Olsen: Obituaries; Producer Who Turned Fleetwood Mac into Superstars Only to Have a Falling Out When He Banned Taking Drugs in the Studio," *Times* (London), March 18, 2020, 51.

88. 60sgaragebands, "Music Machine: 'Talk Talk,'" YouTube video, 2:06, September 12, 2011, www.youtube.com/watch?v=iZExWt-bj-k.

89. Gallagher, "Studio Legends."

90. David N. Howard, *Sonic Alchemy: Visionary Music Producers and Their Maverick Recordings* (Milwaukee: Hal Leonard, 2004), 78, Kindle.

91. Rick Krueger, "Rick's Retroarchy: Emerson, Lake and Palmer in the 1990s," Progarchy, August 4, 2017, https://progarchy.com/2017/08/04/ricks-retroarchy-emerson-lake-and-palmer-in-the-1990s/.

92. "Keith Olsen."

93. The grime and glory of the place is celebrated in Dave Grohl, dir., *The Sound City Studios,* Documentary Tube video, 1:47:16, January 18, 2013, www .documentarytube.com/videos/dave-grohl-the-sound-city-studios. My thanks to Tony Berg and Sandy Skeeter for hosting me there on May 19, 2021.

94. Kent Hartman, *Goodnight, L.A.: The Rise and Fall of Classic Rock; The Untold Story from Inside the Legendary Recording Studios* (New York: Da Capo, 2017), 5–7.

95. "Keith Olsen."

96. Matthew T. Hough, "Elements of Style in Three Demo Recordings by Stevie Nicks," *Music Theory Online* 21, no. 1 (2015), https://mtosmt.org /issues/mto.15.21.1/mto.15.21.1.hough.html.

97. The harmonies on "Races Are Run" have been called "divine," "heavenly," and "timeless" by devotees. The praise extends to the demo of the song, which dates from the end of the run for Fritz. See the comments for Tehwaesle, "Buckingham Nicks: Races Are Run," YouTube video, 4:14, May 23, 2013, www.youtube.com/watch?v=UrMyQ6odUic.

98. Matt Wake, "45 Years Later Buckingham Nicks Album Still Casts Spell," AL, October 25, 2018, www.al.com/life-and-culture/erry-2018/09/da850ca1cf6155 /45-years-later-buckingham-nick.html.

99. Rob Sheffield, "Stevie Nicks on Twirling, Kicking Drugs and a Lifetime with Lindsey," *Rolling Stone,* October 2, 2014, www.rollingstone.com/music /music-news/stevie-nicks-on-twirling-kicking-drugs-and-a-lifetime-with-lindsey-176143/.

100. Steve Pond interview with Nicks in *Us Weekly,* July 9–23, 1990, Nicks Fix, http://rockalittle.com/us1.htm. Davis, *Gold Dust Woman,* 42–43, sensationalizes the story of the cover shoot.

101. See, for example, Joellen A. Meglin, "Behind the Veil of Translucence: An Intertextual Reading of the Ballet Fantastique in France, 1831–1841; Part

One: Ancestors of the Sylphide in the Conte Fantastique," *Dance Chronicle* 27, no. 1 (2004): 67–129.

102. Pat Morgan, "Classic Stars Led Way in Men's-Wear Look," *Gazette*, October 8, 1991, 27.

103. Laura, "Marlene Dietrich on Greta Garbo," YouTube video, 1:10, March 16, 2017, www.youtube.com/watch?v=JTJJ5oRSgYk.

104. Elton John sings these words in the 1973 song "Candle in the Wind."

105. Mike Bise, "Garbo 08-14-1998 Woodstock," YouTube video, 4:10, June 8, 2017, www.youtube.com/watch?v=4lTogVF5Joo.

106. *Queen Christina* refers to the 1933 Garbo film about the Swedish monarch. Kapaudio, "Fleetwood Mac: Backstage *Rumours* Tour," YouTube video, 2:00:42, August 15, 2015, www.youtube.com/watch?v=eImVJZnrL8Y, 56:20.

107. Pond interview, http://rockalittle.com/us1.htm.

108. Robert Hilburn, "Prine, Browne: Bond of Craftsmanship," *Los Angeles Times,* October 20, 1973, B6.

109. The dates and venues of the *Buckingham Nicks* tour are listed on "Tour Archive: 1969–1974," Changing Times: Stevie Nicks, accessed December 26, 2020, stevienicks.bellaillume.com/her-music/tour-archive/1969-1974/.

110. Wake, "45 Years Later."

111. Schruers, "Fleetwood Mac."

112. Wake, "45 Years Later."

113. Rob Trucks, *Tusk* (New York: Bloomsbury, 2011), 43.

114. Information and quotations in this paragraph are from Jefferson Cowie, *Stayin' Alive: The 1970s and the Last Days of the Working Class* (New York: New Press, 2010), 178–79, Kindle.

115. See Carrie Courogen, "On Buckingham Nicks, 44 Years Later," Tumblr, accessed September 17, 2021, https://carriecourogen.tumblr.com/post/164937197480/on-buckingham-nicks-44-years-later.

CHAPTER 2. STEVIE

1. "Stevie: Behind the Music (11.01.1998)," Buckingham Nicks Info, accessed December 26, 2020, www.buckinghamnicks.info/quotes/2016/3/6/stevie-behind-the-music-11011998; Lesley A. Thode, "Keith Olsen," *Penguin Biographies,* May 13, 2019, https://web.archive.org/web/20130921142613/http://www.fleetwoodmac.net/penguin/olsen.htm.

2. Dave Grohl, dir., *The Sound City Studios,* Documentary Tube video, 1:47:16, January 18, 2013, www.documentarytube.com/videos/dave-grohl-the-sound-city-studios, 17:10.

3. "The Stevie Nicks and Lindsey Buckingham Guide to Los Angeles," Curbed LA, March 17, 2015, https://la.curbed.com/maps/stevie-nicks-lindsey-buckingham-los-angeles.

4. She recalled her ire in a 1980 interview:

In 1971 I was cleaning the house of our producer Keith Olsen for $50 a week. I come walking in with my big Hoover vacuum cleaner, my Ajax, my toilet brush, my cleaning shoes on. And Lindsey has managed to have some idiot send him eleven ounces of opiated hash. He and all his friends—Warren Zevon, right?—are in a circle. They smoked hash for a month, and I don't like smoke because of my voice. When you don't smoke there's something that makes you really dislike other people smoking. I'd come in every day and have to step over these bodies. I'm tired; I'm pickin' up their legs and cleaning under them and emptying out ashtrays. A month later all these guys are going, "I don't know why I don't feel very good." I said, "You wanna know why you don't feel very good? I'll tell you why—because you've done nothing else for weeks but lie on the floor and smoke and take my money." (Chris Salewicz, "Fleetwood Mac: Can't Go Home Again," *Trouser Press*, April 1980, 29)

5. Crystal Zevon, *I'll Sleep When I'm Dead: The Dirty Life and Times of Warren Zevon* (New York: Harper, 2008), 78.

6. Stevie Nicks, "The Stevie Nicks Special," broadcast on NBC Radio network's The Source, 1981; quoted in "Landslide," Stevie Nicks: In Her Own Words, accessed December 26, 2020, www.inherownwords.com/landslide.htm.

7. "I guess it was about September 1974, I was home at my Dad and Mom's house in Phoenix, and my father said, 'You know, I think that maybe . . . you really put a lot of time into this [her singing career], maybe you should give this six more months, and if you want to go back to school, we'll pay for it and uh, basically you can do whatever you want and we'll pay for it'—I have wonderful parents—and I went, 'Cool, I can do that.'" Ibid.

8. The song features two verses and a chorus, a guitar-solo bridge that introduces a suspended pitch above the tonic (Ebsus2), the chorus again, and a return of the first verse in variation before the outro. The verses unfold with slight distress, the bass line descending in Eb major from the tonic down to D, C, and D again in the first inversion of the dominant. Alternately, it can be heard as the first inversion of the tonic in Bb. The vocal lines are more conducive to the key of Bb, but the guitar holds on to Eb. In the chorus, however, the two parts agree on Bb, just as getting older agrees with getting bolder. The transition is marked by the appearance of A natural. The chordal outline in the chorus is I (Bb major) V6/5 vi (G minor) for the first line, then IV I6/3 ii7 V6/5, followed by I (Bb major) V6/5 vi7 (G minor 7), and, for the fourth line, IV I6/3 ii7 I6/3.

9. Mitchell Morris, *The Persistence of Sentiment: Display and Feeling in Popular Music of the 1970s* (Berkeley: University of California Press, 2010), 10.

10. Bill DeMain, "Fleetwood Mac: The Story behind 'Rhiannon,'" Louder, September 4, 2015, www.loudersound.com/features/the-story-behind-the-song-rhiannon-by-fleetwood-mac. For her claim that she bought the novel in an airport, see Stephen Bishop, *Songs in the Rough* (New York: St. Martin's, 1996), quoted in "Rhiannon," Stevie Nicks: In Her Own Words, accessed December 26, 2020, www.inherownwords.com/rhiannon2.htm.

11. Mary Bartlet Leader, *Triad: A Novel of the Supernatural* (New York: Coward, McCann and Geoghegan, 1973), 185.

12. I am immensely indebted for the following information to Helen Fulton, an expert on English medieval culture and literature at the University of Bristol.

13. The eleven tales have been translated by Sioned Davies, *The Mabinogion* (Oxford: Oxford University Press, 2018). In her introduction Davies explains the difference between *Mabinogion* as the collective name for all eleven tales and *Mabinogi*, referring only to the four branches (ix–x). A detailed study of the figure of Rhiannon as an ancient deity was undertaken by William John Gruffydd,

Rhiannon: An Inquiry into the Origins of the First and Third Branches of the Mabinogi (Cardiff: University of Wales Press, 1953).

14. DeMain, "Fleetwood Mac."

15. Evangeline Walton, *The Song of Rhiannon* (New York: Ballantine Books, 1972).

16. The silver nitrate tincture she was given as a child for treatment of bronchitis caused her skin to darken as she aged.

17. DeMain, "Fleetwood Mac."

18. As Amy Kaufman explains, "Because of the scope of the story, it was later decided that the movie should be a television miniseries, and earlier this year [2020] Nicks says she finally signed a deal with a studio to make it. She has 10 songs that she's never released, still on cassette tapes in a suitcase, set aside specifically for the project." "The Moonlit Confessions of Stevie Nicks," *Los Angeles Times*, September 30, 2020, www.latimes.com/entertainment-arts/music /story/2020–09–30/stevie-nicks-fleetwood-mac-solo-concert-film.

19. "Rhiannon by Fleetwood Mac," Songfacts, 2020, www.songfacts.com /facts/fleetwood-mac/rhiannon.

20. Stephen Davis, *Gold Dust Woman: The Biography of Stevie Nicks* (New York: St. Martin's Griffin, 2017), 59.

21. Mitch Gallagher, "Studio Legends: Keith Olsen," Premier Guitar, November 5, 2012, www.premierguitar.com/articles/Studio_Legends_Keith_Olsen. "The Green Manalishi (with the Two Prong Crown)" was the last song Peter Green wrote for Fleetwood Mac.

22. Zevon, *I'll Sleep*, 76.

23. Davis, *Gold Dust Woman*, 63.

24. David Wild, "Landslides, Goose Bumps, and Other First Initial Feelings," Essential Fleetwood Mac, January 19, 2018, https://fleetwoodmac.rocks /category/fleetwood-mac-1975/.

25. Ann Powers, "Stevie Nicks: 'When We Walk into the Room, We Have to Float in Like Goddesses,'" NPR, March 17, 2013, www.npr.org/sections/therecord /2013/03/17/174494011/stevie-nicks-when-we-walk-into-the-room-we-have-to-float-in-like-goddessses.

26. Matt Wake, "45 Years Later Buckingham Nicks Album Still Casts Spell," AL, October 25, 2018, www.al.com/life-and-culture/erry-2018/09/da850ca1cf6155 /45-years-later-buckingham-nick.html; Lindsey Buckingham Gems, "Buckingham Nicks: Lola (My Love); Alabama Live 1974," YouTube video, 4:36, February 22, 2009, www.youtube.com/watch?v=C9EYjYfbWko&feature=emb_logo.

27. Wake, "45 Years Later"; Opalstardream, "Buckingham Nicks: Rhiannon 1974," YouTube video, 3:31, May 18, 2014, www.youtube.com/watch?v= nDHpcnHGYkM&feature=youtu.be.

28. "Buckingham Nicks and Murphy Perform," *Chanticleer*, February 3, 1975, 8.

29. Jan Susina, "Buckingham Nicks: Goodbye to the First Eight Years," *Birmingham after Dark* 1, no. 4 (1975): 1.

30. Powers, "Stevie Nicks."

31. Rob Sheffield, "Stevie Nicks on Tom Petty, Drag Queens, 'Game of Thrones' and Missing Prince," *Rolling Stone*, February 28, 2019, www

.rollingstone.com/music/music-features/stevie-nicks-interview-tom-petty-drag-queens-game-of-thrones-prince-801112/. John Byrne Cooke's *On the Road with Janis Joplin* (2014) is one of Nicks's favorite books.

32. Mark Paytress, *The Rolling Stones: Off the Record* (New York: Omnibus, 2009), 181.

33. Such is how Pense is described in a 1969(?) press release from the band's manager Bill Graham: "Cold Blood," Museum of the City of San Francisco, www.sfmuseum.org/hist5/cblood.html.

34. Ken Garcia, "Funk Band Singer Keeps It Positive," SFGate, February 3, 2012, www.sfgate.com/news/article/Funk-Band-Singer-Keeps-It-Positive-Local-3002548.php.

35. "Rock Hall Nominee Stevie Nicks Empowers through Her Songs," Cleveland.com, November 14, 2018, www.cleveland.com/metro/2018/11/stevie_nicks.html.

36. Kent Hartman, *Goodnight, L.A.: The Rise and Fall of Classic Rock; The Untold Story from Inside the Legendary Recording Studios* (New York: Da Capo, 2017), 17.

37. Amanda Petrusich, "The Resurgent Appeal of Stevie Nicks," *New Yorker*, November 21, 2016, www.newyorker.com/magazine/2016/11/28/the-resurgent-appeal-of-stevie-nicks.

38. Gallagher, "Studio Legends."

39. Stephen Thomas Erlewine, "Fleetwood Mac, *Fleetwood Mac*," Pitchfork, January 27, 2018, https://pitchfork.com/reviews/albums/fleetwood-mac-fleetwood-mac/.

40. Nigel Williamson, "Fleetwood Mac: 'Everybody Was Pretty Weirded Out'; The Story of *Rumours*," *Uncut*, January 29, 2013, www.uncut.co.uk/features/fleetwood-mac-everybody-was-pretty-weirded-out-the-story-of-rumours-26395/.

41. Fleetwood Mac advertisement, *Circus*, July 11, 1975, Pinterest, https://in.pinterest.com/pin/467107792602293289/.

42. Nick Collier, "Mick, Mac: Indisputably Fleetwood," *Vancouver Sun*, August 8, 1975, 31. Collier writes about the clone: the band "had been around under the leadership of Mick for years, but, during a period of inactivity, an ex-manager of the group decided to help himself to the name. He put together a number of musicians and attempted an American tour. The result was uproar. Fans went wild when they discovered that they had been bilked, and legal battles went on in all quarters." The biggest lawsuit, the real band contra the fake band, lasted through 1975.

43. Elliot Cahn, "Fleetwood Mac: Instinct for Survival," *Courier News*, September 8, 1975, 2.

44. Dave Wagner, "Two Newcomers Are Lucky Fleetwood Mac Additions," *Capital Times*, September 18, 1975, 42.

45. Rob Sheffield, "17 Reasons This 'Rhiannon' Clip Is the Coolest Thing in the Universe," *Rolling Stone*, May 26, 2020, www.rollingstone.com/music/music-news/17-reasons-this-rhiannon-clip-is-the-coolest-thing-in-the-universe-61514/. Consider the source. Judith A. Peraino blasts *Rolling Stone* as "notoriously sexist"

in "Reviewed Works: *Madonna: Bawdy and Soul* by Karlene Faith; *Scars of Sweet Paradise: The Life and Times of Janis Joplin* by Alice Echols; *Frock Rock: Women Performing Popular Music* by Mavis Bayton; *Girls Will Be Boys: Women Report on Rock* by Liz Evan," *Journal of the American Musicological Society* 54, no. 3 (2001): 693. She also endorses a collection of articles, not favorable to Nicks, by female music critics. Ann Powers describes Nicks's voice as "a Southern bleat with one of the most insane vibratos known to pop" ("Bohemian Rhapsodies," in *Trouble Girls: The Rolling Stone Book of Women in Rock,* ed. Barbara O'Dair [New York: Random House, 1997], 328).

46. ARN Radio, "No, We Had No Idea That Stevie Nicks Did Ballet Either," 96FM Perth, December 17, 2018, https://www.96fm.com.au/entertainment /stevie-nicks-hall-fame-fleetwood-mac-ballet-rare-photos/.

47. Pete Bishop, "Jefferson Starship Launches 2 New Stars," *Pittsburgh Press*, October 16, 1975, 15.

48. Wake, "45 Years Later," reproduces the contract.

49. Davis, *Gold Dust Woman,* 65.

50. Ken Caillat with Steven Stiefel, *Making Rumours: The Inside Story of the Classic Fleetwood Mac Album* (Hoboken, NJ: Wiley, 2012), 44.

51. Nicks moved that year, 1976, to 6684 Bonair Place in Hollywood Heights.

52. Walter Egan, telephone interview with the author, December 26, 2020. *Fundamental Roll* means "basic rock"; it's also a play on "fun" and "mental."

53. Chip Schell, "Walter Egan: Staying Young at Heart through Music," 9 *Years of Rock* (blog), March 23, 2015, https://eriecountyfieldhouse.wordpress .com/2015/03/23/walter-egan-staying-young-at-heart-through-music/.

54. Walter Egan, email communication with the author, December 28, 2020.

55. Two Beverly Hills High School cheerleaders appear with him on the cover of *Fundamental Roll*; the photographs of Nicks in the BHHS costume were taken, for fun, at the house of his manager, Greg Lewerke. Egan explains that commercial photographer Moshe Brakha "had just done a portfolio for *Rolling Stone* called 'High School' and that's how the two 14-year-olds, Tammy and Selma, got on the cover [of *Fundamental Roll*]. Although Stevie wasn't considered for the role, the car on the cover, a Mercedes 280SL, did belong to her" (email communication, December 27, 2020).

56. Egan, telephone interview, December 26, 2020.

57. "Through the years," he recalled, "the sustaining remnant of that infatuation continues to be a centerpiece in my life and career." Egan, email communication, December 28, 2020. Elsewhere he is misquoted as saying, "I'm not sure if Stevie is as 'mystical' as she seems, but she certainly is mystifying." The remark implies a disgruntled inamorato, which he's never been. "Walter Egan, October 13–26, 1999," sec. 2, Penguin Q&A Sessions, March 18, 2012, https://web .archive.org/web/20120318165236/http://www.fleetwoodmac.net/penguin/qa /walteregan_qa2.htm.

58. Jessica Hopper, "Fleetwood Mac: *Rumours*," Pitchfork, February 8, 2013, https://pitchfork.com/reviews/albums/17499-rumours/.

59. Mel Evans, "Mick Fleetwood Confirms Infamous '7-Mile Cocaine Line' Tale as Band Plays London," Metro, June 17, 2019; https://metro.co.uk/2019/06/17/mick-fleetwood-confirms-infamous-7-mile-cocaine-line-tale-band-plays-london-9975764/.

60. Edward Huntington Williams, "Negro Cocaine 'Fiends' Are a New Southern Menace; Murder and Insanity Increasing among Lower Class Blacks Because They Have Taken to 'Sniffing' Since Deprived of Whisky by Prohibition," New York Times, February 8, 1914, sec. M, p. 12.

61. Robert Sabbag, Snowblind: A Brief Career in the Cocaine Trade (Edinburgh: Canongate, 1998), 62–70, esp. 70. I also draw from J. Bryan Page, "Coca, Cocaine, and Consumption: Trends and Antitrends," in Drug Trafficking, Organized Crime, and Violence in the Americas Today, ed. Bruce M. Bagley and Jonathan D. Rosen (Gainesville: University Press of Florida, 2017), 27–42.

62. Page, "Coca, Cocaine, and Consumption," in Bagley and Rosen, Drug Trafficking, 35.

63. Aldo Civico, The Para-State: An Ethnography of Colombia's Death Squads (Oakland: University of California Press, 2015), 129; William Overend, "Adventures in the Drug Trade: How 4,000 Colombians Took the 'Champagne Drug' to the Inner City and Turned L.A. into a Cocaine Capital," Los Angeles Times, May 7, 1989, www.latimes.com/archives/la-xpm-1989-05-07-tm-3315-story.html.

64. Mick Wall, "Stevie Nicks: All of Us Were Drug Addicts, but I Was the Worst," Louder, March 20, 2020, www.loudersound.com/features/stevie-nicks-all-of-us-were-drug-addicts-but-i-was-the-worst.

65. Will Kaufman, American Culture in the 1970s (Edinburgh: Edinburgh University Press, 2009), 121. Singer-songwriter Jude Johnstone, a friend of Eagles founder Don Henley, affirms the song's decadence. "Every time I heard 'Hotel California'" on the radio in 1976, "I wanted to tell [Henley], 'Dude, write something real.'" Jude Johnstone, telephone interview with the author, December 1, 2020.

66. Barbara Lebrun and Catherine Strong, "The Great Gig in the Sky: Exploring Popular Music and Death," in Death and the Rock Star, ed. Catherine Strong and Barbara Lebrun (Farnham: Ashgate, 2015), 5–6.

67. Wall, "Stevie Nicks."

68. "500 Greatest Albums of All Time (2003)," Rolling Stone, May 31, 2012, www.rollingstone.com/music/music-lists/500-greatest-albums-of-all-time-156826/.

69. Rob Sheffield, "Why Fleetwood Mac's 'Rumours' Hits Home Right Now," Rolling Stone, February 3, 2017, www.rollingstone.com/music/music-features/why-fleetwood-macs-rumours-hits-home-right-now-121403/.

70. The personal drama behind the album is related in a multitude of contemporary and retrospective sources. Donald Bracket glosses it in Fleetwood Mac: 40 Years of Creative Chaos (Westport, CT: Praeger, 2007), 117–20.

71. Carol Ann Harris, Storms: My Life with Lindsey Buckingham and Fleetwood Mac (Chicago: Chicago Review Press, 2007), x.

72. Jordan Runtagh, "Fleetwood Mac's 'Rumours': 10 Things You Didn't Know," *Rolling Stone*, February 3, 2017, www.rollingstone.com/feature /fleetwood-macs-rumours-10-things-you-didnt-know-121876/.

73. Williamson, "Fleetwood Mac."

74. "The outcome of the various separations and emotional upheavals in the band that caused so many rumors are in the songs," Christine McVie recounted. "We weren't aware of it at the time, but when we listened to the songs together, we realized they were telling little stories. We were looking for a good name for the album that would encompass all that *and* the feeling the band had 'given up' (the most active rumor flying about). And, I believe it was John, one day, who just said we should call it *Rumours*. He didn't *state* that, but rumors kept cropping up." Quoted in Salley Rayl, "The Truth Will Tell," *Circus*, March 31, 1977, 32.

75. Caillat, *Making Rumours*, 115.

76. Ibid., 122.

77. Jancee Dunn, "A Trip to Stevieland," *Harper's Bazaar*, November 1997, Nicks Fix, http://rockalittle.com/bazaar1.htm.

78. Runtagh, "Fleetwood Mac's 'Rumours.'"

79. Tim McPhate, "Fleetwood Mac 'Rumours' Producer on Making an Iconic Album," Recording Academy, May 15, 2017, www.grammy.com/grammys /news/fleetwood-mac-rumours-producer-making-iconic-album.

80. "Ken Caillat: Listening to Rumours," Recording Academy, March 27, 2015, www.grammy.com/grammys/videos/ken-caillat-listening-rumours.

81. Stevie Nicks, *Crawdaddy*, November 1976, quoted in "Gold Dust Woman," Stevie Nicks: In Her Own Words, accessed December 23, 2020, www.inherownwords.com/golddust.htm.

82. Chameleon, "Dreaming of the Gold Dust Woman: Stevie Nicks as a Feminine Icon," uga.digication.com, accessed September 3, 2021, https://uga .digication.com/chameleon2/Dreaming_of_the_Gold_Dust_Woman_Stevie_ Nicks_as_a_.

83. Mary Celeste Kearney, *Gender and Rock* (Oxford: Oxford University Press, 2017), 222, Kindle.

84. Tim Sommer, "How Fleetwood Mac's 'Rumours' Became One of the Best Albums Ever," *Observer*, February 3, 2017, https://observer.com/2017/02 /fleetwood-mac-rumours-album-anniversary-review/.

85. Caillat, *Making Rumours*, 131–32.

86. Ibid., 29.

87. Gino Sorcinelli, "Stevie Nicks Wrote 'Dreams' in 10 Minutes over a Drum Loop," Medium, December 14, 2018, https://medium.com/micro-chop /stevie-nicks-wrote-dreams-in-10-minutes-over-a-fender-rhodes-drum-pattern-703ec19c6426.

88. Matthew T. Hough, "Elements of Style in Three Demo Recordings by Stevie Nicks," *Music Theory Online* 21, no. 1 (2015), https://mtosmt.org /issues/mto.15.21.1/mto.15.21.1.hough.html.

89. Caillat, *Making Rumours*, 146–48; Ken Caillat, email communication with the author, September 13, 2020.

90. John Rockwell, "Fleetwood Mac Finds the Combination," *New York Times,* June 26, 1977, 55.

91. Caillat, *Making Rumours,* 308–12. Judy Wong, a longtime manager of the band employed by Mick Fleetwood, proposed the accepted final order of songs.

92. Mikiandemma, "Go Your Own Way (Early Take)," YouTube video, 4:10, May 1, 2013, www.youtube.com/watch?v=LWm8HnsVdTE, 00:53.

93. TikTok brought the song back into vogue in 2020, thanks to Idaho laborer Nathan Apodaca, aka Doggface, lip-synching the second phrase with perfect cool while riding his longboard and drinking cranberry juice. The clip spawned numerous imitations, and even Mick Fleetwood and Stevie Nicks herself responded to it on TikTok. Lisa Respers France, "Stevie Nicks Wins the 'Dreams' Tik Tok Challenge," CNN Entertainment, October 14, 2020, www.cnn .com/2020/10/14/entertainment/stevie-nicks-tik-tok-dreams-trnd/index.html.

94. Richard Buskin, "Fleetwood Mac 'Go Your Own Way,'" Sound on Sound, August 2007, www.soundonsound.com/people/fleetwood-mac-go-your-own-way.

95. Caillat, *Making Rumours,* 130, 312, 131.

96. Andrew Underberger, "Every Song on Fleetwood Mac's 'Rumours' Ranked," *Billboard,* February 4, 2017, www.billboard.com/articles/columns /rock/7678007/fleetwood-mac-rumours-stevie-nicks-ranked-anniversary.

97. Caillat, *Making Rumours,* 119.

98. Ibid., 122–23, 250–51.

99. Brittany Spanos, "'Silver Springs': Inside Fleetwood Mac's Great Lost Breakup Anthem," *Rolling Stone,* August 17, 2017, www.rollingstone.com/feature /silver-springs-inside-fleetwood-macs-great-lost-breakup-anthem-201303/.

100. Davis, *Gold Dust Woman,* 106–7.

101. Fleetwood Mac, "Silver Springs (Official Music Video)," YouTube video, 4:47, September 27, 2018, www.youtube.com/watch?v=eDwi-8n054s, 2:03.

102. Spanos, "'Silver Springs.'"

103. Chris13345, "Fleetwood Mac (Stevie Nicks): Silver Springs Live 2004," YouTube video, 5:28, October 21, 2007, www.youtube.com/watch?v=_ DNZWFqTU38, 2:38.

104. Caillat, *Making Rumours,* 252.

105. Brad Pack, "40 Years of Excess: The Making of Fleetwood Mac's Rumours," Vintage King, November 15, 2017, https://vintageking.com/blog /2017/11/fleetwood-mac-rumours/.

106. Caillat, *Making Rumours,* 130.

107. Ibid., 204.

108. Davis, *Gold Dust Woman,* 96.

109. Harris, *Storms,* 362.

110. Buskin, "Fleetwood Mac."

111. As Caillat explains:

Tape machines will never run at the same speed twice. So this guy put a pair of head-phones on, and put the hi-hat and snare from the original tape in his left ear, and the hi-hat and snare from the "safety master" in his right ear. We kept marking the tape and hitting "start" on both machines at the same time until it was close enough at the beginning. Then he would use the VSO [varispeed oscillator] on one of the machines, carefully adjusting the speed slightly and basically playing it like an instrument. He did that all night long and saved our butts. (Quoted in Buskin, "Fleetwood Mac")

112. Caillat, email communication, August 31, 2020.

113. Caillat, *Making Rumours,* 213.

114. Runtagh, "Fleetwood Mac's 'Rumours.'"

115. Caillat, *Making Rumours,* 38.

116. Ibid., 103.

117. According to John Swenson, "The formula is vintage Byrds: Christine sings the verse simply, with sparse instrumental background, and the chorus comes on like an angelic choir—high harmonies soaring behind her with 12-string electric guitar counterpoint ringing against the vocals." "Rumours," *Rolling Stone,* April 21, 1977, www.rollingstone.com/music/music-album-reviews/rumours-189491/.

118. Jones, a self-described "bodyguard to the stars," worked for Fleetwood Mac in the late seventies. Hoping to promote his freestyle martial arts methods (and a technique called "environmental defense awareness") to women, he asked Nicks to participate in a photo shoot for his book *Hands Off! A Unique New System of Self-Defense against Assault for the Women of Today* (Sydney: Bay Books, 1983). Half in jest, and after snubbing her publicist's efforts to contract a quarter-million-dollar photo shoot for *Playboy,* Nicks agreed to demonstrate her back-kicks on the terrace of her home in Beverly Hills. She did so "artistically," Jones commented in *Australasian Martial Arts* magazine, wearing a diaphanous dress, high-heeled suede boots, and "hair done to resemble the mane of a lion." "Fleetwood mac, 1980s," bobjones.com, accessed February 4, 2022, www.bobjones.com.au/1980s?limitstart=0.

119. Rockwell, "Fleetwood Mac Finds the Combination."

120. John Rockwell, "Fleetwood Mac in Nassau," *New York Times,* March 26, 1977, 10.

121. Rockwell, "Fleetwood Mac Finds the Combination."

122. Peter Herbst, "Fleetwood Mac Not Hurt by Stevie Nicks," *Rolling Stone,* August 25, 1977, www.rollingstone.com/music/music-news/fleetwood-mac-not-hurt-by-stevie-nicks-199673/.

123. Quoted in Bracket, *Fleetwood Mac,* 119.

124. The number ninety-eight includes two shows that were canceled to allow Nicks to treat her voice. Kapaudio, "Fleetwood Mac: Backstage Rumors Tour," YouTube video, 2:00:42, August 15, 2015, www.youtube.com/watch?v=eImVJZnrL8Y, 45:10.

125. Sam Anderson, "Letter of Recommendation: Fleetwood Mac's 'Tusk,'" *New York Times Magazine,* February 18, 2015, www.nytimes.com/2015/02/22/magazine/letter-of-recommendation-fleetwood-macs-tusk.html.

126. Ryan Reed, "Fleetwood Mac's 'Tusk': 10 Things You Didn't Know," *Rolling Stone,* October 11, 2019, www.rollingstone.com/music/music-features/fleetwood-mac-tusk-things-you-didnt-know-896796/.

127. Rob Trucks, *Tusk* (New York: Bloomsbury, 2011), 74.

128. Jeff Giles, "When Fleetwood Mac Made a Masterpiece That Flopped," UCR, October 12, 2015, https://ultimateclassicrock.com/fleetwood-mac-tusk/.

129. I visited the studio on August 28, 2020.

130. S. Anderson, "Letter of Recommendation."

131. Ibid.

132. Jon Pareles, "Peter Green, Fleetwood Mac's Founder, Is Dead at 73," *New York Times,* July 26, 2020, www.nytimes.com/2020/07/26/arts/music/peter-green-dead.html. Green occasionally turned up for the *Tusk* recording sessions, semi-interested in the proceedings, and contributed to Christine McVie's song "Brown Eyes." Hints of his slow-hand masterpiece "Albatross," from 1969, can be heard on the alternate version of this song in particular, which has different lyrics and an altogether different, black magic feel.

133. Giles, "When Fleetwood Mac."

134. Stephen Holden, "Tusk," *Rolling Stone,* December 13, 1979, www.rollingstone.com/music/music-album-reviews/tusk-2-191586/.

135. Amanda Petrusich, "Fleetwood Mac: *Tusk*," Pitchfork, July 17, 2016, https://pitchfork.com/reviews/albums/21924-tusk/.

136. Ken Caillat and Hernan Rojas, *Get Tusked: The Inside Story of Fleetwood Mac's Most Anticipated Album* (Guilford, CT: Backbeat Books, 2019).

137. The cover is slower and more homophonic than the original. Some "live" applause is heard at the end, but "Farmer's Daughter" is definitely a studio product, as I confirmed with producer Ken Caillat (email communication, October 25, 2020). The band started singing the song impromptu, and Caillat grabbed it on tape. The clapping is a postproduction add-on.

138. Haunted Song, "Fleetwood Mac: Angel; Stevie Nicks," YouTube video, 9:49, April 21, 2006, www.youtube.com/watch?v=3A6ICAlcREw&app=desktop, 3:33. Nicks said, "I honestly don't know what the hell this song ["Sisters of the Moon"] is about. It wasn't a love song, it wasn't written about a man. . . . It was just about a feeling I might have had over a couple of days, going inward in my gnarly trollness. Makes no sense. Perfect for this record." Christopher R. Weingarten, David Browne, Jon Dolan, Corinne Cummings, Keith Harris, Rob Sheffield, "Fleetwood Mac's 50 Greatest Songs," *Rolling Stone,* September 22, 2019, www.rollingstone.com/music/music-lists/fleetwood-macs-50-greatest-songs-192324/sisters-of-the-moon-115300/.

139. Tlcarpenter3, "Fleetwood Mac Tusk Documentary 1981," YouTube video, 40:22, February 29, 2020, www.youtube.com/watch?v=Y1uYfJfTFog&t=1254s, 24:38.

140. "Tusk (1979)," Buckingham Nicks Info, accessed December 26, 2020, www.buckinghamnicks.info/words-tusk#angel. Aaron is the first name of Nicks's grandfather and the middle name of her brother.

141. Ibid.

142. Caillat and Rojas, *Get Tusked,* 37–39.

143. Caillat's "preferred hours were noon to midnight, but many times we went later and that meant we didn't start the next session until another 12 hours had passed. If this cycle started, we usually had to stop early one night so we could get back to the preferred schedule" (email communication, August 1, 2020).

144. Caillat, email communication, August 2, 2020.

145. The "fat box" was the "best sounding" direct box of the time, according to Caillat, whose friend Larry Comara invented it (email communication, August 1, 2020).

146. Caillat, email communication, August 1, 2020.

147. Nicks dated Souther before the song was written. In 1991, Don Henley of the Eagles disgracefully went public with details about his affair with Nicks and an aborted pregnancy. Nicks long avoided reacting to his remarks about a traumatic episode in her life, and then only pithily, noting that she had Sara in mind as the child's name. Roy Tannenbaum, "Stevie Nicks Admits Past Pregnancy with Don Henley and More about Her Wild History," *Billboard*, September 26, 2014, www.billboard.com/articles/news/6266329/stevie-nicks-interview-on-don-henley-fleetwood-mac-24-karat-gold-album.

148. Sophie Gee, *Scandal of the Season* (New York: Scribner, 2007).

149. Recor was born Sara Lynn Jones in 1953 and married James Recor in 1972. He managed Loggins and Messina, for whom Fleetwood Mac opened in 1975, just before the release of *Rumours*, and he introduced his wife to Nicks, a "funny little chick singer who would twirl round and round." See comments by Recor, writing as "Sara from Pasadena," at "Sara, by Fleetwood Mac," Songfacts, www.songfacts.com/facts/fleetwood-mac/sara, accessed November 30, 2020; and Leah Greenblatt, "Stevie Nicks on Her Favorite Songs: A Music Mix Exclusive," *Entertainment Weekly*, March 31, 2009, https://ew.com/article/2009/03/31/stevie-nicks-in/.

150. Recor left her husband for Fleetwood. The two were married in Malibu in 1988 and later divorced.

151. Sara, epigraph, "Innocence," *366 Days of Sara*, Tumblr, accessed November 30, 2020, https://366daysofsara.tumblr.com/post/22391938192/innocence-a-few-years-ago-sara-recor-apparently.

152. Greenblatt, "Stevie Nicks."

153. Fleetwood Mac, "Fleetwood Mac: Sara (Official Music Video)," YouTube video, 4:09, September 27, 2018, www.youtube.com/watch?v=9bWGyoK5VFo.

154. Stevie Nicks, "Sara," Stevie Nicks: In Her Own Words, accessed December 26, 2020, www.inherownwords.com/sara.htm.

155. Tonally, the opening alternates between F and G major, the Bb and B contrast giving the ear a hint of F Lydian. The vocal line settles into C, with F as antipode, defined by a traditional rock progression of I vi IV V.

156. Mary Oliver, *Owls and Other Fantasies: Poems and Essays* (Boston: Beacon, 2003), 56; Brendan Kennelly, "A Glimpse of Starlings," 1968, in *New Oxford English 3*, ed. Anne Powling, John O'Connor, and Geoff Barton (Oxford: Oxford University Press, 1997), 44.

157. Roy Tannenbaum, "Stevie Nicks Admits Past Pregnancy with Don Henley and More about Her Wild History," *Billboard*, September 26, 2014, www.billboard.com/articles/news/6266329/stevie-nicks-interview-on-don-henley-fleetwood-mac-24-karat-gold-album.

158. Davis, *Gold Dust Woman*, 133.

159. Caillat, email communication, August 3, 2020.

160. Madison Bloom, "Storms," *Stevie Nicks: Her Art and Life in 33 Songs,* Pitchfork, April 6, 2020, https://pitchfork.com/features/lists-and-guides/stevie-nicks-in-33-songs/.

161. I quote from the description of the $1,095 necklace on Kent's website, www.margikent.com.

162. Kristen Sollée, email communication with the author, August 8, 2020.

163. Perry Anderson, "A Day at the Races," *London Review of Books,* February 7, 1991, www.lrb.co.uk/the-paper/v13/no3/letters.

164. Holden, "Tusk."

165. Davis, *Gold Dust Woman,* 133. *Indovina zingara* is Italian for "gypsy fortune teller," making "Gypsy queen" superfluous, also questionable.

166. Andy Leo, "Sisters of the Moon: Tusk Tour '79/'80; Fleetwood Mac Stevie Nicks," YouTube video, 7:49, October 5, 2013, www.youtube.com /watch?v=Sujmxj9TmDY.

167. Caillat and Rojas, *Get Tusked,* 66–67.

168. Egan, email communication, December 29, 2020.

169. S. Anderson, "Letter of Recommendation."

170. Kandrews, "Stevie Nicks: In Your Dreams" Q&A, March 31, 2013, Landmark Cinema, YouTube video, 22:21, April 1, 2013, www.youtube.com /watch?v=G5EJEM70bA4, 14:50.

171. Popular music in general makes special use of the added sixth as a so-called functional consonance (whether placed against the tonic or as the ninth of a dominant chord).

172. Caillat and Rojas, *Get Tusked,* 109.

173. Reed, "Fleetwood Mac's 'Tusk.'" Caillat considers the connection "very possible" (email communication, August 8, 2020).

174. Buckingham relies on occasional chromatic shifts between chords, but the movement is nowhere near as amorphous as on "Our Prayer," the opening track on Wilson's *Smile.* "That's All for Everyone" relies on a simple progression of F7, D, F7, D, A, E, and A, inexplicably likened to "blues and folk" by Hernan Rojas (Caillat and Rojas, *Get Tusked,* 90).

175. Marcel Cobussen, "Music, Deconstruction, and Ethics" (PhD diss., Erasmus University, 2001), https://deconstruction-in-music.com/outwork/music-deconstruction-and-ethics/110.

176. Paul McGrath, "Inside the Sleeve: Tusk Fleetwood Mac Warner Bros. 2 HS 3350," *Globe and Mail,* October 20, 1979, F4.

177. Minna Bromberg and Gary Alan Fine, "Resurrecting the Red: Pete Seeger and the Purification of Difficult Reputations," *Social Forces* 80, no. 4 (2002): 1140–41.

178. Robert Cantwell, *When We Were Good: The Folk Revival* (Cambridge, MA: Harvard University Press, 1996); Benjamin Filene, *Romancing the Folk: Public Memory and American Roots Music* (Chapel Hill: University of North Carolina, 2000).

179. "John Stewart: Interviewed by Rich Wiseman," *Omaha Rainbow* 22 (Autumn 1979), http://bitemyfoot.org.uk/omaha/or23/or23_19.html. The title of the magazine comes from a song on Stewart's album *California Bloodlines.*

180. "John Stewart: Interviewed by Spencer Leigh," *Omaha Rainbow* 35 (Autumn 1984), http://bitemyfoot.org.uk/omaha/or35/or35_03.html.

181. Peter O'Brien, "Obsessions with John Stewart: Interview with Tom De Lisle; Part 2," *Omaha Rainbow* 20 (Spring 1979), http://bitemyfoot.org.uk /omaha/or20/or20_02.html.

182. "John Stewart: Interviewed by Peter O'Brien," *Omaha Rainbow* 22 (Autumn 1979), http://bitemyfoot.org.uk/omaha/or22/or22_12.html.

183. Egan, telephone interview, December 26, 2020.

184. "John Stewart: Interviewed by Peter O'Brien."

185. "John Stewart: Interviewed by Rich Wiseman."

186. "John Stewart: Interviewed by Peter O'Brien."

187. R. Ferrera, "John Stewart: 'Gold' (1980) (Solid Gold '79)," YouTube video, 4:24, June 5, 2016, www.youtube.com/watch?v=Wii-IYfkLto.

188. "John Stewart: Interviewed by Rich Wiseman."

189. Mick Fleetwood and Anthony Bozza, *Play On: Now, Then and Fleetwood Mac* (New York: Little Brown and Company, 2014), 243.

190. Associated Press, "Rock Music, Vodka Tend toward Détente," *San Mateo Times,* July 15, 1977, 43.

191. Mickey Shapiro, telephone interview with the author, June 20, 2021. Shapiro landed Nicks and Buckingham the deal for their album, after which, through Bob Welch, he started working for Fleetwood Mac, lasting with the band until 1987.

192. Wall, "Stevie Nicks."

193. Cameron Crowe, "They Call Him Big Shorty," *Rolling Stone,* June 15, 1978, www.theuncool.com/journalism/rs267-irving-azoff/.

194. Danny Goldberg, email communication with the author, September 28, 2020.

195. Danny Goldberg, *Bumping Into Geniuses: My Life inside the Rock and Roll Business* (New York: Gotham Books, 2008), 134.

196. Danny Goldberg, email communication, September 28, 2020.

197. Ibid. The cute song can be heard at WildHeart1983, "Stevie Nicks: Goldfish and the Ladybug," YouTube video, 4:40, December 8, 2010, www .youtube.com/watch?v=22iHU1Ppk-0.

198. Goldberg, *Bumping Into Geniuses,* 144. Goldberg recalls hostilities between him and "Fleetwood Mac's lawyer, Mickey Shapiro, who explained that our contract with Stevie was blocking Fleetwood Mac from getting an increased royalty rate. He tried to strong-arm me, saying, 'You can't expect [Warner record executive] Mo Ostin to create a new label around an artsy-crafty album that Stevie is going to make on her own.' Fleetwood called Stevie and yelled at her, but she started crying and told him to talk to me. This time the politeness was gone and he was screaming at me at the top of his lungs, 'Danny, you didn't tell me she had signed a piece of paper.' As calmly as I could I reminded him that I had told him we had made a deal with her. 'But you didn't tell me she had *signed*'" (ibid., 142). Shapiro, for the record, claims no recollection of this event (email communication with the author, January 17, 2022).

CHAPTER 3. BELLA DONNA

1. Robert Christgau, *Rock Albums of the Seventies: A Critical Guide* (New York: Da Capo Press, 1981), 120; also quoted in Jefferson Cowie, *Stayin' Alive: The 1970s and the Last Days of the Working Class* (New York: New Press, 2010), 186, Kindle.

2. Danny Goldberg, email communication with the author, November 15, 2020.

3. Iovine eventually joined Dr. Dre in creating Beats Electronics, which Apple acquired from them for a colossal sum.

4. Leah Fessler, "Apple's Top Music Exec, the Man behind Eminem and U2, Wants You to Stop Believing Your Bullshit," *Quartz*, June 16, 2017, https://qz.com/1004860/jimmy-iovine-the-man-behind-apple-music-and-eminem-wants-you-to-stop-believing-your-bullshit/.

5. Goldberg, email communication, November 15, 2020.

6. Azoff and Kaufman worked together at Front Line Management. After Azoff became president of MCA Records, Kaufman bought Front Line and renamed it H.K. Management. The two joined forces again in 2005 as part of a larger corporate entity. Kaufman represented Nicks until his death in 2017. She is currently managed by a former Kaufman employee, Sheryl Louis of CSM Management.

7. Annie Zaleski, "Leather and Lace: How Stevie Nicks Created a New Musical Language," *Guardian*, April 17, 2019, www.theguardian.com/music/2019/apr/17/leather-and-lace-stevie-nicks-bella-donna-fleetwood-mac-solo-debut.

8. Justin Graci, "Tom Petty: A Good Man to Ride the River With," Medium, October 3, 2017, https://medium.com/@jgraci07/tom-petty-a-good-man-to-ride-the-river-with-397c27c65fdd.

9. Rachel Chang, "How Stevie Nicks' Obsession with Tom Petty Turned into a 40-Year Friendship," Biography, September 8, 2020, www.biography.com/news/tom-petty-stevie-nicks-friendship; Annie Zaleski, "Tom Petty and Stevie Nicks: A History of Their Friendship and Musical Collaborations," UCR, October 4, 2017, https://ultimateclassicrock.com/tom-petty-stevie-nicks-friendship/.

10. Stephen Davis, *Gold Dust Woman: The Biography of Stevie Nicks* (New York: St. Martin's Griffin, 2017), 155.

11. Bill DeMain, "The Story behind Stevie Nicks and Tom Petty's Stop Draggin' My Heart Around," Louder, August 19, 2020, www.loudersound.com/features/the-story-behind-stevie-nicks-and-tom-pettys-stop-draggin-my-heart-around.

12. Laura Snapes, "Fleetwood Mac: *Mirage*," Pitchfork, September 26, 2016, https://pitchfork.com/reviews/albums/22134-mirage/.

13. Gerrick D. Kennedy, "Essay: A Former Sound City Engineer Details How Tom Petty and Stevie Nicks' 'Duet' Came to Be," *Los Angeles Times*, October 4, 2017, www.latimes.com/entertainment/music/la-et-ms-tom-petty-engineer-20171004-story.html.

14. Ann Powers, "Stevie Nicks: 'When We Walk into the Room, We Have to Float in Like Goddesses,'" NPR, March 17, 2013, www.npr.org/sections/therecord

/2013/03/17/174494011/stevie-nicks-when-we-walk-into-the-room-we-have-to-float-in-like-goddessses.

15. Dwight Garner, "Living with Music: A Playlist by Camille Paglia," *New York Times*, July 16, 2008, https://artsbeat.blogs.nytimes.com/2008/07/16/living-with-music-a-playlist-by-camille-paglia/.

16. Timothy White, "Stevie Nicks' Magic Act," *Rolling Stone*, September 3, 1981, www.rollingstone.com/music/music-news/stevie-nicks-magic-act-242776/. The "Sara" lawsuit ended when Nicks proved that she had demoed the song before the litigant, Carol Hinton, submitted a song of her own with similar lyrics to Warner Brothers. Nicks later made a point of never reading poems sent to her by fans. Undeterred, fans instead began to send her personal stories, or entire collections of them, like Linda Iorio's 1989 *A Book of Legends*. My thanks to Roland Hui for this information.

17. Nicks's uncle ran a construction business in suburban Phoenix in the sixties and seventies. He was her father's oldest brother.

18. Jeva Lange, "Stevie Nicks Finally Learned What a Dove Sounds Like," *Week*, April 7, 2020, https://theweek.com/speedreads/907406/stevie-nicks-finally-learned-what-dove-sounds-like.

19. White, "Stevie Nicks' Magic Act."

20. David Simons, "Waddy Wachtel," *Musician*, no. 245 (April 1999): 14; Nathan Hesselink, "Rhythmic Play, Compositional Intent and Communication in Rock Music," *Popular Music* 33, no. 1 (January 2–14): 74–75.

21. The single is 4:10.

22. DeMain, "Story"; Vaughn Schmutz and Alison Faupel, "Gender and Cultural Consecration in Popular Music," *Social Forces* 89, no. 2 (December 2010): 694.

23. Danny Goldberg, *Bumping Into Geniuses: My Life inside the Rock and Roll Business* (New York: Gotham Books, 2008), 150.

24. White, "Stevie Nicks' Magic Act."

25. Michael H. Little, "Graded on a Curve: Stevie Nicks, *Bella Donna*," Vinyl District, June 20, 2018, www.thevinyldistrict.com/storefront/2018/06/graded-on-a-curve-stevie-nicks-bella-donna/.

26. Stevie Nicks, interview by WLIR New York, 1981, quoted in "After the Glitter Fades," accessed December 2, 2020, Buckingham Nicks Info, www.buckinghamnicks.info/words-belladonna#aftertheglitterfades.

27. Marcel Pariseau (Dolly Parton's publicist), email communication with the author, December 15, 2020.

28. Jessi Colter with David Ritz, *An Outlaw and a Lady: A Memoir of Music, Life with Waylon, and the Faith That Brought Me Home* (Nashville: Nelson Books, 2017), 165.

29. Christopher Myers, "Leather and Lace (Acoustic Demo), Stevie Nicks, Don Henley (Duet)," YouTube video, 3:44, December 9, 2013, www.youtube.com/watch?v=g90Tuzs1hMA.

30. Jeremy Doe, "Stevie Nicks: Leather and Lace (Live Studio Demo Takes)," YouTube video, 10:26, March 1, 2011, www.youtube.com/watch?v=BSJtDjfA2 4E&list=PLIPQoDoePzmXw86zu3d-SATqooTn1JTkB&index=151.

31. "Don Henley," Walden Woods Project, accessed December 3, 2020, www.walden.org/biographies/don-henley/.

32. The concert was held on April 16, 1998.

33. "Sharon Celani," Nicks Fix Singers' Pages, accessed July 5, 2020, http://rockalittle.com/SingerPage/singers/SharonCelani.html.

34. "Renaissance Five Will Perform Two Nights in Glendale," *Valley News,* December 1, 1972, 35.

35. "Blue Max Staff Remember Magical Elton John Concert in Lahaina," *Lahaina News,* February 7, 2011, www.lahainanews.com/news/local-news /2011/02/17/blue-max-staff-remember-magical-elton-john-concert-in-lahaina/.

36. She lent a hand on "Here Comes the Moon," Harrison's parody of "Here Comes the Sun." Graeme Thomson, *George Harrison: Behind the Locked Door* (London: Omnibus Press, 2017), 379–80, Kindle.

37. Stevie Nicks, Jim Ladd interview, 1983, quoted in "Lori and Sharon," Stevie Nicks: In Her Own Words, accessed January 8, 2021, www.inherown words.com/girls.htm.

38. "Lori Nicks," Nicks Fix Singers' Pages, accessed December 31, 2020, http://rockalittle.com/SingerPage/singers/LoriNicks.html.

39. See *Lori Perry Nicks* (blog), LiveJournal, accessed December 16, 2020, mamatojessi.livejournal.com.

40. Peter Cashwell, "Records: Bella Donna (Modern)," *Daily Tar Heel,* September 10, 1981, 20.

41. Davis, *Gold Dust Woman,* 172; Goldberg, email communication, November 22, 2020.

42. I borrow from Sheila Whiteley, *Women and Popular Music: Sexuality, Identity and Subjectivity* (Abingdon: Routledge, 2013), 120, Kindle, on the essentializing of women as "passive, receptive, nurturant, emotional."

43. Mick Fleetwood and Anthony Bozza, *Play On: Now, Then and Fleetwood Mac* (New York: Little Brown and Company, 2014), 249.

44. Hugo Wilcken, *David Bowie's Low* (New York: Continuum, 2011), 37–41; Hugh Schofield, "The Return of the Honky Chateau," BBC News, December 27, 2015, www.bbc.com/news/magazine-35152716.

45. Davis, *Gold Dust Woman,* 177.

46. White, "Stevie Nicks' Magic Act."

47. David Wild, "'The Beautiful Blur' That Is Mirage," Stevie Nicks Info, September 24, 2016, https://stevienicks.info/2016/09/the-beautiful-blur-that-is-mirage/.

48. Snapes, "Fleetwood Mac."

49. Ibid.

50. Compare MayEmeraldsCT, "Buckingham Nicks: Designs of Love," YouTube video, 3:15, May 9, 2008, www.youtube.com/watch?v=ZhVNbisc3Sg; Stephanie Riccelli, "Designs of Love: Buckingham-Nicks," YouTube video, 3:21, September 5, 2008, www.youtube.com/watch?v=YxxBHYfp5v4; and Fleetwood Mac, "That's Alright (2016 Remaster)," YouTube video, 3:10, September 29, 2016, www.youtube.com/watch?v=voop7zHKi_k.

51. I am immensely indebted to Elizabeth DiSavino, an expert on American folk music at Berea College, for information in this paragraph.

52. The phrase belongs to Timofey Agarin and his review article of books on the Roma in Europe, "Angels with Dirty Faces? European Identity, Politics of Representation and Recognition of Romani Interests," *Ethnicities* 14, no. 6 (December 2014): 849–60.

53. Elizabeth Hollerith, "Behind the Song: Fleetwood Mac, 'Gypsy,'" *American Songwriter,* February 2020, https://americansongwriter.com/behind-the-song-fleetwood-mac-gypsy-stevie-nicks/.

54. She responds to being abandoned by "the handsome man" by doing "what any true diva would do," Michael Montlack continues. "She will create her *own* image, painstakingly and independently, before lifting the considerably large painting to lug it across the dunes . . . to an unclear destination that you *just know* will be as surreal and beautiful as this one she is leaving." "Stevie Nicks," in *My Diva: 65 Gay Men on the Women Who Inspire Them,* ed. Michael Montlack (Madison: Terrace Books, 2000), loc. 2378, Kindle.

55. He described the shoot as "a fucking nightmare, a horrendous day in the desert. John McVie was drunk and tried to punch me. Stevie Nicks didn't want to walk on the sand with her platforms. Christine McVie was fed up with all of them. Mick thought she was being a bitch; he wouldn't talk to her. They were a fractious bunch." Craig Marks and Rob Tannenbaum, *I Want My MTV: The Uncensored Story of the Music Video Revolution* (New York: Dutton, 2011), 99.

56. This moment in the video might be likened to Madonna's "submitting," "controlling" stare into the camera in the admittedly more provocative video for the 1990 song "Justify My Love." Whiteley, *Women and Popular Music,* 149.

57. Songery, "Stevie Nicks: Wild Heart; Live Demo: 1981," YouTube video, 4:11, July 28, 2011, www.youtube.com/watch?v=S2rOh6dCwao; Andy Cush, "Wild Heart," *Stevie Nicks: Her Art and Life in 33 Songs,* Pitchfork, April 6, 2020, https://pitchfork.com/features/lists-and-guides/stevie-nicks-in-33-songs/.

58. Stevie Nicks, liner notes, *Timespace,* 1991, quoted in "Beauty and the Beast," Stevie Nicks: In Her Own Words, accessed December 8, 2020, www.inherownwords.com/beauty_beast.htm.

59. Jean Cocteau, *The Art of Cinema,* trans. Robin Buss (New York: Boyars, 1994), 34.

60. "Notes," Stevie Nicks: The Wild Heart Press Kit, quoted in "Beauty and the Beast," Stevie Nicks: In Her Own Words, accessed September 8, 2020, www.inherownwords.com/beauty_beast.htm.

61. Dennis Grunes, "Beauty and the Beast (Jean Cocteau, 1946)," WordPress, March 22, 2007, https://grunes.wordpress.com/2007/03/22/beauty-and-the-beast-jean-cocteau-1946/.

62. Cocteau, *Art of Cinema,* 141.

63. Ibid.

64. To assert the influence of "pulsing Juju music then being introduced from Nigeria" in those stomps, as Stephen Davis does, is at best nonsensical (*Gold Dust Woman,* 186).

65. Doug Jessop, "Stevie Nicks Telling Story behind the Song Stand Back," YouTube video, 5:10, February 26, 2017, www.youtube.com/watch?v=8mikCI3sdlY.

66. Martin Kielty, "Stevie Nicks Recalls Prince's Surprise Appearance on 'Stand Back,'" UCR, November 18, 2018, https://ultimateclassicrock.com /stevie-nicks-stand-back-prince/; Duane Tubahl, *Prince and the Purple Rain Era Studio Sessions: 1983 and 1984* (Lanham: Rowman & Littlefield, 2018), 28–29. Prince's producer David Z confirms that "Stand Back" was done at A&M Studios, not Sunset, and that this happened after Nicks asked Prince to write a song for her using the same chords as "Little Red Corvette" (David Z via Paul Camerata, email communication with the author, February 3, 2022).

67. "Fairy Sightings," *Fairyist,* Fairy Investigation Society, accessed December 31, 2020, www.fairyist.com/fairy-sightings/.

68. Jack Hamilton, "Prince Was Our Bard of One-Night Stands, and 'Little Red Corvette' Was His Masterpiece," *Slate,* April 21, 2016, https://slate.com /culture/2016/04/little-red-corvette-by-prince-the-greatest-song-ever-about-one-night-stands.html.

69. Marks and Tannenbaum, *I Want My MTV,* 110.

70. Goldberg, *Bumping Into Geniuses,* 152–53.

71. Flamingcrystal, "Stevie Nicks: Stand Back Live 1983 with 'Elaine,'" YouTube video, 7:44, February 19, 2008, www.youtube.com/watch?v=cR8Zshu W8vE.

72. Tubahl, *Prince,* 40–41.

73. Emma McKee, "Stevie Nicks and Prince Had a Falling Out over a Scene from 'Purple Rain,'" *Showbiz Cheatsheet,* December 27, 2021, https://www .cheatsheet.com/entertainment/stevie-nicks-prince-falling-scene-purple-rain.html/.

74. Rick Nowels, email communication with the author, January 27, 2022. Munday's model seems to have been Prince's "She's Always in My Hair," which Prince worked on by himself at Sunset Studios. "All Over You" involves Prince-style distorted guitar and pitch-shifting but it is less showy than typical of him. Munday and Stewart do the singing. I am grateful to Dana Baitz for her analysis of the bootleg (email communication with the author, January 23, 2022).

75. Angie Martoccio, "'RS Interview: Special Edition' with Joe Walsh," *Rolling Stone,* December 3, 2020, www.rollingstone.com/music/music-news /joe-walsh-rs-interview-special-edition-1098225/.

76. "Stevie Nicks Thought She Still Had a Chance with Lindsey Buckingham 30 Years after Their Split (Exclusive)," *Closer Weekly,* October 25, 2017, www .closerweekly.com/posts/stevie-nicks-heartbreaks-regrets-145065/. Davis, *Gold Dust Woman,* provides additional details about the tour that brought Nicks and Walsh together and their subsequent relationship (192–97).

77. Stevie Nicks, *MTV Storytellers,* 1998, quoted in "Has Anyone Ever Written Anything for You," Stevie Nicks: In Her Own Words, accessed September 18, 2020, www.inherownwords.com/hasanyone.htm.

78. Marie Johnson, "Joe Walsh Stevie Nicks 2012," interview with Howard Stern," YouTube video, 10:24, March 14, 2018, www.youtube.com/watch?v= KN7ppI-vxrM.

79. My thanks to Roland Hui for this information.

80. Henri David operates a boutique called Halloween on Philadelphia's Pine Street. I quote a customer.

81. Stephen Holden, "Folk-Rock: Stevie Nicks," *New York Times,* June 30, 1983, sec. C, p. 18, and "Stevie Nicks and Rickie Lee Jones Carry the Torch," *New York Times,* June 12, 1983, sec. B, p. 25.

82. Ken Tucker, "Eccentric Nicks Gives Delicate Concert," *Philadelphia Inquirer,* June 28, 1983, in Stevie Nicks Info, https://stevienicks.info/1983/06/review-eccentric-nicks-gives-delicate-concert/.

83. "Stevie Nicks Thought."

84. Johnson, "Joe Walsh."

85. Kristin Casey, *Rock Monster: My Life with Joe Walsh* (Los Angeles: Rare Bird, 2018), 60.

86. Kristin Casey, email communication with the author, December 18, 2020.

87. Stevie Nicks, "Has Anyone Ever Written Anything for You," *Live at Red Rocks,* 1986, quoted in "Has Anyone Ever Written Anything for You," Stevie Nicks: In Her Own Words, accessed January 8, 2021, www.inherownwords.com/hasanyone.htm.

88. George Piggford, "'Who's That Girl?' Annie Lennox, Woolf's 'Orlando,' and Female Camp Androgyny," *Mosaic: An Interdisciplinary Critical Journal* 30, no. 3 (September 1997): 40; also Gillian Rodger, "Drag, Camp and Gender Subversion in the Music Videos of Annie Lennox," *Popular Music* 23, no. 1 (January 2004): 19–20.

89. Rodger, "Drag," 22; email exchange with the author, August 30, 2021.

90. Dave Stewart, *Sweet Dreams Are Made of This: A Life in Music* (New York: New American Library, 2016), 123–25, Kindle.

91. Ibid., 125.

92. Sunset's owner, Paul Camarata, confirmed billing Tom Petty for studio time in 1984. These billed hours don't specifically mention the song, however (email communication with the author, October 26, 2020).

93. Nick Thomas, *Tom Petty: A Rock and Roll Life* (Green, OH: Guardian Express Media, 2018), 101.

94. Michael Washburn, *Southern Accents* (New York: Bloomsbury, 2019), loc. 722, Kindle.

95. T. M. L. Price, Reginald Lightwood, and Selwyn H. Goodacre, "Did the Mad Hatter Have Mercury Poisoning?," *British Medical Journal* 288, no. 6413 (1984): 324–25.

96. Stewart, *Sweet Dreams,* 125.

97. Hallie Cantor and Rebecca Caplan, "Every Prime-Time Special about a Female Celebrity from the Two Thousands," *New Yorker,* February 19, 2021, https://www.newyorker.com/humor/daily-shouts/every-prime-time-special-about-a-female-celebrity-from-the-two-thousands.

98. "Rock Star Stevie Nicks, in Her Own Words," CBS, October 25, 2020, www.cbsnews.com/news/stevie-nicks-fleetwood-mac-interview/.

99. Jeff Giles, "Why Stevie Nicks Found Completing 'Rock a Little' So Difficult," UCR, November 18, 2015, https://ultimateclassicrock.com/stevie-nicks-rock-a-little/.

100. Michael Hampe, *The Crafty Art of Opera,* trans. Chris Walton (Woodbridge, NJ: Boydell and Brewer, 2016), 99.

101. Giles, "Why Stevie Nicks."

102. Christopher Kelly, "A Nightclub Reflecting '80s Dallas Is Revisited," *New York Times,* April 12, 2014, www.nytimes.com/2014/04/13/us/the-starck-club-documents-rise-and-fall-of-dallas-nightclub.html.

103. "Hearts of Stone," *Backstreets Magazine* 28 (Spring 1989): 5.

104. William Defebaugh, "Dreams Unwind: Lana Del Rey in Conversation with Stevie Nicks," *V Magazine,* June 27, 2017, https://vmagazine.com/article/lana-del-rey-stevie-nicks-cover-story/.

105. Rick Nowels, telephone interview with the author, December 14, 2020.

106. Ibid.

107. Ibid.

108. Ibid.

109. Andy Newmark, email communications with the author, July 10 and November 16, 2020.

110. 1MAG3, "Stevie Nicks: Has Anyone Written Anything for You," YouTube video, 6:22, November 21, 2012, www.youtube.com/watch?v=-Uyn-f4ofTCk.

111. Davis, *Gold Dust Woman,* 201.

112. Information in the preceding paragraphs from Chas Sandford, telephone interview with the author, May 21, 2021.

113. Mark Coleman, "Album Review: Rock a Little," Stevie Nicks Info, January 30, 1986, https://stevienicks.info/1986/01/album-review-rock-a-little-2/.

114. Matthew T. Hough, "Elements of Style in Three Demo Recordings by Stevie Nicks," *Music Theory Online* 21, no. 1 (2015), https://mtosmt.org/issues/mto.15.21.1/mto.15.21.1.hough.html.

115. Stevie Nicks, "Off the Record," interview by Mary Turner, 1986, quoted in "Rock a Little," Stevie Nicks: In Her Own Words, accessed October 17, 2020, www.inherownwords.com/rockalit.htm. *Julia* is based on a chapter from Hellman's *Pentimento: A Book of Portraits* (1973) and stars Vanessa Redgrave, whom Robin resembled.

116. Nowels, telephone interview, December 14, 2020.

117. SisterNightroad, "*Rock a Little* Sessions (1981–1986)," *Ledge Rumours* (blog), November 19, 2015, www.ledge.fleetwoodmac.net/showthread.php?t=55700, originally posted by Ivory Keys, http://stevienicksivorykeys.blogspot.com/2015/11/rock-little-sessions-1981-1986.html (site discontinued).

118. Paul Johnson, "The Night Gallery Intro," YouTube video, 1:53, May 8, 2012, www.youtube.com/watch?v=8rjIm4mcw3w; Mike Bise, "Stevie Nicks: Night Gallery (Rock a Little Demo 1985)," YouTube video, 2:28, January 19, 2019, www.youtube.com/watch?v=97SkKuoocoo.

119. Alfred Soto, "The Cars: *Shake It Up,*" Pitchfork, March 31, 2018, https://pitchfork.com/reviews/albums/the-cars-shake-it-up-heartbeat-city/.

120. Coleman, "Album Review."

121. Davis, *Gold Dust Woman,* 208.

122. Marty Callner, dir., *Stevie Nicks: Live at Red Rocks* (New York: Lightyear Entertainment, CD-ROM, 1987; DVD, 2007). The choreography is credited to Brad Jeffries and Stevie Nicks, and Mick Fleetwood and Peter Frampton are listed as special guests.

123. Ibid.

124. Jeffrey Christ, "Music Box: Stevie Nicks Rocks a Little," My New Boyfriend, September 27, 2010, https://mynewboyfriend.com/2010/09/27/women-in-rock-stevie-nicks/.

CHAPTER 4. SARA

1. "Stevie Nicks: Betty Ford Saved My Life," CNN, July 11, 2011, https://marquee.blogs.cnn.com/2011/07/11/stevie-nicks-betty-ford-saved-my-life/.

2. Steve Hochman, "Stevie Nicks: 'The Other Side of the Mirror,'" Los Angeles Times, May 28, 1989, www.latimes.com/archives/la-xpm-1989-05-28-ca-1371-story.html.

3. Brad Nelson, "Fleetwood Mac: Tango in the Night," Pitchfork, March 11, 2017, https://pitchfork.com/reviews/albums/22976-tango-in-the-night-deluxe-edition/.

4. Nikki Darling, "Revisiting LA Music History: Guns N Roses' 'Appetite for Destruction' Studio," LA Weekly, May 14, 2009, www.laweekly.com/revisiting-la-music-history-guns-n-roses-appetite-for-destruction-studio/.

5. The "bachelor pad" he bought in the late eighties for $2 million no longer exists; Buckingham claims he had it "bulldozed," along with the rest of his past, after he married his current wife, interior designer Kristin Messner, and relocated to Brentwood. Julia St. Pierre, "Lindsey Buckingham," Los Angeles Magazine, May 23, 2013, www.lamag.com/lastory/lindsey-buckingham/.

6. Nelson, "Fleetwood Mac."

7. Ann Powers, Good Booty: Love and Sex, Black and White, Body and Soul in American Music (New York: HarperCollins, 2017), loc. 3744, Kindle.

8. Annie Zaleski, "'He Could Be Brash; He Could Be Harsh. He Was Very Motivated': The Real Story behind Fleetwood Mac's 'Tango in the Night,'" Salon, April 2, 2017, www.salon.com/2017/04/02/he-could-be-brash-he-could-be-harsh-he-was-very-motivated-the-real-story-behind-fleetwood-macs-tango-in-the-night/.

9. Sandy Stewart (via Anita Kruse), email communication with the author, November 10, 2020.

10. My thanks to John Pendergast, an expert on Joan of Arc, for the following information.

11. "Your Money or Your Wife!," Q 72 (September 1992): 47.

12. Mick Fleetwood with Stephen Davis, Fleetwood: My Life and Adventures in Fleetwood Mac (New York: Avon, 1990), 276.

13. "Your Money or Your Wife!"

14. Fleetwood, Fleetwood, 276; Jarmila Mildorf, Storying Domestic Violence: Constructions and Stereotypes of Abuse in the Discourse of General Practitioners (Lincoln: University of Nebraska Press, 2007), 104.

15. Dee Ann Rexroat, "Stand Back: Stevie Nicks a Chum after Her Bath," Cedar Rapids Gazette, November 20, 1987, 32.

16. Stevie Nicks, liner notes, Timespace, 1991, quoted in "Rooms on Fire," Stevie Nicks: In Her Own Words, accessed November 3, 2020, www.inherownwords.com/rooms.htm.

17. Adam Sweeting, "Rupert Hine Obituary," *Guardian,* June 11, 2020, www.theguardian.com/music/2020/jun/11/rupert-hine-obituary.

18. Paul Tingen, "Rupert Hine: Les Negresses Vertes," Sound on Sound, February 1995, https://web.archive.org/web/20150924104054/http:/www.soundonsound.com/sos/1995_articles/feb95/ruperthine.html.

19. Jon Pareles, "Rupert Hine, Synth-Pop Music Producer, Dies at 72," *New York Times,* June 15, 2020, www.nytimes.com/2020/06/15/arts/music/rupert-hine-synth-pop-music-producer-dies-at-72.html; "Things We'd Like to Hold," Kilometre Paris, November 16, 2019, www.kilometre.paris/post/things-we-d-like-to-hold.

20. Tingen, "Rupert Hine."

21. Stephen Davis, *Gold Dust Woman: The Biography of Stevie Nicks* (New York: St. Martin's Griffin, 2017), 229. Karen Johnston started working for Nicks in 1996, taking over from her sister Kelly, who had held the position for ten years. Before that, Rebecca Alvarez, Debbie Alsbury, and Robin Snyder assisted Nicks.

22. Paul Tingen, "Secrets of the Mix Engineers: Chris Lord-Alge," Sound on Sound, May 2007, www.soundonsound.com/techniques/secrets-mix-engineers-chris-lord-alge#para3.

23. Davis, *Gold Dust Woman,* 234.

24. Stevie Nicks, "Rooms on Fire (Official Music Video)," YouTube video, 4:26, May 28, 2019, www.youtube.com/watch?v=KUhBc35T-e4.

25. Jude Johnstone, telephone interview with the author, December 1, 2020.

26. Rob Sheffield, "How Stevie Nicks' Lost Masterpiece 'Ooh My Love' Became a Cult Fan Favorite," *Rolling Stone,* May 30, 2019, www.rollingstone.com/music/music-features/steve-nicks-ooh-my-love-rob-sheffield-841005/.

27. Michael Wood, "Quashed Quotatoes," *London Review of Books* 32, no. 24 (2010), www.lrb.co.uk/the-paper/v32/n24/michael-wood/quashed-quotatoes.

28. Lewis Carroll, *Through the Looking-Glass: And What Alice Found There* (Philadelphia: Altemus, 1897), 70, 186.

29. Lewis Carroll, *Alice's Adventures in Wonderland* (Stockholm: Wisehouse Classics, 2016), 113.

30. Alice specifically says, "'There ought to be a book written about me, that there ought! And when I grow up, I'll write one—but I'm grown up now,' she added in a sorrowful tone." Carroll, *Alice's Adventures,* 33.

31. "Mirror Writing," *Guardian,* December 19, 2003, reprint from December 27, 1871, www.theguardian.com/books/2003/dec/20/fromthearchives.lewiscarroll.

32. Jeff Giles, "When Stevie Nicks Released the Introspective 'The Other Side of the Mirror,'" UCR, May 11, 2014, https://ultimateclassicrock.com/stevie-nicks-other-side-of-mirror/.

33. Rob Harvilla, "Oh My God, They Resurrected Kenny: On Kenny G's Show-Stealing Kanye Guest Spot," Ringer, October 29, 2019, www.theringer.com/music/2019/10/29/20937160/kenny-g-kanye-west-use-this-gospel-clipse-jesus-is-king.

34. Giles, "When Stevie Nicks."

35. Kate Bradshaw, "Remembering Mr. Clements," *Almanac*, February 1, 2018, www.almanacnews.com/news/2018/02/01/remembering-mr-clements.

36. This same period brought the pitiful case of a Nicks impersonator named Cheryl Cusella (aka Britney Marx) to an inglorious head. After singing Nicks's songs for a few years and boasting on *The Sally Jessy Raphael Show* about their supposed mystical connection, Cusella was convicted of fraud in a concert promotion scheme; in 1990, she self-published a book called *Sweet Poison: A Heartfelt Diary*, describing her rise and fall and time in jail along with the "lies and deception of friends and lovers" that turned "instant glamor" into "a life of pure hell." Cusella was subsequently charged, repeatedly, for bilking investors in an animal rescue organization. Recently, she claims to have attended Bible school and, "forever changed," has tried preaching and singing gospel for profit. My thanks to Roland Hui for bringing her story to my attention and providing images from her book.

37. Sheffield, "Stevie Nicks' Lost Masterpiece."

38. Jack Whatley, "Stevie Nicks Once Made Her PA Take Her Prescription Drugs and It Saved Her Life," *Far Out Magazine*, August 23, 2020, https://faroutmagazine.co.uk/stevie-nicks-fleetwood-mac-saved-her-life-pa-prescription-drugs/.

39. Shelly Bobbins, "Goodbye to Daniel Freeman Marina Hospital," *Acupuncture Today* 3, no. 8 (August 2002), https://www.acupuncturetoday.com/mpacms/at/article.php?id=28020.

40. Olivia Carter Mather, "Taking It Easy in the Sunbelt: The Eagles and Country Rock's Regionalism," *American Music* 31, no. 1 (Spring 2013): 38–41.

41. Cobius, "Stevie Nicks: Street Angel Interview, 05/13/1994," interview with Robin Ross DJ, YouTube video, 41:58, September 29, 2020, www.youtube.com/watch?v=XHxUXppoY8Y, 6:20.

42. WildHeart1983, "Stevie Nicks off the Record with Mary Turner Street Angel 1994 Pt 2," YouTube video, 8:06, August 24, 2010, www.youtube.com/watch?v=c4-LIXT7iKs, 7:47.

43. Glyn Johns, *Sound Man* (New York: Penguin, 2014), 237; Larry Rohter, "What He Saw from the Control Room," *New York Times*, December 19, 2014, www.nytimes.com/2014/12/21/arts/music/glyn-johns-on-recording-rock-greats.html.

44. WildHeart1983, "Nicks off the Record," 5:24.

45. Ethan Johns, email communication with the author, December 5, 2020.

46. Allen Sides, email communication with the author, November 30, 2020.

47. Stevie Nicks, WMMR, July 31, 1994, quoted in "Street Angel (1994)," Buckingham Nicks Info, accessed September 18, 2020, www.buckinghamnicks.info/words-streetangel.

48. Marceline Thompson and Carol L. Thompson, "Changing Gender Images in Rock and Roll: An Analysis of the Songs and Image of Stevie Nicks," *American Communication Journal*, accessed January 3, 2021, http://ac-journal.org/journal/vol2/Iss1/essays/thompson.htm.

49. Gary Graff, "Stevie Nicks, Now a Solo Act," *Detroit Free Press*, August 19, 1994, quoted in Stevie Nicks Info, https://stevienicks.info/1994/08/thinking-about-tomorrow-stevie-nicks-now-a-solo-act-sees-her-music-as-her-life/.

50. Roger Catlin, "Nicks' Hip Return," *Hartford Courant,* July 21, 1994, https://stevienicks.info/1994/07/album-review-nicks-hip-return/; "Stevie Nicks: Street Angel," *New Jersey Record,* July 10, 1994, https://stevienicks.info/1994/07/album-review-stevie-nicks-street-angel-2/; Tracy Collins, "Stevie Nicks: Street Angel," *Pittsburgh Post-Gazette,* July 8, 1994, https://stevienicks.info/1994/07/album-review-stevie-nicks-street-angel-3/, all quoted in Stevie Nicks Info.

51. "Stevie Nicks: Street Angel; Original Version," Steve Hoffmann Music Forums, May 17, 2020, https://forums.stevehoffman.tv/threads/stevie-nicks-street-angel-original-version.959902/.

52. Davis, *Gold Dust Woman,* 247.

53. Frank Bruni, "After the Show with Stevie Nicks: Going Her Own Way, but Slowly This Time," *New York Times,* November 25, 1997, www.nytimes.com/1997/11/25/arts/after-the-show-with-stevie-nicks-going-her-own-way-but-slowly-this-time.html. Nicks also repaid a favor to saxophonist Dave Koz, who had played on "Unconditional Love" on *Street Angel.* Producer Thom Panunzio reached out to her to provide vocals for "Let Me Count the Ways," a 1996 song written for Koz's *Off the Beaten Path* disc, which embeds his smooth saxophone sound in contrasting textures. Nicks was scheduled to arrive at Jackson Browne's studio in Santa Monica at eight thirty on the night of March 26. She intentionally turned up late, toward midnight, with a giant cake to celebrate Koz's March 27 birthday (Dave Koz, telephone interview with the author, January 13, 2021).

54. Stevie Nicks, digibook liner notes, "Enchanted," track 1 on *Enchanted,* EMI 7243 5 21085 2 7 3 × CD, 1998.

55. Neil Lerner, "Copland's Music of Wide Open Spaces: Surveying the Pastoral Trope in Hollywood," *Musical Quarterly* 85, no. 3 (2001): 477–515.

56. Davis, *Gold Dust Woman,* 257.

57. Aidin Vaziri, "'Trouble' and Paradise," *San Francisco Chronicle,* May 13, 2001, quoted in Nicks Fix, http://rockalittle.com/article_sf_chronicle_may13_2001.htm.

58. Ibid.

59. Maggie Gruber, "Paradise Found: An Interview with Stevie Nicks," *Borders,* June 2001, quoted in Nicks Fix, http://rockalittle.com/interview_borders_june2001.htm.

60. Bobbie Jean Sawyer, "'Landslide': The Story behind the 1975 Fleetwood Mac Classic and the Chicks' Country Cover," Wide Open Country, July 8, 2020, www.wideopencountry.com/landslide-dixie-chicks/.

61. Stevie Nicks, *Q,* May 2001, quoted in "Bombay Sapphires," Stevie Nicks: In Her Own Words, accessed August 1, 2020, www.inherownwords.com/bombay.htm.

62. Stevie Nicks, VH1 interview, April 14, 2001, quoted in "Bombay Sapphires," Stevie Nicks: In Her Own Words, accessed October 5, 2020, www.inherownwords.com/bombay.htm.

63. Maura Johnston, "Lilith Fair at 20: The Legacy of a Tour That Put Women First," *Rolling Stone,* July 24, 2017, www.rollingstone.com/feature/lilith-fair-at-20-the-legacy-of-a-tour-that-put-women-first-203195/.

64. Mike Ross, "Solo Stevie a Singular Pleasure," *Edmonton Sun,* October 2001, quoted in "Trouble in Shangri-La: Reviews," Nicks Fix, http://rockalittle.com/reviews_tisl.htm; Lucy O'Brien, *She Bop: The Definitive History of Women in Music* (New York: Continuum, 2002), 108, Kindle.

65. O'Brien, *She Bop,* 108.

66. Fleetwood Mac, "Planets of the Universe (Demo) (2013 Remaster)," YouTube video, 4:27, October 5, 2015, www.youtube.com/watch?v=TNioe WZiUDE, 4:07.

67. Wayland D. Hand, "California Miners' Folklore: Below Ground," *California Folklore Quarterly* 1, no. 2 (1942): 134.

68. Mark Guarino, "Nicks Faithful Offered Big Hits, Little Spark," *Chicago Daily Herald,* July 11, 2001, 9.

69. Mickey Shapiro, interview with the author, August 20, 2021.

70. Arion Berger, "Say You Will," *Rolling Stone,* May 1, 2003, www.rollingstone.com/music/music-album-reviews/say-you-will-112089/.

71. Dave Stewart, dir., *Stevie Nicks: In Your Dreams,* Tubi video, 1:40:46, 2013, https://tubitv.com/movies/501868/stevie-nicks-in-your-dreams, 23:02–24:12.

72. Stephen Holden, "Stevie Nicks and Rickie Lee Jones Carry the Torch," *New York Times,* June 12, 1983, sec. B, p. 25.

73. "The Nobel Prize in Literature 2016," Nobel Prize, December 11, 2020, www.nobelprize.org/prizes/literature/2016.summary/.

74. Moncrieff had roomed with Nicks in 1976. He and McLoone both toured with Egan in 1977.

75. Ken Caillat and Hernan Rojas, *Get Tusked: The Inside Story of Fleetwood Mac's Most Anticipated Album* (Guilford, CT: Backbeat Books, 2019), 159, 213.

76. Stevie Nicks, Queen of Rock interview, 2003, quoted in "Illume," Stevie Nicks: In Her Own Words, accessed January 8, 2021, www.inherownwords.com/illume.htm.

77. Sylvie Simmons, "Rock Sweetheart, Soldiers' Angel," Fleetwood Mac News, May 13, 2007, www.fleetwoodmacnews.com/2007/05/rock-sweetheart-soldiers-angel.html.

78. Sara Ahmed, *The Promise of Happiness* (Durham: Duke University Press, 2010), 61.

79. Simon Smith, telephone interview with Violet Prete, January 8, 2021.

80. Jonathan Keafe, "Review: Stevie Nicks, *In Your Dreams,*" *Slant,* May 2, 2011, www.slantmagazine.com/music/stevie-nicks-in-your-dreams/.

81. Jenny Turner, "The Beautiful Undead," *London Review of Books* 31, no. 6 (2009), www.lrb.co.uk/the-paper/v31/no6/jenny-turner/the-beautiful-undead.

82. Ibid.

83. Dave Stewart, *Sweet Dreams Are Made of This: A Life in Music* (New York: New American Library, 2016), 280, Kindle.

84. Nicks has lived on or near the Pacific Ocean for decades, both on the estate in Pacific Palisades referenced here, which she purchased in 2005, and in a condominium in Santa Monica, acquired in 2004.

85. Davis, *Gold Dust Woman,* 300.

86. Stewart, *Stevie Nicks.* The detail about the bracelet is at 4:45.

87. Stewart, *Sweet Dreams,* 288.

88. Rob Sheffield, "In Your Dreams," *Rolling Stone,* April 27, 2011, www
.rollingstone.com/music/music-album-reviews/in-your-dreams-113794/.

89. John Seger, "(Fan Reviews) Stevie Nicks 'In Your Dreams': 'Ms. Stevie
Nicks Is Back in Peak Form,'" Fleetwood Mac News, April 28, 2011, www
.fleetwoodmacnews.com/2011/04/fan-reviews-stevie-nicks-in-your-deams.html.

90. The film dates from 1993. Marjorie Hernandez, "The 'Best' Is Yet to
Come for Stevie Nicks," *Ventura County Star,* July 29, 2010, http://archive
.vcstar.com/entertainment/the-best-is-yet-to-come-for-stevie-nicks-ep-368090933-
348624231.html/.

91. Lynne Margolis, "Gold Dust Woman: Q&A with Stevie Nicks," Stevie
Nicks Info, September 1, 2011, https://stevienicks.info/2011/09/gold-dust-
woman-a-qa-with-stevie-nicks/.

92. Jean Rhys, *Wide Sargasso Sea* (London: Random House, 1966), 12.

93. Jancee Dunn, "A Trip to Stevieland," *Harper's Bazaar,* November 1997,
Nicks Fix, http://rockalittle.com/bazaar1.htm.

94. Stewart, *Stevie Nicks,* 25:43.

95. Mary-Kay Wilmers, "Narcissism and Its Discontents," *London Review
of Books* 2, no. 3 (1980), www.lrb.co.uk/the-paper/v02/n03/mary-kay-wilmers
/narcissism-and-its-discontents.

96. Randy Lewis, "Tom Petty's Death Is Still a Hard Reminder for Aging
Rockers about the Downside of Life on the Road," *Los Angeles Times,* October
5, 2018, www.latimes.com/entertainment/music/la-et-ms-tom-petty-death-
anniversary-20181006-story.html; Grunge, "Everything That's Come Out
about Tom Petty since He Died," YouTube video, 4:42, February 19, 2019,
www.youtube.com/watch?v=hvEzSEbh-sY.

97. Lewis, "Tom Petty's Death."

98. Ari Shapiro, "Stevie Nicks on TikTok, Tom Petty and Claiming What's
Yours," NPR, November 4, 2020, www.npr.org/2020/11/04/930448701/stevie-
nicks-on-tiktok-tom-petty-and-claiming-whats-yours.

99. Historic Films Stock Footage Archive, "Stevie Nicks Interview," YouTube
video, 8:47, March 27, 2020, www.youtube.com/watch?v=-9XMiHElino,
5:10, 4:35.

100. "Quotes from Ann Richards," *New York Times,* September 14, 2006,
www.nytimes.com/2006/09/14/us/richards_quotes.html.

101. Tavi Gevinson, "Stevie Nicks Is Still Living Her Dreams," *New Yorker,*
February 15, 2022, www.newyorker.com/culture/the-new-yorker-interview
/stevie-nicks-tavi-gevinson-conversation.

102. My thanks to John Collins for his account of the evening.

103. Madison Vain, "Fleetwood Mac Shine at 2018 MusiCares Person of the
Year Benefit," *Entertainment Weekly,* January 27, 2018, https://ew.com/music
/2018/01/27/fleetwood-mac-2018-musicares/. Sam Roche, "Lindsey Buckingham: 'Pretty Much Everyone Would Love to See Me Come Back to Fleetwood
Mac,'" *Guitar World,* August 3, 2021, https://www.guitarworld.com/news
/lindsey-buckingham-fleetwood-mac-reunion.

104. Sam Moore, "Stevie Nicks Says Fleetwood Mac and Lindsey Buckingham 'Haven't Had Any Communication' since His Heart Attack," NME, October 15, 2020, www.nme.com/en_asia/news/music/stevie-nicks-fleetwood-mac-lindsey-buckingham-havent-had-any-communication-since-his-heart-attack-2786628.

105. Amy Kaufman, "Fleetwood Mac Fired Lindsey Buckingham. So Why Won't He Let Them Go?," Los Angeles Times, September 8, 2021, https://www.latimes.com/entertainment-arts/music/story/2021-09-08/lindsey-buckingham-fleetwood-mac-stevie-nicks; Lindsay Zoladz, "Lindsey Buckingham Has Survived It All," New York Times, September 8, 2021, https://www.nytimes.com/2021/09/08/arts/music/lindsey-buckingham.html; Stephen Rodrick, "Lindsey Buckingham Won't Stop," Rolling Stone, September 9, 2021, https://www.rollingstone.com/music/music-features/lindsey-buckingham-fleetwood-mac-stevie-nicks-new-album-1221755/.

106. Rodrick ("Lindsey Buckingham") solicited a statement from Nicks through her manager:

> It's unfortunate that Lindsey has chosen to tell a revisionist history of what transpired in 2018 with Fleetwood Mac. His version of events is factually inaccurate, and while I've never spoken publicly on the matter, preferring to not air dirty laundry, certainly it feels the time has come to shine a light on the truth. Following an exceedingly difficult time with Lindsey at MusiCares in New York, in 2018, I decided for myself that I was no longer willing to work with him. I could publicly reflect on the many reasons why, and perhaps I will do that someday in a memoir, but suffice it to say we could start in 1968 and work up to 2018 with a litany of very precise reasons why I will not work with him. To be exceedingly clear, I did not have him fired, I did not ask for him to be fired, I did not demand he be fired. Frankly, I fired myself. I proactively removed myself from the band and a situation I considered to be toxic to my well-being. I was done. If the band went on without me, so be it. I have championed independence my whole life, and I believe every human being should have the absolute freedom to set their boundaries of what they can and cannot work with. And after many lengthy group discussions, Fleetwood Mac, a band whose legacy is rooted in evolution and change, found a new path forward with two hugely talented new members.
>
> Further to that, as for a comment on "family"—I was thrilled for Lindsey when he had children, but I wasn't interested in making those same life choices. Those are my decisions that I get to make for myself. I'm proud of the life choices I've made, and it seems a shame for him to pass judgment on anyone who makes a choice to live their life on their own terms, even if it looks differently from what his life choices have been.

107. Aisling O'Connor, "Former Fleetwood Mac Member Lindsey Buckingham Reportedly Wants to Deny Estranged Wife Kristen Messner Spousal Support," Ok!, July 27, 2021, https://okmagazine.com/p/fleetwood-mac-lindsey-buckingham-deny-estranged-wife-kristen-messner-spousal-support/.

108. Anne Steele, "Stevie Nicks Sells Stake in Songwriting Catalog," Wall Street Journal, December 4, 2020, www.wsj.com/articles/stevie-nicks-sells-stake-in-songwriting-catalog-11607095635.

CHAPTER 5. 24 KARAT GOLD

1. As Nicks explained to Tavi Gevinson,

I just said, "You know what? We need to get a divorce. " I left, and he just decided to clean out the whole house, and there was a suitcase of cassettes—I don't really know that he knew what was on all these cassettes. He had, like, a yard sale, and I don't think that the people who bought it necessarily even knew what was exactly on it either. But somebody [eventually] figured out what it was, and then all of a sudden all these demos were out there in the world. So some fans who found out about this bought them and sent them back to me. That's how cool my fans are. And then I took a lot of the great demos to Nashville and said I want to record these songs, but I want it exactly as they are. And they did it. And that's why I love that record so much, because the songs on there are really close to how I wrote them. (Tavi Gevinson, "Stevie Nicks Is Still Living Her Dreams," *New Yorker,* February 15, 2022, www .newyorker.com/culture/the-new-yorker-interview/stevie-nicks-tavi-gevinson-conversation)

2. Nicks's "singing dominates as easily now as it ever did": Mikael Wood, "Stevie Nicks Looks Back on Shimmering '24 Karat Gold,'" *Los Angeles Times,* October 6, 2014, www.latimes.com/entertainment/music/posts/la-et-ms-stevie-nicks-looks-back-on-shimmering-24-karat-gold-20141006-story.html. Holly Gleason found "vexation and amazement" in the album's "frozen-in-amber" reality. For as much as her acolytes wish they could twirl in chiffon scarves and platforms, few remain as ageless or beyond the clock as Nicks; in that gap ripples the nostalgia that stains these songs" ("Stevie Nicks: 24 Karat Gold; Songs from the Vault Review," *Paste,* October 15, 2014, www.pastemagazine.com/music /stevie-nicks/stevie-nicks-24-karat-gold-songs-from-the-vault-re/). Dave Dimartino of *Rolling Stone* seemed primed to dismiss the album but settled instead for qualifiers. It's "quite good actually: the songs seem like genuine works of their time—heartfelt lyrics rather than effort-laden approximations of former glories—and Nicks still sings very well" ("All Eyes on Prince!," *Rolling Stone,* October 1, 2014, www.rollingstone.com/music/music-news/all-eyes-on-prince-180689/). Darryl Sterdan took the kitchen-confidential route in assessing the singer's "leftovers": "Surprisingly, they're far from half-baked ideas and failed experiments. In fact, at least half a dozen of these songs . . . are so good they'll make you wonder what she was thinking by not recording them sooner" ("Stevie Nicks' 'Songs from the Vault' Plus P!nk and Dallas Green Top This Week's New Music," *Toronto Sun,* October 9, 2014, www.torontosun.com/2014/10/09/stevie-nicks-songs-from-the-vault-plus-pnk-and-dallas-green-top-this-weeks-new-music). John Murphy added that it "doesn't sound like a hotch-potch of songs all thrown together either, as you may expect from that description"; "most of the songs that Nicks has resurrected are strong enough to make you wonder why she scrapped them in the first place." (The simple answer: she didn't.) It's a "cohesive album," Murphy decides, despite some anachronistic cuteness in "Hard Advice" about hanging around in a record store ("Stevie Nicks—24 Karat Gold: Songs from the Vault," Music OMH, October 9, 2014, https://www.musicomh.com/reviews /albums/stevie-nicks-24-karat-gold-songs-vault).

3. Ed Masley, "Stevie Nicks Launches 24K Gold Tour in 'My Hometown' of Phoenix with Pretenders' Chrissie Hynde," *Arizona Central,* October 26, 2016, www.azcentral.com/story/entertainment/music/2016/10/26/stevie-nicks-tour-launch-phoenix-pretenders/92775652/.

4. Brittany Spanos, "Stevie Nicks Announces '24 Karat Gold' Concert Film, Live Album," *Rolling Stone*, September 16, 2020, www.rollingstone.com/music/music-news/stevie-nicks-concert-film-24-karat-gold-1060201/.

5. Tom Grater, "'Stevie Nicks 24 Karat Gold' Doc Heads to PVOD as Distributor Trafalgar Releasing Adapts to Pandemic Era," Deadline, October 26, 2020, https://deadline.com/2020/10/stevie-nicks-24-karat-gold-pvod-trafalgar-adapts-pandemic-1234603233/.

6. Skylar De Paul, "'Stevie Nicks 24 Karat Gold the Concert' Is Too Long, but Worth a Cozy Sit-Down," *Daily Californian*, November 2, 2020, www.dailycal.org/2020/11/02/stevie-nicks-24-karat-gold-the-concert-is-too-long-but-worth-a-cozy-sit-down/.

7. Markos Papadatos, "Stevie Nicks Releases Masterful '24 Karat Gold' Concert Film," *Digital Journal*, October 25, 2020, www.digitaljournal.com/entertainment/music/review-stevie-nicks-releases-masterful-24-karat-gold-concert-film/article/580047.

8. Jim Farber, "'24 Karat Gold: Songs from the Vault,' Music Review," *Daily News*, October 7, 2014, www.nydailynews.com/entertainment/music/24-karat-gold-songs-vault-music-review-article-1.1965210.

9. Michel de Montaigne, "All Things Have Their Season," in *Quotidiana*, ed. Patrick Madden, October 2, 2006, http://essays.quotidiana.org/montaigne/all_things_have_their_season/.

10. UCR, "Stevie Nicks Talks Future Plans, Life after Music," YouTube Video, 4:24, February 8, 2014, www.youtube.com/watch?v=kvmuYPKR1sg, 4:00.

11. SisterNightroad, "Stevie Nicks: G#2–F6," *Ledge Rumours* (blog), August 18, 2017, https://ledge.fleetwoodmac.net/showthread.php?t=57431. Despite exaggerating Nicks's overall range, this blog provides a useful outline of changes in her voice, reproduced here in abbreviated form:

1973–1978: Her prime years; husky voice; comfortable lower register and powerful fourth and fifth octave climaxes; head voice seldom used, though when it is, she reaches into the fifth octave, including ghostly "wails" in live performances of "Gold Dust Woman." She is a low(ish) mezzo-soprano singing with ease in both her upper and lower registers.

1979–1983: Largely the same, but with a rougher edge, lowering her range slightly. No head voice on *Bella Donna*, and some slurred diction.

1985–1989: Lower. The upper register is much less comfortable than on *Rumours*, and rougher overall.

1990–1998: Solid lower register; unused higher register. She becomes a contralto. She finds comfort in the third octave while the upper fourth sounds strained.

2001–2009: Contralto. She seldom reaches above A4, with notes in the fifth octave rare and uncomfortable. Her lower register sounds strong—she reaches into the second octave with notes in the lower third octave beginning to sound like mid-range for her.

2011–2017: Contralto; notes in the mid-fourth octave sounding raspier. Her lower register is still strong. She avoids singing upper parts and lowers the keys of her older songs in performance (by five half-steps in one case). While her voice has lost much of its power, her tone [timbre] is essentially unchanged.

12. Phil Audibert, "Is It a Fiddle or a Violin?," *Orange County Review inSIDEr,* June 7, 2007, www.audibertphoto.com/articles/2007-06-07_Ann%20 Marie%20Calhoun.pdf.

13. Farber, "'24 Karat Gold.'"

14. "Annenberg Inclusion Initiative's Annual Report on Popular Music Reveals Little Progress for Women," USC Annenberg School for Communication and Journalism, March 8, 2021, https://annenberg.usc.edu/news/research-and-impact /annenberg-inclusion-initiatives-annual-report-popular-music-reveals-little.

15. Information and quotations in these two paragraphs come from "Who Exactly Was Mabel Normand?," pt. 1, *The Keystone Girl Blogs* (blog), February 23, 2018, https://thekeystonegirlblogs.wordpress.com/2018/02/23/who-exactly-was-mabel-normand-part-1/.

16. Jon Boorstin, "In on the Big Bang: Why I Love the Queen of Slapstick," *Los Angeles Review of Books,* March 11, 2014, https://lareviewofbooks.org /article/big-bang-love-queen-slapstick/.

17. Kathleen Phalen Tomaselli, "Saving Mabel Normand," Fix, February 24, 2015, www.thefix.com/content/saving-mabel-normand.

18. Jeff Nilsson, Andy Hollandbeck, and William McAdoo, "The Other Prohibition: Opiate Addiction in the Roaring '20s," *Saturday Evening Post,* September 6, 2016, www.saturdayeveningpost.com/2016/09/prohibition-opiate-addiction-roaring-20s/.

19. "Mabel and the Dines Affair," *The Keystone Girl Blogs* (blog), August 30, 2018, https://thekeystonegirlblogs.wordpress.com/2018/08/30/mabel-and-the-dines-affair/.

20. This quotation comes from the script of the Normand film *Tillie's Punctured Romance* (1914): "Tillie, the pride of Yokeltown and the apple of her papa's eye." "Tillie's Punctured Romance (1914) Analysis," *One Movie Blog,* October 7, 2013, http://onemovieblog.blogspot.com/2013/10/tillies-punctured-romance-1914-analysis.html.

21. Jon Blistein, "Stevie Nicks Details Release Plan for New Solo Album '24 Karat Gold,'" *Rolling Stone,* July 24, 2014, www.rollingstone.com/music /music-news/stevie-nicks-details-release-plan-for-new-solo-album-24-karat-gold-246502/.

22. Jessica Goodman, "Stevie Nicks' New Track 'Mabel Normand' Is a Brutal Look at 'What Drugs Can Do to You,'" Huffpost, October 1, 2014, www .huffpost.com/entry/stevie-nicks-mabel-normand_n_5912492.

23. Roy Tannenbaum, "Stevie Nicks Admits Past Pregnancy with Don Henley and More about Her Wild History," *Billboard,* September 26, 2014, www .billboard.com/articles/news/6266329/stevie-nicks-interview-on-don-henley-fleetwood-mac-24-karat-gold-album. The demo of "Mabel Normand" dates from 1984 and the *Rock a Little* sessions. No docudrama or biopic was made about Mabel Normand in that year or 1985, according to Betty Harper Fussell, author of *Mabel* (Boston: Ticknor and Fields, 1982), with whom I communicated by email on December 18, 2020. Her claim was corroborated by William Thomas Sherman, author of the self-published *Mabel Normand: A Source Book on Her Life and Films* (2019), and Bruce Long (creator of www.taylorology.com), each of whom I also communicated with by email on December 18, 2020. (Fussell noted

that she was personally "thrilled that Stevie carries on the Mabel torch.") The most probable source is a magazine program about the Taylor murder, *The Dark Side of Hollywood,* shown on KABC Los Angeles on June 1, 1984. Less probable is the 1982 stage musical *Keystone,* which focuses on Normand's relationship with Sennett. Normand's putative biography was the subject of an October 18, 1999, episode of *Mysteries and Scandals* on the E! network. The biopic *Looking for Mabel Normand* (Anthony Mercaldi, dir.) postdates *24 Karat Gold* by a year.

24. Michael Martin, "Edge of Everything," *Out,* September 11, 2014, www .out.com/entertainment/music/2014/09/11/inevitable-return-stevie-nicks.

25. Boorstin, "Big Bang."

26. Stevie Nicks, "Mabel Normand," accessed January 20, 2021, https:// genius.com/Stevie-nicks-mabel-normand-lyrics. The line "Haven't much faith in her talent" refers to the founder of Vitagraph Studios, producer Albert Edward Smith, who belittled Normand, questioning her talent.

27. Parke Godwin, *Beloved Exile* (New York: Bantam, 1984), 34.

28. Roberta Davidson, "Parke Godwin and the Lessons of History," *Arthuriana* 20, no. 4 (2010): 25.

CONCLUSION

1. Roberta Davidson, "Parke Godwin and the Lessons of History," *Arthuriana* 20, no. 4 (2010): 25; Rob Sheffield, "Stevie Nicks on Tom Petty, Drag Queens, 'Game of Thrones' and Missing Prince," *Rolling Stone,* February 28, 2019, www.rollingstone.com/music/music-features/stevie-nicks-interview-tom-petty-drag-queens-game-of-thrones-prince-801112.

2. Fans have also organized Fleetwood Mac/Stevie Nicks conventions, the first in the US taking place at a hotel in Winston-Salem, North Carolina, on August 6–7, 1988. It included a charity auction, and Christopher Nicks turned up to complain about the proliferation of unlicensed Stevie Nicks merchandise. The hotel suffered minor damage from the partying.

3. "NOTS 30: Book of Stevie," Night of 1000 Stevies, accessed January 19, 2021, http://1000stevies.com/nots30/.

4. Susan Sontag, "Notes on Camp," 1964, in *Against Interpretation: And Other Essays* (New York: Picador, 2001), 283.

5. Hilary Mantel, "The Perils of Antoinette," *New York Review,* January 11, 2007, www.nybooks.com/articles/2007/01/11/the-perils-of-antoinette/.

6. Sheffield, "Nicks on Tom Petty."

7. *Rolling Stone,* "Night of 1000 Stevies: Inside the Most Twirltastic Tribute Show in NYC," YouTube video, 6:09, May 8, 2015, www.youtube.com/watch ?v=xSZCEjFGS5k&feature=youtu.be, 0:17, 1:23, 4:39.

8. Lucy O'Brien, *She Bop: The Definitive History of Women in Music* (New York: Continuum, 2002), 108, Kindle.

9. Madison Moore, *Fabulous: The Rise of the Beautiful Eccentric* (New Haven: Yale University Press, 2018).

10. Jason Lee Oakes, "Queering the Witch: Stevie Nicks and the Forging of Femininity at the Night of a Thousand Stevies," in *Queering the Popular Pitch,* ed. Sheila Whiteley and Jennifer Rycenga (Abingdon: Routledge, 2006), 50–52.

In a related article, Rachel Devitt disputes Oakes's characterization of Nicks impersonators' "ambiguousness" in terms of gender and sexuality. Rather, she writes, the impersonators "firmly" plant "a fastidiously pedicured foot in more than one spot." ("Keep the Best of You, 'Do' the Rest of You": Passing, Ambivalence and Keeping Queer in Gender Performative Negotiations of Popular Music," *Popular Music* 32, no. 3 [October 2013]: 440.)

11. Michael Montlack, "Stevie Nicks," in *My Diva: 65 Gay Men on the Women Who Inspire Them,* ed. Michael Montlack (Madison: Terrace Books, 2000), loc. 2403–15, Kindle.

12. Sheffield, "Nicks on Tom Petty."

13. I borrow philosopher Arthur Schopenhauer's formulation. See Jordi Fernández, "Schopenhauer's Pessimism," *Philosophy and Phenomenological Research* 73, no. 3 (2006): 646–47.

14. Ray Rogers, "A Storm Called Stevie," *Interview,* July 1998, Go Your Own Way, www.fleetwoodmac-uk.com/articles/archive/SNart009.html.

15. Quoted in Kristen J. Sollée, *Witches, Sluts, Feminists: Conjuring the Sex Positive* (Berkeley: ThreeLMedia, 2017), 126, 8.

16. Stevie Nicks, "Cathouse Blues," accessed January 20, 2021, https://genius.com/Stevie-nicks-cathouse-blues-lyrics.

17. GM Admin, "Real Life Rock (01/83)," Greil Marcus's online archive, July 27, 2014, https://greilmarcus.net/2014/07/27/real-life-rock-0183/.

18. "Q&A: Stevie Nicks," Stevie Nicks Info, August 1, 1994, https://stevienicks.info/1994/08/qa-stevie-nicks-4/.

19. James [Jacob] Sprenger and Henry [Heinrich] Kramer, *Malleus maleficarum,* trans. Montague Summers, accessed June 12, 2021, www.sacred-texts.com/pag/mm/.

20. "20 Questions: Stevie Nicks," *Playboy* 29, no. 7 (1982), Nicks Fix, www.stevienicks.net/playboy1.htm.

21. Liz Derringer, "Stevie Nicks' First Interview without Fleetwood Mac," *High Times,* March 1982, Nicks Fix, http://rockalittle.com/hightimes3-82.htm.

Index

Founded in 1893,
UNIVERSITY OF CALIFORNIA PRESS
publishes bold, progressive books and journals
on topics in the arts, humanities, social sciences,
and natural sciences—with a focus on social
justice issues—that inspire thought and action
among readers worldwide.

The UC PRESS FOUNDATION
raises funds to uphold the press's vital role
as an independent, nonprofit publisher, and
receives philanthropic support from a wide
range of individuals and institutions—and from
committed readers like you. To learn more, visit
ucpress.edu/supportus.